# *Just-in-Time Quality*

## *A Practical Approach*

Arnaldo Hernandez

PTR  Prentice Hall
Englewood Cliffs, New Jersey 07632

**Library of Congress Cataloging-in-Publication Data**

Hernández, Arnaldo.
   Just-in-time quality : a practical approach / by Arnaldo
Hernandez.
     p.  cm.
   Includes bibliographical references and index.
   ISBN 0–13–512203–1
   1. Just-in-time systems.  2. Quality control.  I. Title.
TS157.H468   1993
658.5′6—dc20                     92–46069
                                        CIP

Acquisitions Editor: Michael Hays
Editorial/production supervision: Tally Morgan, WordCrafters Editorial Services, Inc.
Cover design: Karen Marsilio
Cover photo: C. Orrico/Superstock
Buyer: Mary Elizabeth McCartney

 © 1993 by P T R Prentice-Hall, Inc.
A Simon & Schuster Company
Englewood Cliffs, New Jersey 07632

Printed in the United States of America
10  9  8  7  6  5  4  3  2  1

ISBN 0-13-512203-1

Prentice-Hall International (UK) Limited, *London*
Prentice-Hall of Australia Pty. Limited, *Sydney*
Prentice-Hall Canada Inc., *Toronto*
Prentice-Hall Hispanoamericana, S.A., *Mexico*
Prentice-Hall of India Private Limited, *New Delhi*
Prentice-Hall of Japan, Inc., *Tokyo*
Simon & Schuster Asia Pte. Ltd., *Singapore*
Editora Prentice-Hall do Brasil, Ltda., *Rio de Janeiro*

**To my wife Barbara—
true love is all quality**

# Contents

Contents

# *Preface*

---

The concept of quality is not new to manufacturing. Most manufacturers claim they have a quality organization and a quality system in place. But most of the time their system consists of the old practice of using inspectors to inspect or reject materials to produce a quality product at the end of the production line. This system is wasteful, operates in a reacting mode, and in all ways is obsolete in today's manufacturing environment. A successful quality system puts emphasis on prevention, rather than correction. It also assigns responsibility for quality to the makers of the part. This is the main idea behind Just-in-Time quality: Workers are directly responsible for the quality of the parts they produce, including the monitoring of quality. This book will explain in detail the steps necessary to implement such a system.

A manufacturer using Just-in-Time will not succeed without a first-class quality system in place. Just-in-Time reduces the inventories required to support a production line. In a Just-in-Time system, there are no extra parts to cover for defective ones. Parts should arrive at the process precisely at the moment they are needed, and they should have perfect quality. The manufacturer has no choice but to procure quality parts and to solve quality problems before continuing to build a product. A first-class quality system is critical to the success of a Just-in-Time system. This book presents a down-to-earth guide to implementing a quality system that complements a Just-in-Time system.

Another obsolete concept is that the quality department is the group primarily responsible for safeguarding quality in a manufacturing organization. This concept couldn't be more wrong. Quality is everybody's business. The responsibility for quality is shared equally by all people in the organization, including management and the president of the company. Quality should start at the top. One of the main thrusts of this book is to show how to implement a quality system that crosses departmental boundaries in both a horizontal and vertical way. The book will show how to implement the concept of total quality control using a company-wide approach.

No manufacturer is self-sufficient; in a normal production environment, there is a selected group of suppliers that constantly ship parts to the manufacturer's production line to keep the process flowing. In a Just-in-Time system, these parts should arrive in the smallest possible quantity, exactly at the time when they are needed, and they should be of perfect quality. No supplier will provide that kind of service unless there is a close partnership between the supplier and the manufacturer, as well as a first-class Just-in-Time quality system in place. The supplier's workers are the makers of the parts; they should be responsible for delivering quality-perfect parts to the supplier's customers. This is one of the most critical aspects of Just-in-Time quality. This book will discuss the steps required to implement a successful supplier quality program.

The main thrust of a Just-in-Time system is to eliminate all forms of waste in manufacturing. Poor-quality parts are the worse of them. Inspecting parts is also a waste. Inspection doesn't add any value to the part—it only verifies what should have been clear to begin with: that the part was quality perfect. This book departs from other books on the subject by addressing the issue of waste in a quality system. A streamlined, dynamic, and wasteless quality system is crucial to obtaining quality-perfect parts.

Finally, I want to address the issue of measuring quality. No matter how perfect a quality system is, the ultimate judge of the quality of a product is the customer. If a product performs to the expectations of the customer and does so reliably for the length of time the customer expects it to work, then the product is of good quality. The hidden message here is that any other measurement is of no value to the manufacturer of the product. A first-class quality system should set the customer's expectations right as they relate to the performance, reliability, and life of the product. Ultimately, customer satisfaction is the criterion for quality. We will review how to measure customer satisfaction and how to make sure customer expectations are in tune with the product being bought.

The importance of quality was discovered in the United States many years ago. We never took it seriously until Japan started to compete with us with high-quality products that grabbed a large portion of the U.S market share. Manufacturers in the United States are badly behind the quality curve; unfortunately, only a few are winning that battle to become equal in quality. There are many companies struggling hopelessly to hit the moving target of Japanese quality standards. I hope this book will help them to improve the odds in that battle. Because, in the end, the quality business is nothing but a never-ending war for continuous improvement.

Arnaldo Hernandez

# Acknowledgments

I want to thank Michael Hays, Executive Editor and Assistant Vice-President at Prentice-Hall. Michael's support and patience have been invaluable to this project. He believed, as I do, that this book would be an excellent companion for my other book, *Just-in-Time Manufacturing,* providing manufacturing practitioners with a complete set of references for achieving excellence in their profession.

I also want to thank Terry Farlow, Director of Quality Assurance, and Mike Carney, Director of Process Engineering, at Relevant Technologies for reading the manuscript and providing many valuable suggestions. Thanks are also extended to Rick Jernberg, Manager of Quality Control, and Martin Anvieh, Senior Supplier Quality Engineer, for volunteering to read the manuscript and offering important comments.

Finally, I want to thank my wife, Barbara, for her support and encouragement during the writing of this book. Barbara's love and patience have taught me that there is quality in everything we do in our lives. Thank you.

# 1★

# *A Case for Quality: Survival*

After a manufacturer ships a product to a customer, there is nothing he or she can do to change the quality of that product. At that moment the product's fate is sealed: The satisfaction of the customer will depend on how well the product meets expectations. This is the value the product offers to the customer, value that will influence that customer to buy more or to recommend the product to someone else.

Before shipping, a manufacturer spends a considerable amount of effort solving quality issues related to the product. These issues are normally addressed by a quality organization and corrected by the workers on the production line. Sometimes, the manufacturer ends up shipping a quality product. To accomplish this, however, the manufacturer has invested large amounts of resources and money—a wasteful approach.

Many times a defective product slips through quality checks in the process and is shipped in spite of all efforts spent on detecting and correcting its defects. This is a worst case. No manufacturer ships a defective product without gambling with the survival of his or her business. The key to quality is to manufacture quality-perfect parts the first time, investing a reasonable amount of effort monitoring the system that produces such a quality part. Manufacturers who achieve this goal are very successful and will have an edge on the competition. They are also long-term survivors.

## 1.1  THE NEED FOR QUALITY

The need for quality in manufacturing is obvious. In the manufacturing business, the strongest competitors get all the orders because they are shipping a quality product that performs to customer specifications.

Quality is also a moral issue. If we tell the customer that a product conforms to certain specifications when it doesn't, this deception will ruin our business enterprise. Companies cannot survive without a working quality system in place.

Price is not always the deciding factor in the purchase of a product. Quality should always be that factor. The idea that a quality product is more expensive is erroneous. A low-cost quality product can use a good quality process to assure that the product meets low cost specifications.

This brings up the concept of quality in design. The level of quality a product is going to have at the end of the production line is defined during its design phase. Design engineers share most of the responsibility for it, second only to manufacturing engineers. Both groups must use quality practices to design the product and define the manufacturing process. A design lab is the place where quality for a particular product starts taking form. There is a definitive need for quality in the design of products. A poorly designed product will never reach a sufficient level of quality to satisfy a customer no matter how hard the manufacturing organization tries.

Quality is a discipline that covers many complex areas in the life of a product; it should not be limited to the factory only. Quality commitment is a company-wide effort.

## 1.2  WORLD COMPETITION AND QUALITY

Advances in communication and transportation have opened the world to international business. The aggressive Japanese market penetration in the United States and the recent common market trends in Europe are proof of that. World competition means a business opportunity for every U.S. enterprise, but it also opens the door to companies competing to sell their products in the United States.

This competitive environment offers consumers more products to choose from, with a wide range of performance and price. The world market produces a product for every need and budget. The price and performance of a product being equal, the primary factor in the customer's decision to buy a particular product is its quality. This is a lesson that has taken U.S. manufacturers many years to learn and has cost them many losses in their businesses.

The challenge to U.S. business is not world competition. The challenge is to produce a product that matches or surpasses the quality of foreign products at a cost that makes good business sense. The challenge is not to invest a certain amount of money in quality and wait to see what comes out at the end of the production line. The challenge is to strive for perfect-quality products efficiently and with a minimum amount of investment. Companies that meet this challenge have nothing but success ahead of them. They will be world competitors. Companies that fail to achieve this goal will be history.

## 1.3 THE VALUE OF QUALITY TO THE CUSTOMER

How much more should a customer pay for quality in a product? The answer is: nothing. When customers buy a product, they expect the product to work and to do the things the manufacturer has claimed. Good quality is taken for granted, and every manufacturer should understand that. The product should work and it should meet customer expectations. This effort should be supplied to the customer free. Anything less is unacceptable.

Products don't work forever, or have all the features a customer needs. The job of the manufacturer is to adjust the customer's expectations properly as they relate to the performance of a product. There are always tradeoffs that should be pointed out before the sale. The job the manufacturer does in presenting these tradeoffs reflects the overall quality of the company. Some companies are very good at explaining the performance and features of their products. These companies succeed in setting the customer's expectations at a certain level, but later defraud the customer by shipping a product that fails to attain that level.

There are other companies that do a poor job of describing a product to the customer, but ship a first-rate quality product that performs better than expectations. In this case the customer is better off buying this product, but the company is not quality perfect across all its departments.

Quality is the ultimate value to a customer. Value doesn't mean just a product that works when the customer receives it. There is quality in the documentation that accompanies the product. There is also quality in the service that a company gives in training a customer and supporting the product. There is also quality in the information that describes the product. The sum of all these services is what makes a customer satisfied and ready to purchase other products from the same company. The sum of these services is what differentiates a successful company from one that is not.

## 1.4 QUALITY AND THE JAPANESE

Most people in the United States perceive Japanese cars as being of better quality than their U.S. counterparts. Japanese companies didn't earn that reputation by fancy, expensive advertising campaigns, telling people in the United States that their cars had great quality. Japan earned its reputation by working hard for many decades to overcome obstacles that stood in the way of shipping quality cars. They didn't tell customers they had great quality: They showed it.

Japan's evolution in quality is something that requires study and admiration. Right after World War II, all Japanese industries were destroyed and near bankruptcy. The industrial might of the United States was at its peak; it seemed invincible. Forty-five years later, the U.S. automobile and electronic industries are struggling to survive Japan's industrial invasion—not because Japanese products are cheaper than U.S. products, but because they are of better quality.

Ironically, Japanese awareness of quality is due principally to the United States. It all started with occupation forces teaching Japanese workers the newly developed concepts of statistical quality control; later came the history-making visits and lectures of the U.S. quality gurus Dr. W. Edwards Deming and Dr. J. M. Duran. Japan was awakened to the need for quality and brought it to all levels of management and worker participation.

There is no need to blame the United States for Japan's quality and competitive stand in today's world market. But there is no question that we *can* blame U.S. corporations for the lack of quality in their products which caused their market shares to decline to a point where they are no longer competitive.

It took Japanese companies many years to reach the quality levels of today, and they are still improving. The challenge to U.S. manufacturers is to match those quality levels, and then reassert their leadership. Time will not tell the winner; customers buying products will.

## 1.5 DEFINITION OF A QUALITY SYSTEM

There is no simple way to define a quality system. In general, a quality system is part of overhead. The system doesn't add any value to the product. It only ensures that the product works and meets customer expectations. If a manufacturer uses perfect parts and a perfect process with perfectly trained workers, however, the product should come out of the production line being of perfect quality, without the need of a quality system. Of course, this is not true in a manufacturing environment. Suppliers don't always ship quality parts. The process is never constant: It can be random. Then there are people. People are not perfect. Workers make mistakes inadvertently.

A quality system is a process that combines with the manufacturing process to ensure that a manufacturing process produces quality-perfect products. The scope of a quality system is more broad than a manufacturing process. A quality system covers areas related to the suppliers that produce parts for the process. It also covers other departments in the company to ensure that customers are properly informed, trained, and serviced whenever problems are presented. Finally, it covers the design department to ensure that products are designed to specifications and perform as intended.

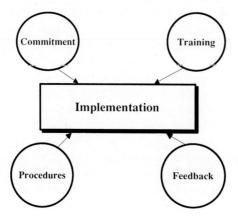

**Figure 1.1**   The Quality System Areas of Operation

Figure 1.1 shows the four components of a quality system. All four areas are needed: Without one of them, the system will not be successful. First, we need the procedures to define the quality system. These procedures should be simple, clear, and cover all areas of concern. Procedures are not cast in concrete; they should be modified as experience in their use produces new suggestions to improve them. Procedures should include goals that with time should evolve into tighter and more aggressive ones, so the quality system is always stretching to its limits to meet them.

Once the procedures are put in place, the next step is to train all the people involved in their use. This is a good test of the clarity of the procedures. Training is an activity that should never end, even after the trainers believe the workers clearly understand the implementation and goals of the procedures.

The third component of a quality system is information and feedback. A quality system needs a sensitive mechanism for monitoring and feedback, usually one of the most ineffective parts of the system. Most manufacturers create quality procedures that define their quality systems, then burden the system by creating voluminous reports designed to please upper management by showing that a quality system is in place—reports that nobody reads or uses. The information and feedback mechanism of a quality system is the most important part of the system. Incomplete procedures with a good feedback mechanism are more desirable than good procedures with no feedback information.

The last important aspect of the quality system is commitment. To succeed, a quality system needs a strong commitment—commitment at all levels of the organization, including top management. A company should be serious about quality, and showing strong management and worker commitment is the best way to prove it.

## 1.6 QUALITY AND SURVIVAL

Quality can be the Achilles heel of a company. There are cases in which a company has an excellent product idea which meets a market need. The company invests in a manufacturing line to produce the product and in a marketing and sales department to introduce the product into the market. But the product is ill designed and shows poor quality after it is shipped to customers. This product is far from satisfying customers' needs and it will fail.

In general, it doesn't matter how many features a product has. If a product lacks quality, there will be no buyers for it in the long run. It is true that the manufacturer will fool a few customers when the product is introduced, but once the word is out, buyers will abandon the product for a less fancy one of better quality. Quality is a survival feature that has to be designed into every product.

Quality does not guarantee the long-term survival of a manufacturer. There are cases where manufacturers ship a product of quality, but only after they have invested a large amount of inefficient labor to overinspect and reject a great percentage of their products. This shotgun approach to quality is a slow cancer that will kill the manufacturer. A good quality system should be efficient, not a financial burden to a manufacturer. This delicate balance between perfect quality and the burden the system imposes is the difference between a struggling manufacturer and a very successful one.

## 1.7 QUALITY STRATEGY

Most companies have a product strategy, a sales and marketing strategy, perhaps a manufacturing strategy, but not a quality strategy. The first step is to develop a strategy that everyone in the organization understands and supports. This is the aspect most critical to the introduction of a quality program. The strategy should be developed by departments primarily responsible for implementing the system, and it should have management support. Once the quality strategy is drafted, it should be reviewed and approved at all levels of the organization. Strong management support should be evident during this stage of development.

The quality strategy should clearly state the importance of delivering quality products to customers, and the company's commitment to making this happen. It also has to declare that quality is everybody's responsibility, including the suppliers of the material used to build the product. Figure 1.2 shows the key areas the quality strategy should cover to specify the quality environment in which the company will operate. The strategy should cover not only the operational areas in manufacturing, but it should also postulate quality standards for all departments that are associated with the customer and the general operation of the company. This is a very important point to consider because most quality organizations believe their responsibilities are only concerned with manufacturing.

The following chapters of this book will present the different elements required to formulate a company-wide quality strategy. These chapters will provide a clear picture of

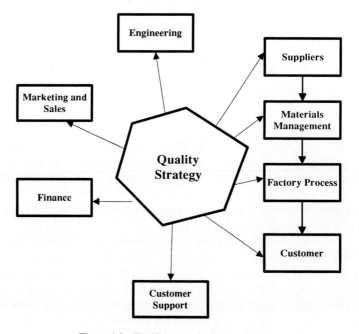

**Figure 1.2**   The Universe of a Quality Strategy

the issues that are important to readers. The postulation of the quality strategy should be short, clear, and not burdened with tactical issues that can be addressed during implementation. The strategy should be understood by everyone in the organization and it should be presentable to customers as well.

## 1.8 COMMITMENT TO QUALITY

The most important aspect of a quality program is the company's resolve to improve the program as it develops. This level of commitment should be shown in actions rather than words. This obligation should be present at all levels of the organization, with no exceptions. Workers should show their commitment to quality by practicing the quality system in every aspect of their manufacturing activities. They should also provide feedback on how to improve the system. Middle managers and supervisors should show their commitment by working closely with the workers. They should provide the necessary training and tools to make the system successful. Finally, upper management should show its support by allocating the resources necessary to get the job done. This concerted effort should never stop: It should become a natural way for the organization to operate.

In any organization, commitment without persistence will make the quality system fail. Quality is a business of small details and a business of extreme persistence. Any problem can be corrected, but if the organization lowers its guard, the problem will return. The best way to maintain a high level of commitment is to create new goals as soon as the old ones are met. Then the organization should be engaged in meeting the new goals again. This never-ending resolve to achieve higher goals should be the engine that drives a company to higher levels of accomplishment and satisfaction.

## 1.9 SUMMARY

There is very little question about the need for quality. Poor quality performance in a product is sure death. Poor quality not only involves manufacturing, but other operational aspects of the company. Quality is a people business, because people cause most of the problems that lead to poor quality. Furthermore, it is only people who can fix quality problems. Many companies have been wrong about this, as upper management erroneously concluded that automation was the solution to its quality problems. A first-class quality system will not work without people's involvement and commitment. No level of automation can provide that.

The following chapters will present the practical basis for designing a quality system that encompasses manufacturing and other departments in a company. The chapters are broad in scope, to fit the general needs of every company. Every product, process, and manufacturer is different and each has particular needs, but all have the same basic need for quality. The information presented in this book is of a practical nature and is easily adaptable to the needs of different companies. It offers a framework in which companies seriously interested in improving their quality can formulate their own custom systems.

# REFERENCES

CROSBY, PHILIP B. *Quality Is Free: The Art of Making Quality Certain.* New York: New American Library, 1979.

HALL, ROBERT W. *Attaining Manufacturing Excellence.* Homewood, Ill.: Dow Jones-Irwin, 1987.

"Quality: Approaching the Myth." *Industry Week*, 7 October 1991, 12–25.

ROBSON, ROSS E., ed. *The Quality and Productivity Equation.* Cambridge, Mass.: Productivity Press, 1990.

"The Quality Imperative." *Business Week*, 25 October 1991, 7–169.

# 2★

# Just-in-Time and Quality: A Marriage for Success

Manufacturing companies embrace Just-in-Time intending to increase efficiency and reduce costs. Once started, manufacturers realize that operational habits that have been used for years must change before the new system can help to achieve their goals. Just-in-Time will also force manufacturers to improve quality. Nothing makes quality problems with suppliers and in the factory more evident than a Just-in-Time system.

One key goal in a Just-in-Time system is to eliminate the buffer inventories used to feed a production line. Every part counts toward meeting the production schedule; there are no additional parts to replace the bad ones. Just-in-Time will not succeed without the implementation of a parallel quality program. A Just-in-Time manufacturer has no choice but to procure quality parts for the company's process. The manufacturer also has to run a quality process in his or her operation; otherwise, Just-in-Time will bring the production line to a screeching halt.

The best way to accommodate all these requirements is to plan the implementation of both systems concurrently. This approach will allow the two programs to be closely coupled so they will help each other in areas that require management attention and intervention. For example, a Just-in-Time supplier's program requires a supplier to ship small lots, on a pull basis, that arrive exactly at the point in the process where the parts are needed. These parts will bypass the receiving inspection stations and go directly to the manufacturing floor without the need for any buffer to cover irregularities in the delivery rate. The job of a Just-in-Time quality program is to ensure that those parts are of perfect quality and that no waste is incurred in receiving inspection efforts, line part rejections, or shutdowns for lack of material.

## 2.1 THE JUST-IN-TIME SYSTEM

The Just-in-Time system evolved in Japan. After World War II, most Japanese companies started a crusade to improve productivity and to eliminate waste in their manufacturing facilities. This effort was led by Toyota, where most Just-in-Time concepts were first used. Just-in-Time is a crusade to increase productivity by eliminating waste in all its forms. This is the key concept of the system. The immediate result of this effort is an increase in worker productivity and the reduction of the material used to support a process.

Just-in-Time considers excess inventory as waste and focuses on reducing all types of inventories used in the factory. Reducing inventories, however, is not the primary goal of Just-in-Time. The primary goal is to increase the productivity of a manufacturing system by eliminating all kinds of activities that add no value to a product. Just-in-Time also forces the manufacturer to improve the quality level of the product produced. All these improvements in productivity and quality translate into larger profit margins for the manufacturer and an increase in customer satisfaction.

## 2.2 ELIMINATION OF WASTE

The typical definition of waste in manufacturing is rework and scrap; these are classes of waste that are very easy to identify. Activities such as inspecting, material travel time, and buffer inventories are not considered waste. Just-in-Time defines waste as any activity that doesn't add any value to the product. When a product is put together in a factory, there is a considerable amount of labor invested in material handling, assembling, and testing of the product. The labor invested in assembling parts into a product is adding value to the product, assuming this is not in excess of the time it will reasonably take to do the job. Testing the product also adds value, because it verifies the integrity of the assembly. Handling material from one location to another doesn't add any value to the parts. The material is still the same at the receiving end of the transfer.

In the case of suppliers, material travel waste will vary depending on their locations relative to the destination of the parts. Material shipped from the East Coast wastes more traveling time than material shipped from a supplier next door to the customer. Just-in-Time calls for the selection of suppliers located close to the manufacturer.

Figure 2.1 shows three activities that are not normally considered waste in manufac-

Traveling              Inspecting              Waiting in Buffers

**Figure 2.1**   Just-in-Time Types of Material Waste

turing. Traveling waste not only relates to the time it takes the material to travel from a supplier to a manufacturer—traveling inside the manufacturing process is also waste and should be minimized. Waiting is normally related to buffer inventories. Material stored in buffers and in stockrooms is wasted.

There is another class of time waste that is related to machine setup time. Material waiting for a machine to be set up is a waste because the activity is not adding any value to the material. Just-in-Time concentrates on reducing the setup times of the machines used in a process.

Finally, inspecting is an activity that doesn't add any value to the parts. All that inspection accomplishes is to prove that a part meets manufacturer specifications. This activity is wasted because the manufacturer of the part should have a good process control system to build quality parts that don't need a double inspection system. First, Just-in-Time strives to reduce the inspection time of the parts, and ultimately to eliminate this activity.

Just-in-Time reduces the traveling time and the waiting time for parts in a manufacturing system. A Just-in-Time quality system reduces, or eliminates, the need for inspecting, shifting the responsibility for quality to the maker of the parts. All three reductions are necessary for the success of the Just-in-Time system.

## 2.3 INVENTORY REDUCTION

Traditionally, inventory levels measure the efficiency of a manufacturing organization in the control of material for a particular production process. High inventories with material buffers stored at different locations in the process are a signal of relaxed planning and lack of control. Just-in-Time considers such buffers a waste and concentrates on eliminating them.

The elimination of buffers helps to improve the quality of the material in two important ways. First, material will not become obsolete or need rework because of engineering changes affecting the parts stored in the buffers. Small buffer inventories will make the implementation of changes faster and will reduce the possibility of using a defective part in the process.

The second benefit of eliminating buffer inventories is that defective parts become more obvious in the system. In most manufacturing lines worker effectiveness is gauged by the amount of production completed. If workers have a large buffer inventory beside them at the work center and they encounter a defective part, the workers most likely will use another part, letting the bad one sit there until they have no more parts to keep the process going. This delay in discovering and removing bad parts will affect the overall quality of the process.

Inventory reduction points up such problems because the system has no extra parts to replace the bad ones. It forces the quality system to monitor the quality of the parts fed into the process. A batch of defective parts will cause the process to stop, requiring immediate response. Just-in-Time without a parallel quality system implemented cannot reduce inventories without causing a major disruption in the process flow.

## 2.4 PUSH/PULL SYSTEMS IN MANUFACTURING

Section 2.2 explained the concept of waste in a Just-in-Time system. The second concept critical to the success of Just-in-Time is the implementation of a pull system, which describes the way material is moved along the process.

Traditional manufacturing organizations use master scheduling and Material Requirement Planning (MRP) to plan the material needed to feed production lines. This system takes into account product demand, material on order, material in different factory inventory locations, lead times of the suppliers to deliver raw material, and lead time of the factory to process the finished product. In general, this system does a good job of keeping a stream of material flowing into a process, but overstocking and preplanned buffer inventories may result. This system pushes the material in the factory without considering actual

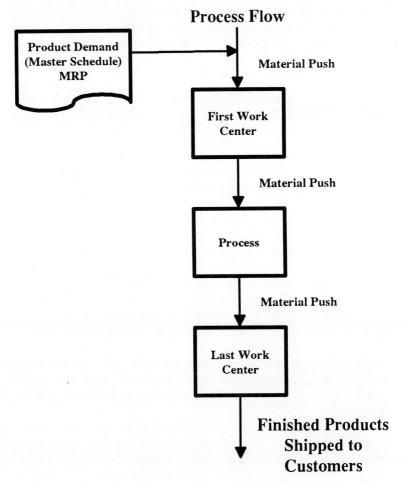

**Figure 2.2**    Material Flow in a Push System

consumption of the material at work center levels. The combination with work orders to schedule the actual production run tends to be wasteful and inefficient. Figure 2.2 shows the flow of material in a push system. The material is driven by the master schedule and MRP at the beginning of the process. This is the place where the demand for the finished product is first introduced into the system.

Figure 2.3 shows a pull system. A pull system only moves material in the process in response to consumption. This means that a part will not move to a new location until the part previously stored in that place was consumed by the process. In this system, the demand schedule is introduced at the end of the process. The demand pulls the need of parts from that work center, which, in turn, pulls from the next one upstream in the process. This produces a demand ripple throughout the factory up to the beginning of the line. Then it will span out the receiving door to reach the suppliers feeding raw material to the manufacturer.

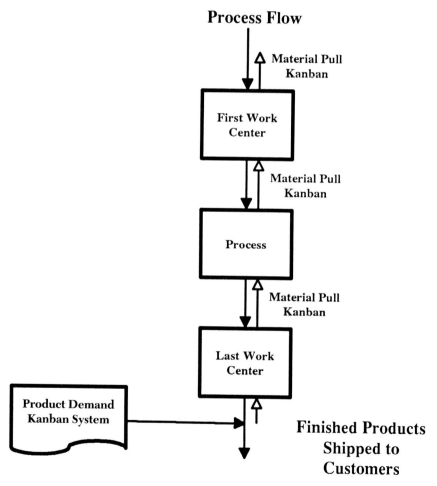

**Figure 2.3**   Material Flow in a Pull System

The role of a Just-in-Time quality system in this operating mode is extremely important. Demand for parts in the process is random and only occurs when there is a need for them. When the demand for a part arrives at a work center, the part requested has to be of perfect quality to fulfill the need of the worker requesting the part. There is no room for parts with poor quality. A problem with a part will cause the line to stop, because there are no buffer inventories to compensate for it.

## 2.5 THE CONCEPT OF SMALL

In a Just-in-Time system the quantity of one is the ideal lot size for a product built through a process. This is the third key principle of Just-in-Time. Normally, in a discrete manufacturing process the parts used to build a product are kitted in lot sizes gauged to match a work order or production flow. Traditional manufacturing cuts these work orders in large sizes to accommodate production schedules. This is wasteful, tending to create inefficiencies in the system when shortages plague the kit and the rest of the parts have to wait until shortages are filled. Just-in-Time calls for reducing the size of the kits, so material is distributed throughout a process in small increments and in a constant flow. The ideal kit size is the one that supplies a work center with the material needed for a day's production work. If a material planner moves material to a work center in excess of a day's workload, the parts are wasted. A worker will only have use for parts that are consumed in one shift schedule. Large kits tend to create small buffer inventories waiting all the time at the beginning of a work center. Figure 2.4 shows this. Waiting a week for materials to be processed in a work center is wasteful and tends to hide quality problems with parts. An efficient quality system not only should monitor the quality of the parts but their consumption in the process. A manufacturer with too many good quality parts waiting to be used is not using

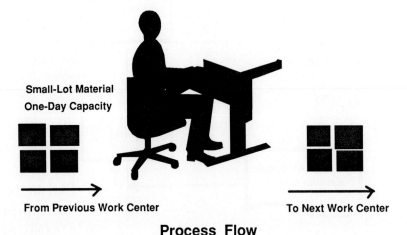

Small-Lot Material
One-Day Capacity

From Previous Work Center

To Next Work Center

**Process Flow**

**Figure 2.4**   Small-Lot-Size Concept in Just-in-Time

the system properly. The quality of the waiting parts is also at risk, because changes in the process or in the product itself could make the parts obsolete.

## 2.6 THE NEED FOR A QUALITY SYSTEM IN A JUST-IN-TIME ENVIRONMENT

Just-in-Time strives to reduce the excess material required to meet the demand of a process. This approach limits the capability of the manufacturer to replace defective parts when they appear in the process. In Just-in-Time a defective part is also a waste and therefore should be minimized. All the effort invested in shipping a bad part from a supplier, receiving it, and moving it to the work center has been wasted. There is also wasted effort in returning the part to the manufacturer for repair or replacement. The Just-in-Time and quality systems should be implemented at the same time. If the manufacturer has no resources with which to implement both systems at the same time, it is better to reduce the scope of the Just-in-Time system and implement the quality system first. The implementation of one without the other will create major interruptions in the manufacturer's process.

## 2.7 QUALITY AT THE SOURCE

It is not difficult to make a case for good quality at the source of the parts. The manufacturer of a part should be responsible for producing quality-perfect parts the first time, and should also be held accountable for wasting customers' time and money processing and returning defective parts. A defective part slipping through a process is a product built incorrectly and will surely produce an unsatisfied customer. A manufacturer burdened with a system constantly rejecting defective parts is doomed to failure. No supplier should burden its customers with this problem; no supplier will survive if it does.

The best way to ensure perfect quality at the source of the part is to implement a program designed to put emphasis on this aspect of quality. Most manufacturers claim the quality systems in their factories are great. But the same manufacturers fail to maintain a quality program with their suppliers to reduce the number of defective parts in the suppliers' process. The main thrust of a Just-in-Time quality system is to solve all quality issues with suppliers before parts are shipped. This is the area where the return on the Just-in-Time quality system will be greatest. It will also help to increase the efficiency of the manufacturer by requiring only a small organization to monitor the quality of its own process.

A first-class supplier quality program is critical to the success of Just-in-Time. Chapter 6 addresses this topic and provides guidelines on how to implement a program that is effective and successful—not a police system that forces a supplier to improve quality, or else. The system will work by implementing the idea of prevention and process control. It will also use the concept of *partnership* between the supplier and the customer.

## 2.8 THE COST OF POOR QUALITY

Very few manufacturers know exactly how much poor quality costs them. A manufacturer with good systems and controls in place normally tracks reject rates, rework, and scrap costs. But this information is only the obvious cost of bad quality. There are many intangible costs that escape the system because they are difficult to measure: for example, customer satisfaction and impact on sales. Chapter 11 will address this topic and will show methods proven to detect the true cost of quality and how to reduce this cost to acceptable levels.

In Just-in-Time, a quality organization that spends its resources inspecting and rejecting parts is adding no value to a product, and is therefore a waste. This effort should be minimized by solving the problems that caused faulty quality, so there is no need to have a large inspecting staff to detect mistakes. The best way to solve this problem is not to increase the inspecting effort at the source of the part, but to improve the supplier's process used to build the part so there are no defects. The supplier is responsible for taking corrective actions and solving quality problems.

## 2.9 QUALITY AND PRODUCTIVITY

Quality and manufacturing productivity are directly related. Poor quality causes low productivity. The best way to improve productivity is to make sure that every worker's activity in the factory produces an added value to the product in the process. A part of poor quality will consume a worker's effort that is wasted.

There are other wasted efforts that are not clearly visible but that affect the productivity of a worker. For example, the layout of a work center will determine whether a worker wastes time reaching for the parts and the tools needed to build the product. If the worker is using a part that is defective and that has to be replaced later when an inspector discovers it, productivity will be further diminished.

In general, poor quality affects productivity by wasting labor and material that has to be replaced or reworked. Quality is essential to operating a productive manufacturing organization. No matter how much automation and labor efficiency the process has in place, the worker or the machines still need to use quality-perfect parts to avoid wasting labor.

A first-class manufacturing team means a productive organization that is lean and effective, including workers' productivity in the quality organization.

## 2.10 SUMMARY

The implementation of a Just-in-Time system and a quality system at the same time could be burdensome for a manufacturer. It is essential that both systems exist at the same time; otherwise, Just-in-Time will fail. If the manufacturer doesn't have sufficient resources to implement both systems at the same time, it is best to reduce the scope of the Just-in-Time program and to implement the quality system first. This setting of priorities will ensure success.

The other choice is to reduce the scope of both systems and apply them on a reduced scale to a product line and to a subset of suppliers. This will give experience in implementing both systems, increasing the confidence of the team implementing them. This approach is the recommended one. Once a product line is under a Just-in-Time system and the proper quality system is implemented, other products can be added to the list, including new suppliers. The experience gained in the first phase will make the second product transition quicker and more effective.

## REFERENCES

HANNAH, KIMBALL H. "Just-in-Time: Meeting the Competitive Challenge." *Production and Inventory Management* 28, no. 3 (1987): 1–3.

HAYES, ROBERT H., and STEVEN C. WHEELWRIGHT. *Restoring Our Competitive Edge: Competing Through Manufacturing.* New York: John Wiley & Sons, 1984.

HERNANDEZ, ARNALDO. *Just-in-Time Manufacturing: A Practical Approach.* Englewood Cliffs, N.J.: Prentice-Hall, 1989.

ROBINSON, ALAN, ed. *Continuous Improvement in Operations: A Systematic Approach to Waste Reduction.* Cambridge, Mass.: Productivity Press, 1991.

SCHONBERGER, RICHARD J. *Japanese Manufacturing Techniques: Nine Hidden Lessons in Simplicity.* New York: The Free Press, 1982.

# 3★

# The Quality System:
# Program Concepts

Implementing a Just-in-Time quality system requires organization, persistence, and attention to detail. The quality department is responsible for implementing such a system, but in order to succeed, the program needs the commitment and assistance of the rest of the company. The first step for such a program is to develop a quality strategy that covers all operational aspects of the company. A clear, well-designed strategy should be viewed as a beacon that will guide quality improvement programs in every department in the company toward the common goal of product excellence and complete customer satisfaction.

The main directive toward developing a quality strategy should come from top management in the company. Management commitment and support should not stop after the strategic goals are defined. Management should be made an integral part of the process, by participating in the implementation of the system. This is a clear departure from cases in which management's lip service is used to support such an effort.

Another important aspect in the implementation of a quality system is the allocation of resources. The program should be properly staffed to achieve the established goals. Conversely, the goals should be adjusted and given priority to match the resources available in the organization. Failure to do this will cause the program either to fail or to be poorly implemented.

A Just-in-Time quality system implemented at the same time as a Just-in-Time system will require two sets of resources working together as a team. The need for a team approach to succeed is critical to both programs. Tasks and goals should be closely coordinated, so that neither will get ahead of the other. For example, the Just-in-Time system can't stop receiving inspection and buffer inventories until the quality system has suppliers already participating in the quality program. The implementation of a Just-in-Time system and a quality system is like laying a railroad track: The rails should be assembled at the same time, and neither track should get ahead of the other.

## 3.1 COMMITMENT TO QUALITY

Many quality books call for the commitment to quality to start at the top of a company. In reality, quality needs more broadly based support to reach the level of excellence that is required in today's market environment. The practice of perfect quality should be embraced by every employee of the company without distinction as to job or rank. This commitment should not be only verbal or implied: It should be continuously proven by actions that every person is responsible. For example, a worker in a production line should show a commitment to quality by consciously following the principles learned in the quality training programs. A middle manager should show commitment to quality by providing workers with all the necessary training and tools required to do a first-class job. The manager should also stick to the rules when quality issues stand in the way of production output. This is one of the most common situations that causes morale problems when implementing a quality program. Quality rules should be firm and not subject to reinterpretation when faced with a conflicting situation of production output versus quality output.

Finally, top management should avoid giving only lip service to a quality program— the kiss of death to the program. Managers should show their commitment by approving adequate resources and giving budgetary support. They should also show commitment by personally participating in some critical areas of the program that are difficult and highly critical.

Nothing more threatens the success of a quality system than apathy and lack of commitment on the part of the team in charge of the implementation. Commitment to a new program doesn't grow overnight, nor is it achieved by just telling the team they are committed. There should be a strategy, a plan, a set of goals, and a clear path of implementation to achieve these. The quality team should have 100 percent ownership of the program to make it successful. Feedback and corrections along the way from the people on the team will also lead to ownership.

The following steps are important to create workers' interest and commitment:

1. Present to workers the strategy for the Just-in-Time quality system and get their input as to what needs to be improved or changed. Define clearly the workers' roles in the implementation.
2. Show workers the training and tools that will be provided to implement the system.
3. During implementation, ask workers for periodic feedback as to the weak points of the program and what has to change in order to increase the probability of success.
4. Schedule periodic progress reviews with top management. Give workers an opportunity to express their opinions to management about possible improvements that need to be made.

A Just-in-Time quality system introduces a diverse set of rules to solve common operational problems, which is very different from the old way of assuring quality. These changes tend to create skeptics among the people affected by the changes, who will stay on the sidelines waiting for the system to fail.

Commitment to a Just-in-Time quality system doesn't occur overnight. The process is one of earning the trust of the people involved in the program rather than imposing acceptance. The system needs to show continuous improvement toward published goals. This is a process of building enthusiasm along the way. The objective is to make every participating worker an individual winner and a proud participant.

## 3.2 STRATEGY FOR A JUST-IN-TIME QUALITY SYSTEM

Developing the strategy for a Just-in-Time quality system should be a cooperative effort among different departments in the company. The postulate of the strategy should be clear and to the point. A one-page strategy should be sufficient for this purpose.

The strategy should reflect the business goals of the company. It should also be clearly understood at all levels of the organization and easily translated into goals that are obtainable. This last point is important because the definition of a strategy for quality should not be a list of goals for workers to meet. In general, quality goals are landmarks that workers have to reach; once reached, the landmarks will be moved further out to challenge workers again. If the strategy is viewed as a set of goals, workers will see changes in these goals as a change in strategy.

Key points that a quality strategy should cover are:

1. The quality strategy of the company should be an extension of its business goals.
2. The strategy should be simple and easily understood by everybody in the organization.
3. The strategy should define the quality of the products as the customers will perceive them.
4. The strategy should be reasonable and easily translated into tactical goals.
5. The strategy should cover a reasonable period of time and it should be reviewed periodically to match company or market needs.
6. The strategy should cover all the areas of the company that directly affect the quality of its products, for example, the engineering department and the field service organization.
7. The quality strategy should be viewed as a competitive business advantage.

The strategy should cover specific areas of responsibility and priorities to guide the implementation effort:

1. Quality should strive for complete customer satisfaction.
2. Quality has overriding power over production output.
3. The makers of the part are the people responsible for its quality.
4. Quality starts at the design phase and it should take priority over design options.
5. The quality system should place emphasis on prevention rather than on inspection.
6. Quality problems should be solved immediately and take priority over anything else.

Management plays a key role in leadership, not only defining the quality strategy but making it believable by allocating the resources necessary to make it happen. The strategy should cover a period of three to five years and it should translate into reasonable tactics and goals that are implemented by middle management and workers. Both—the tactics and the goals—could be reviewed and adjusted at any time as the program advances.

## 3.3 PEOPLE PARTICIPATION TO DEFINE THE PROGRAM'S GOALS

Once the quality strategy has been defined, the next step is to translate it into a set of goals that carries out the implementation. After the strategy definition this effort is the most important. A set of goals is the engine that drives the quality effort in a company. Goals are a yardstick to measure the progress of the effort to implement the strategy. Goals should also be the result of a collective effort on the part of the people responsible for meeting them. To set a series of goals in which only management has participated, later imposing the burden of achieving the goals on workers, is a blueprint for failure.

There are a few important rules to remember when goals are set. The team involved in the effort should stick to these rules to ensure the success of the program.

1. Goals should be an extension of the quality strategy of the company.
2. Goals should challenge the people involved in reaching them, but they should be obtainable.
3. Don't list goals for which there are no resources. Goals should match the resources allocated to reach them.
4. Initial goals should be an improvement on the initial assessment of the item considered in the goal. Section 3.4 deals with this subject.
5. There is no final goal achieved in quality. Once the current goal is reached, new goals should be set, one step beyond the ones just attained.
6. Achievement of the goals should lead toward the full implementation of the company's strategy for quality.

## 3.4 INITIAL GOAL ASSESSMENT

The first step in setting the quality goals in a company is to assess the initial status of the task to be included in the goal. This effort requires an honest self-evaluation by the organization in order to come up with realistic numbers that can be improved. For example, suppose that one of the goals is to improve the final inspection yields at the end of a production line for a particular product. The first step is to verify the value of the yields currently at that point in the process. The next step is to determine what changes in the process are required to improve the yields and which yield level should be the next goal. Figure 3.1 shows the process required for evaluating and setting goals. The process is iterative and requires changes in the system to cause improvements down the line.

Goals should be time phased. Once set, they should be monitored to make sure they are achieved. Going back to the first example, suppose that after an evaluation of the final inspection yields of a product, current yield levels are shown to be 90 percent. Once the process is changed to improve the yields, the new goal could be set to 95 percent in three months and 98 percent in six months. The strategic goal of the company, however, is to achieve 100 percent final inspection yields within one year. This final goal should be the magnet that pulls the progressive goals to higher levels.

Other typical goals for quality improvement could be: reduction of product dead on arrival (DOA) rates; reduction of incoming inspection with a group of suppliers; yield improvements throughout a process for a product; reduction of paperwork in the purchasing department; reduction of the number of engineering changes for new products; reduction of scrap and rework; reduction of line down instances because of material shortages; increase in customer satisfaction by a certain percentage, which should ultimately be 100 percent.

## 3.5 DEFINING THE PRIORITY OF THE GOALS

Once the set of goals is defined, it is important to order goals by priority. Goals related to customer satisfaction should always have highest priority. These are goals that directly affect the quality of the product the customer will receive. For example, a goal that achieves a higher final inspection rate is more important than a goal that looks at the raw material at the beginning of the production line. This doesn't mean the second goal is not important, because increasing the level of the quality of the parts at the beginning of a process will help to increase the yields at the other end. But improving only receiving material, ignoring the process and the final quality of the finished product, will cause immediate customer dissatisfaction.

Achieving goals evenly will improve the quality health of the product and with it the image of the company. It will also reduce the waste produced by rework and scrap. Table 3.1 shows a list of goals that should be included in the quality program and their typical values. The starting point of these goals will depend on their initial assessment for a particular process. The final goal should always be perfection.

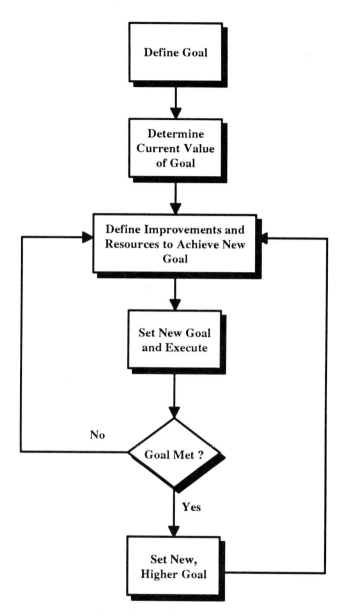

**Figure 3.1**   The Goal-Setting Process

**TABLE 3.1**   TYPICAL VALUES FOR QUALITY GOALS

| Strategic Quality Goals | Areas of Impact | Initial Goal | Final Goal |
|---|---|---|---|
| Dead on arrival (DOA) | Customer satisfaction | 98% | 100% |
| Ship on time | Customer satisfaction | 95% | 100% |
| Infant mortality | Customer satisfaction | 98% | 100% |
| Time to service | Customer satisfaction | 8 hr | 4 hr |
| Suppliers into JIT/TQC program | Supplier program | 20% | 80% |
| Reduce receiving inspection | Supplier program | 10% | 70% |
| Final inspection yields | Customer satisfaction | 95% | 100% |
| Eliminate in-line quality inspectors | Process improvement | 50% | 100% |
| Reduce rework and scrap | Process improvement | 50% | 90% |

## 3.6 PROGRAM DEFINITION AND IMPLEMENTATION STEPS

The first step in defining the Just-in-Time quality program is to select critical areas of implementation. The second step is to select programs and goals to implement within them. Figure 3.2 shows the areas that cover all key activities in a manufacturing organization. The following chapters will present a detailed plan to implement the Just-in-Time quality system in every one of these activities. It is important first to define the areas of activity and the people responsible for implementing the program in them. Then the allocation of adequate resources to get the job done correctly will follow.

The first area requiring priority is the one that relates to the customers of the company. This area should be the driving force that shapes the scope and effort of the quality program. No matter how the quality program is shaped and implemented, the final goal should always be to achieve total customer satisfaction. It is important first to define the customers' requirements for full satisfaction as they relate to the products or services they receive. The following sequence provides customer satisfaction first:

1. Define the quality goals for products delivered to customers in order to achieve their full satisfaction.
2. Define the quality goals for the process to manufacture those products.
3. Define the quality goals for suppliers whose raw materials build those products.
4. Define the quality goals of the field service organization that supports customers.
5. Define the design engineering quality goals to design quality into the product.
6. Define the overall quality goals of the corporation to deal with customer satisfaction and elimination of waste.

Remember, in every one of these cases it is very important that the goals have adequate resources allocated to reach them. These resources not only include people, but equipment and process changes and training. The changes implemented should also be properly budgeted. Expenses should be reasonable and should not burden the financial health of the company.

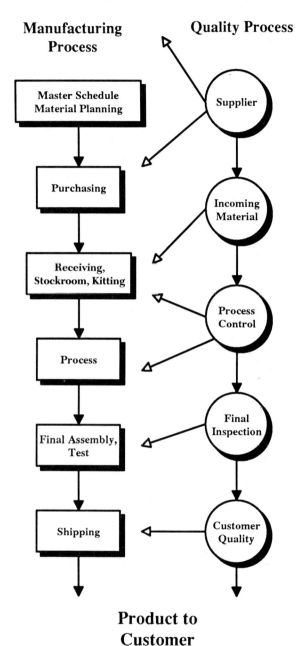

**Product to
Customer**

**Figure 3.2**  Strategic Areas of a Quality
Control Program in Manufacturing

## 3.7 THE QUALITY TEAM

It is well known that quality is everybody's business in a company. This statement is generally true, but the quality department is responsible for making sure the word gets around, and that it is believed and practiced by everyone in the organization.

The job of a quality department in a company is not to police quality—quality can never be policed. The role of the quality department is a missionary one. Its job is to make sure everyone embraces the discipline of doing their jobs with a quality-minded conscience every second of the day. The quality department is the driving force that keeps the goal of perfect quality in front of everyone. The quality department should have total top management support to do its job.

The setting of quality goals should be achieved by quality teams assigned the responsibility for drafting them. These quality teams should include people from different departments involved in achieving the goals. For example, a quality team composed of a quality supplier engineer, manufacturing engineer, and a buyer from the purchasing department should set the goals related to suppliers.

Quality teams should avoid becoming bureaucratic and burdened with red tape. They should be small and composed of a cross section of the workforce and middle management. The leader of the team could be a quality engineer or a person with enough responsibility and authority to make things happen. The quality team is the first step in assigning responsibilities to specific areas of the Just-in-Time quality program. The team will proceed to make a list of goals it wants to achieve to reflect the quality strategy of the company. The next step is to get an initial assessment of these goals before the program is started. The quality team will report to a council in charge of monitoring the quality program across the company. This council for quality should have members at all levels in the organization. The council should also be small and not bureaucratic.

## 3.8 MANAGEMENT INVOLVEMENT

Management involvement in the selection of the quality teams should be minimal. Management's role is support and delegation. Support is provided in different ways. One of the key aspects of support is in the area of resources. Nothing is more frustrating and demoralizing to a quality team than not having adequate resources to implement its program. If the company doesn't have the financial muscle to provide full support to the quality program, it is better to confine the scope of the program to key areas that will maximize return. A narrow, focused quality program with full allocation of resources is much better than a large and ambitious one with a poor allocation of resources; this will cast doubts on the sincerity of top management and its commitment to the program.

Top managers should definitively participate in the definition of the company strategy for quality. Tactical implementation for achieving goals that carry out the strategy is left to middle management and workers. The role of the managers is of support to the program and delegation of authority.

Management should be informed periodically of the progress of the program and should make corrections to the strategy as the implementation progresses and feedback of the program is analyzed. Strategies could change as the internal conditions that contributed to their development change. There could also be changes in strategy as the conditions of the marketplace change. Management feedback and acknowledgment of the program's progress is very important to maintain the morale of the workers involved.

## 3.9 LAUNCHING THE QUALITY PROGRAM

Launching a Just-in-Time quality program should be a big event within the company. All the people involved in the implementation, and the people receiving its benefits, should be gathered in a meeting and presented with the concepts and goals of the program. Nothing will add more credibility to the effort than a description of the resources allocated to make the program successful.

The presentation of the quality plan should start with an overview of the company's strategic goals. The goals should be explained in enough detail to show how they are going to affect the people that do business with the company. Every goal should also have a direct impact on the company's business and should be translated into some measurable return.

Another important aspect of launching a Just-in-Time quality program is related to the suppliers of the company; Chapter 6 addresses this. A good first step is to call a suppliers' day to announce the program and the strategic goals associated with it. The suppliers' day meeting should not be threatening. It should mark the start of a new strategic alliance for quality between the company and its suppliers—a true partnership.

The presence of top management in both meetings is very important. This will give a signal that the program has the support of management. After the program is launched, several review meetings should be scheduled with the same people who attended the launching effort. Periodic reviews will show progress, setbacks and steps taken to correct them, and the intention to get everyone involved. These meetings should be honest and should present successes as well as outstanding problems. A realistic appraisal is very important to make the program believable.

## 3.10 SUMMARY

Defining and launching a quality program is no small task. There should be careful attention to details and the avoidance of too much optimism. It is the job of management to provide guidance and support. It is the job of the workers and first line managers to provide realistic results. Managers don't implement the system, workers do. But workers can't do it without the proper training and allocation of resources. That's the job of management.

The key to a successful Just-in-Time quality program is not just related to the amount of resources that are allocated to do the job. The key is the attention given to using the resources efficiently and the tenacity of the team to succeed no matter what problem is encountered. A quality program never ends. Goals reached are then, by their nature, obsolete. New goals should replace them. The new goals should be more aggressive and challenging than the old ones. This approach will keep workers interested and challenged in achieving this new level of perfection.

Another factor in improving the odds for success is innovation. When a quality team fails to achieve a goal, a detailed analysis of the causes might prove the approach used to achieve that goal is the wrong one and it should be changed. It is very important that the team have an open mind in analyzing results and coming up with changes if the current effort is not yielding the right returns.

# REFERENCES

FEIGENBAUM, ARMAND V. *Total Quality Control*. New York: McGraw-Hill, 1983, pp. 91–108.

HERNANDEZ, ARNALDO. *Just-in-Time Manufacturing: A Practical Approach*. Englewood Cliffs, N.J.: Prentice-Hall, 1989, pp. 123–143.

JURAN, J. M. *Juran on Planning for Quality*. New York: The Free Press, 1988.

KAYDOS, QILL. *Measuring, Managing, and Maximizing Performance*. Cambridge, Mass.: Productivity Press, 1991.

PERIGORD, MICHEL. *Achieving Total Quality Management: A Program for Action*. Cambridge, Mass.: Productivity Press, 1991.

# 4★

# *Quality in the Factory: The First Step*

Once the quality strategy is translated into a quality plan, the first implementation phase should start with the process in the factory. This should precede any attempt to work with suppliers and customers, in an attempt to put your house in order before dealing with external factors. Properly implemented, this will provide valuable information needed in dealing with the outside world during the second phase of the implementation.

The effort to improve the factory process should yield information about the quality of the parts used to build the products. This information will be vital in showing the supplier responsible for the parts the problems the process encounters because of poor quality. Nothing is more effective when working with a troublesome supplier than showing quality data to support your list of problems. This information will help the supplier to focus his or her effort on the corrections required.

Another area that will benefit from an early improvement in the factory process is customer satisfaction. An improved process not only reduces waste and rework, but improves yields by reducing defects. Defective parts are less likely to slip through the system and find their way into a box as part of a product heading for a customer.

Process improvements should be worked out from both ends. First, begin the process with the parts arriving from suppliers. The effort here should focus on evaluating the quality of the parts, giving a clear understanding of which suppliers are causing most of the trouble. The result of this effort should be a suppliers' correction list for the quality team to work on.

The second area that requires immediate attention is the final inspection system at the end of the process. A final inspector is the representative of the customer inside the manufacturing process, and the last person who stands between a bad product and the customer. Effort should be placed on improving this area immediately. Improvements should include yield increases and the reduction of bad products that slip through. This approach should be only temporary, because working on final inspection to improve the quality of a product is a brute-force approach that will not produce consistently high-quality deliveries to customers. Only changes in the process and an increase in the quality of the parts at the beginning of the process will produce consistent results.

## 4.1 DESIGNING A QUALITY SYSTEM FOR A PROCESS

When a product is released to manufacturing, the first step manufacturing engineering takes is to design a process to build it. This should start concurrent with the design phase of the product, so manufacturability is considered at the early stages of the project. A manufacturing process is a series of steps required to build a product. The process is commonly defined by a flowchart that shows a linked series of work centers in the factory. Detailed descriptions of manufacturing tasks are prepared at every work center to inform workers about their jobs. Figure 4.1 shows a typical process flow for an electronic assembly product. Every box in the process represents a work center. A manufacturing process instruction, MPI, will describe the series of tasks the worker has to complete in the process. Figure 4.2 shows a typical MPI used at Relevant Technologies.

The quality system monitors the quality of a product built. The system is a special intensive-care environment designed to read the vital signs of a process. Its job is to flag immediately any deviation from the norm of the process, as products are built. This deviation might occur in the form of a quality problem with parts or some faulty workers' activity that is out of spec with the process. A quality system should be tailored to the needs of the process and the product being built. It should also produce results that match the strategic goals of the company.

A quality system and a process flow for a product should be closely linked. Both systems should meet the requirements for performance and quality the designers of the product had in mind. Figure 4.3 shows a typical flow of a quality system implemented at Relevant Technologies.

There are important guidelines for a quality system to use in monitoring the quality of a process. These guidelines are different for a batch-mode, work-order oriented process. A Just-in-Time production line requires a more integral and faster responding quality system than a work order system. A Just in Time quality system is less wasteful and does not have any inspectors looking over workers' shoulders. Workers are responsible for doing their own inspections. Below are listed several important factors to consider when designing a Just-in-Time quality system for a process:

1. Define the process areas of activity and the work centers assigned to them. Assign the responsibility for quality in those areas to workers.
2. Design the quality system to be responsive, not burdened with unnecessary steps that add no quality value to the process.

## GEM Subassemblies Process Flowchart

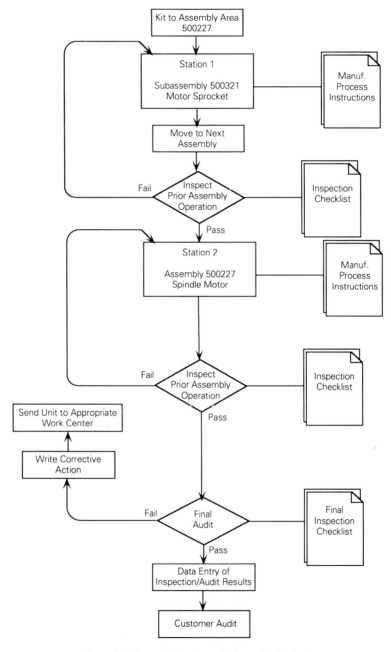

**Figure 4.1**   Process Flowchart at Relevant Technologies

Pg.4
Total Pages: 7
By:  Scott Froelich
Approval:
Effective: 8/1/92

Station:        Stn#1

## RELEVANT
### TECHNOLOGIES

# Manufacturing Instructions
## Assembly

**TITLE:**          Frame

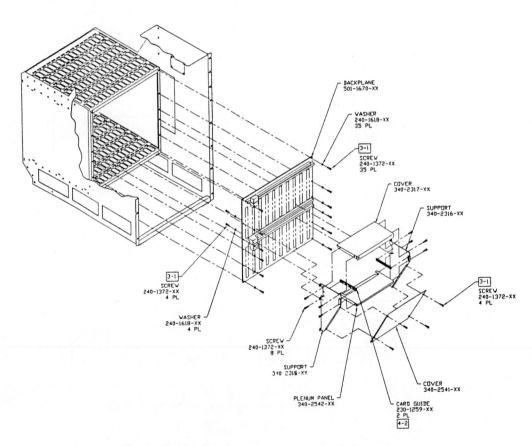

**Figure 4.2**   Manufacturing Instructions at Relevant Technologies

## RELEVANT
TECHNOLOGIES

## Manufacturing Instructions
### Assembly

Total Pages: 7
By:  Scott Froelich
Approval:
Effective: 8/1/92

**TITLE:**           . Frame

Station:           Stn#1

---

| Element No. | Element Description |
|---|---|
| 10 | Install a Plenum onto the left & right cntl bd supports with (4)Screws M4x.7x10 hex sem. |
| 20 | Install (2) Card guides onto the left & right cntl bd support by snapping into hole. Note: Ramped ends of card guides away from the backplane. |
| 30 | Install a Top control bd cover onto the left & right supports with (4)Screws M4x.7x10 hex sem. |
| 40 | Note: Have anti–static wrist strap on at all times while handling the Backplane Assy. Unpackage a Backplane Assy and place on work surface. |
| 50 | Install a Left cntl bd support onto the backplane with (2)Screws M4x.7x10 hex sem & (2)Flat washers M4. |
| 60 | Install a Right cntl bd support onto the backplane with (2)Screws M4x.7x10 hex sem & (2)Flat washers M4. |
| 70 | Unpackage a Card Cage Assy and place on work surface. Remove the slave backplane from the card cage and store for return to the supplier. |
| 80 | Install the Backplane Assy onto the card cage with (35)Screws M4x.7x10 hex sem & (35)Flat washers M4. |
| 85 | Install the Control Board Cover onto the supports with (4) Screws M4x.7x10 hex sem. |

**Figure 4.2**   (Continued)

## ALPHA I/O PANEL

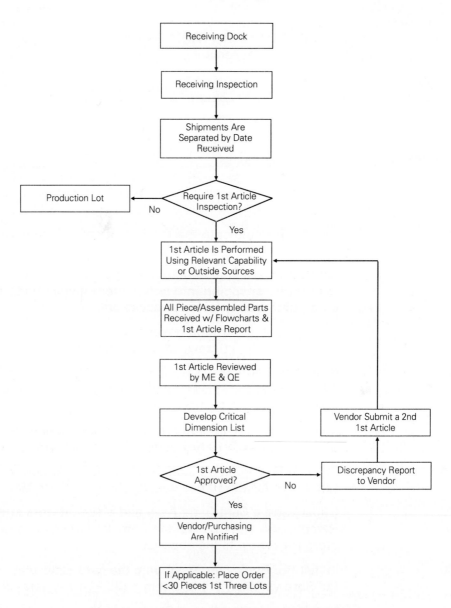

**Figure 4.3**   Quality Process Flowchart at Relevant Technologies

3. Give authority to workers to stop the production line whenever there is a problem that affects the quality of the product.

4. Make the quality data collection at work centers simple and real time. Assign workers to this task.

5. Quality inspection should always precede the work center process steps. This inspection should cover the work completed at the work center upstream in the process flow. Inspection should only take a fraction of the total labor absorbed in the work center.

## 4.2 QUALITY OWNERSHIP IN EVERY STEP OF A PROCESS

In a Just-in-Time quality system, the responsibility for quality is assigned to the makers of the parts. The new system blends the quality inspections in a process with the process itself in such a way that there is no difference between a process step and a quality step. Quality inspectors are eliminated; workers building the product do the inspecting.

Figure 4.4 shows a typical manufacturing flow with quality control inspectors seeded along the process. This approach burdens the process with overhead and lack of ownership on the part of the workers with respect to the quality of the product. A common reaction to quality problems is to blame quality control inspectors for not catching them in their stations. This is wrong and leaves the issue of ownership unresolved. Quality control inspectors are blamed for a problem they didn't cause.

Process bottlenecks are another common problem associated with quality control inspectors. Inspectors are gates through which the process flow has to squeeze in order to get to the next work center. At these gates, quality inspectors delay the flow of parts as they do their inspecting. In general, the inspectors only report defects, with very little authority to stop a line whenever there is a problem that is not catastrophic.

Figure 4.5 shows a system with no quality control inspectors. Workers on the line are trained to do inspections in addition to their jobs. To keep this system honest, workers are assigned to inspect the work done at the upstream work center. The inspecting steps should be taken before workers start their tasks (see Figure 4.6). This approach will reject any faulty part before more labor is invested in it. The faulty part should be returned to where it came from, so the worker who caused the problem fixes his or her own mistakes. Figure 4.3 shows some of the typical inspection steps a worker has to take before proceeding with his or her assigned task at the work center.

## 4.3 ELIMINATION OF QUALITY INSPECTORS

Eliminating quality control inspectors is not an easy task. Production workers' training in inspecting procedures should be in place before a successful transfer can occur. Taking quality inspectors out of a process means the inspecting responsibility is passed to workers building the product. The phaseover should be staged properly to avoid quality and morale

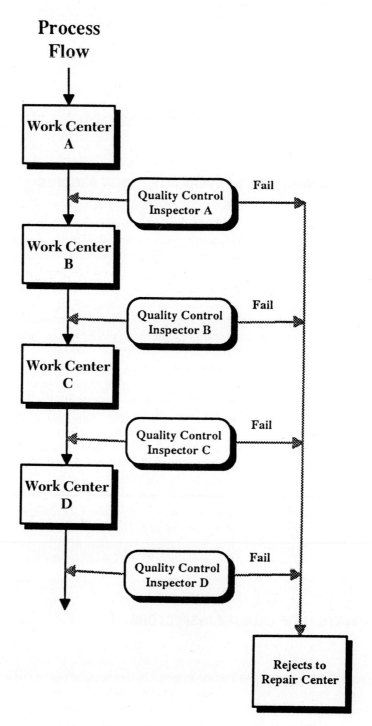

**Figure 4.4**  Process Flowchart with Quality Control Inspectors

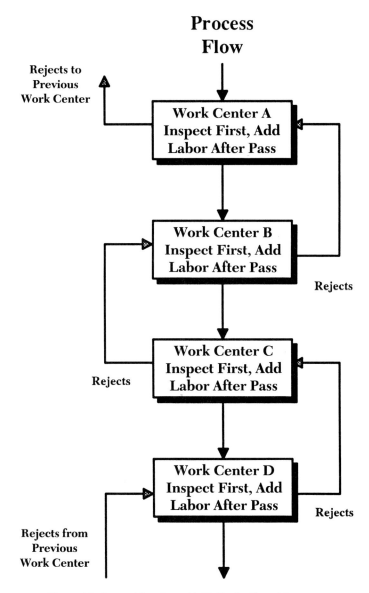

**Figure 4.5**    Process Flowchart with No Quality Control Inspectors

problems. Workers may feel they are burdened with more work, with no pay increase. It should be clearly communicated to workers that the responsibility for quality belongs to them, for they are the builders of the product—nobody knows better when there is a problem in the process than those working there. After all, they are the experts at putting the product together.

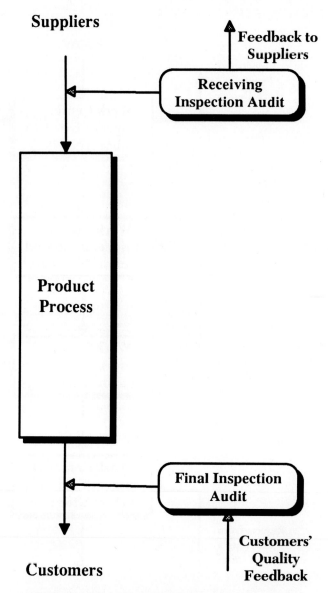

**Figure 4.6**  Checks and Balances in an Internal Quality System

Another problem with the shifting of responsibilities is what to do with the quality control inspectors. In a large manufacturing organization, these people can be absorbed into other jobs not necessarily related to inspection. In small organizations, there may not be any work available to them. This possibility should be considered carefully, and an outplacement program should be in place before removing inspectors from their jobs.

## 4.4 RESPONSIBILITY FOR QUALITY ASSIGNED TO WORKERS

The best way to assign the new task of inspecting a product to line workers is to prove there is no difference in the process between a process step and an inspecting step. Both operations are necessary in building a product and should be completed before the product leaves the work center.

Manufacturing engineers divide a process to build a product into a series of progressive steps that add labor and material value in increments. Quality engineers design inspection steps to ensure that labor and material added meet the quality standards of the product. These two sets of steps should fit like a hand in a glove. Both engineering groups should work closely to make sure that both sets of instructions complement each other to produce a product with perfect quality.

In a Just-in-Time system, process steps add value to a product. Quality steps, however, don't add any value. They merely verify that the process steps are implemented correctly. Inspecting steps should be considered overhead and should be minimized, but without compromising the quality of the process.

A first-class quality process should be composed of effective inspecting steps that address only critical quality issues in the product as they relate to the work center where the steps are included. One way to minimize the labor overhead introduced with the change is to design process steps that are foolproof and don't need workers' inspection. The Japanese have done this with the introduction of the poka-yoke system. Section 4.9 reviews this principle, showing some typical examples.

Most important in the transfer of quality responsibilities to line workers is to have a first-class training program. Normally, line workers are trained to build products, but are not trained to look for defects. A good training program should include a general section on quality, then a section tailored to each work center. The general section on quality is the more important one. The main goal of the training program is to develop a consciousness of quality in every worker attending the classes. It should also make sure workers understand that the responsibility for quality rests on their shoulders 100 percent of the time. A successful training program should produce quality-conscious workers who do nothing but high-quality work.

## 4.5 QUALITY TEAMS IN THE FACTORY

Just-in-Time calls for a reduction of buffer inventories and small-lot production runs. This operating mode eliminates the waste use of material on the production floor, but creates the need for fast responses, to solve quality problems when they occur. The system provides no replacement parts to cover for the defective ones to keep the process going. This characteristic of the Just-in-Time system forces the manufacturer to improve quality and reduce the level of rework on defective material. This approach requires a quick response on the part of technical people in charge of solving quality or process problems.

Quality teams in the factory are the first line of defense against quality problems that can stop a production line. Quality teams are doctors on duty call, ready to treat patients, and committed to staying with them until they are cured. Quality teams are normally composed of quality and manufacturing engineers who understand the technical variables of the process. The team should be available during the time the line is producing and, more importantly, as long as there is a problem causing a line stop.

In a manufacturing organization with several products in a process, there may be separate quality teams in charge of each one of them. This approach ensures that product support is available when it is needed. Quality teams should include supplier quality engineers who can work with suppliers in cases where a problem is related to a particular part procured from an outside source.

The job of a quality team should be preventing rather than reacting. One way to accomplish this is to have the quality team monitor process performance using a Statistical Process Control (SPC) system, then taking corrective action before the process reaches the limits specified to cause a line stop. Some of the key functions and responsibilities of the quality teams are:

1. The primary responsibility of quality teams is to support a process.
2. Quality teams should be composed of quality engineers, manufacturing engineers, and design engineers as backup for design-related problems.
3. Quality teams should operate on a preventive, rather than a reactionary, basis.
4. Quality teams should also work with suppliers to improve their quality.
5. Quality teams should understand the process, the product, and the SPC system that monitors process performance.
6. Solving a quality problem permanently should take priority over production output.
7. A goal of a quality team is to improve a process until workers can produce a product with zero defects.
8. The role of the quality teams is to provide tools, procedures, and process improvements, and to troubleshoot problems when they occur. The role of workers is to produce products with no defects.

## 4.6 PROBLEM DETECTION AND CORRECTION

Manufacturing is nothing but the efficient orchestration of subtasks leading to the completion of a product. But manufacturing is never free from problems, and success will depend on its ability to prevent problems before they occur. Long-term success will also depend on the organization's ability to solve problems permanently.

Problems need to be reported in order to solve them as soon as they happen, avoiding further quality damage. Workers are responsible for this task because they are the ones who are building the product. This responsibility, however, creates a conflict with workers. In manufacturing, worker performance is generally measured by the output produced, rather than the problems reported. The normal tendency of a worker is to overlook a problem until it is so evident that it has to be reported. A good training program will correct this problem by changing the mentality of workers. The training should emphasize that the quality of output is more important than the level of output. Quality should always take priority over volume. Chapter 7 will show how to set up a problem detection and correction system in manufacturing.

## 4.7 THE ROLE OF MANUFACTURING ENGINEERING

A common misunderstanding in many manufacturing organizations is that manufacturing engineering is only responsible for the design of the process that builds a product; then the responsibility for quality is assigned to the quality department. In a Just-in-Time system, every person who works in the company is responsible for the quality of the products the company produces. *No one is exempt from this responsibility.*

Manufacturing engineers influence the quality of the product by designing a process that produces a quality product. A quality process should produce a quality product at a reasonable cost. A process is defined by a flowchart showing the different steps required to build the product. Figure 4.1 shows a typical process chart. The chart includes a detailed description of the steps assigned to every work center involved in the process. Below are some of the key considerations a manufacturing engineer should take into account when designing a process:

1. Process instructions should be simple, pictorial, and easily understood by the workers.
2. A set of process instructions for a work center should be subdivided into small, simple steps that could be reassigned to other work centers in case of line imbalances.
3. Process instructions should be implemented without the possibility of ambiguous interpretation on the part of the worker.
4. Process instructions should specify setup times and associated overhead, at the same time minimizing these activities.
5. Process instructions should specify data collection and paperwork requirements. These should also be minimized.
6. Process instructions that require testing should include simple go/no-go checks with no debugging. All debugging functions should be performed outside of the main flow of the process.
7. A process instruction should specify an output goal for the work center. This goal should not be static and it should increase as the worker progresses on his or her learning curve.
8. The material called by the process instruction should be clearly identified. The process definition should also call for bins or feeding mechanisms needed to make material available in the work center. Ergonomics should also be considered.

9. A process should specify the minimal inventory required between two work centers to keep workers busy without any idle time. Any inventory over this limit is wasted.

10. Process instructions should track the revision level of the documentation that defines the product. Engineering changes to the original documentation should be recorded on the process instructions, even if they do not change the process.

11. The definition of the process should include labor standards to complete tasks.

12. The process should have a defined floor flow, a work center layout, and a description of any special tooling, or tools, that are required to do the job.

13. No one is authorized to change a process unless it is done with an engineering change control.

14. Process instructions should identify the training needed to perform functions at the work center.

## 4.8 QUALITY COMPLIANCE AND LINE STOP

Line stop is a powerful tool in assuring quality in a process. In a traditional manufacturing system, whenever there is a quality problem discovered by quality control inspectors, line workers continue producing bad parts until somebody with authority stops the line. The result is that bad parts accumulate while the decision to stop is being made. A Just-in-Time quality system produces different results. Line workers realize that something is wrong because they are the ones inspecting the parts. They stop the line, avoiding the accumulation of bad parts.

Authority to stop a production line is an important tool in a Just-in-Time system, but it should be properly exercised. Worker training and quick technical support are required to make this option work. Nothing is more demoralizing for a worker than to stop a line because he or she thinks there is a quality problem, then to find out that there is nothing wrong or nothing is being done about the problem. Workers must be properly trained and a set of clear rules on how to stop the line should be in place before the system is put to work. Below are some of the key points to consider before setting up a line stop procedure in a process:

1. Define clear rules for workers to follow in a line stop. Train the workers carefully to understand the rules and conditions that will lead to a line stop.

2. Once the line is down, there must be a technical team on site immediately to work on the problem that caused the line to stop.

3. Never restart a line without creating a corrective action of the problem that caused the line to stop. Workers will lose confidence in a system that ignores their calls for help.

4. Give authority to line supervisors to keep the line down until the cause of the problem has been determined and it has been solved. Never restart a line just to continue the production process. Line stop is the highest of all priorities.

5. If a worker makes a mistake and stops a line for an invalid reason, teach the worker

his or her error in judgment and never punish a worker for the mistake. When in doubt, workers should be encouraged to stop a line rather than to continue building a suspect product.

## 4.9 INSPECTION AND THE POKA-YOKE SYSTEM

An inspection step doesn't add any value to the process. It only verifies that the product inspected either meets some criteria or doesn't. In Just-in-Time this effort is considered a waste. The elimination of quality inspectors in a process adds a new burden on workers because it takes time away from their productive tasks. An efficient process should minimize the time workers spend inspecting a product in a work center. A good rule of thumb is to keep the inspecting process between 5 and 7 percent of the total time available in the work center. A process that requires inspecting time beyond this is nonproductive, and it should be redesigned. Conversely, a process that invests less than 5 percent of its time inspecting is more productive, but runs the risk of overlooking quality defects. The dilemma is to determine the amount of inspecting that should be designed into a process, what system is the best to use for inspections, and the return in quality that results from this effort. When the variables are sorted out and a system is in place, the human factor takes over and there are still defects that sneak through. Workers are human, and humans make mistakes.

Selecting an inspection system is important from two points of view: the amount of overhead the system imposes on the process and how accurately it measures the quality of the product passing through. This brings up the controversy between sampling inspections and 100 percent inspections. Sampling inspections use extrapolating methods to come up with a picture of the quality of the lot going through. This method is low in overhead because it doesn't require inspecting every part of a lot to come up with a quality opinion. One hundred percent inspections, on the other hand, tend to be monotonous, causing oversights on the part of the workers. A compromise would be to sample a large number of units, but reduce the number of inspections per unit to those critical inspections that accurately measure the quality of the product.

The previous approach presents the risk that minor defects might pass through the system, affecting the overall quality of the product. The Japanese solved this problem with the creation of the poka-yoke system. Poka-yoke in Japanese means "mistakeproofing." The idea originated in Japan in the early 1960s to prevent small mistakes in a manufacturing process by making it foolproof.

A poka-yoke system is a collection of devices that eliminate defects in the manufacturing process. These devices are generally mechanical, but they can also be procedural in nature. Their intent is to make manufacturing process steps simple and error free.

A poka-yoke device constantly checks a particular task for a preset criterion and will take some action when this criterion is not met. Poka-yoke devices operate independently of the control of a worker. The device can either stop the process if it detects something wrong or it can ring an alarm. Poka-yoke devices are simple in nature and very dedicated to the task they are designed to accomplish. There are no general rules for their design, other than they have the common goal of making a system foolproof.

A poka-yoke device is a dedicated inspector that will stop the process if it detects something wrong. This inspector makes no mistakes and will inspect 100 percent of the time. A combination of poka-yoke devices foolproofing most of the small steps in the process, coupled with 100 percent inspection of critical aspects of a part, could produce an excellent quality system with zero defects.

Examples of poka-yoke devices include magnetic sensors, limit switches, dispensing devices, or changes in the way a process step is implemented. A typical example is a process task in which a worker has to assemble two subassemblies using 15 screws. Normally, the worker fetches the screws from a bin containing a large number of screws. The job is monotonous and the worker can miss one or more screws if he or she is not attentive. A poka-yoke device would be a screw dispenser, so that every time the worker starts the task, the dispenser will supply the exact number of screws needed. At the end of the assembly job, the worker will check the dispenser to make sure there are no screws left, then the worker will fetch the next 15 screws for the next job.

Another example is when a stream of work centers uses electric or pneumatic screwdrivers to assemble products in a process. In general, manufacturers have a calibration procedure for the screwdrivers that follows a timetable. The tools are calibrated after a determined number of hours of use. This system doesn't take into consideration the actual usage of the tool. A poka-yoke device would be one that monitors the usage of the tool and then activates a timer. When the timer reaches the limit preset by the calibration procedure, the tool becomes inoperable until it is calibrated again.

Some key rules used to implement a poka-yoke system are:

1. Run a pilot process and make a list of the most common mistakes workers make while building the product.
2. Prioritize these mistakes in order of occurrence.
3. Prioritize the mistakes in order of importance.
4. Design a poka-yoke device for the top mistakes on both lists.
5. Always weigh the mistake frequency and cost before deciding whether it should be eliminated by a poka-yoke device or an inspection step. When economical, decide to implement a poka-yoke device instead of an inspection step.

## 4.10 QUALITY PERFORMANCE AND MEASUREMENT

Quality performance is difficult to measure. A manufacturer could have the most sophisticated system to control quality in a factory, but if the customer is not satisfied with the product, the effort is wasted. A good internal quality system that measures quality in a product doesn't necessarily guarantee customer satisfaction. There are too many subjective variables that are not measurable in defects per million or by an SPC chart. A first-class quality system should be tuned to the level of satisfaction of customers and the critical features of the product that are important to them. This is a difficult task because different customers have different opinions about what is important in a product.

Measuring quality in a factory is not independent from customers' needs, and it should be carefully correlated with the outside world, so no surprises will occur when a quality-perfect product is shipped and does not satisfy customer expectations.

## 4.11 MANAGEMENT SUPPORT

Quality systems need management support to be effective. Nothing is worse for a manufacturing organization than to get lip service from management. Support for quality must be shown by actions. Manager support is important at all times, and extremely important during trying times. For example, ordering a line stop at the end of the month because there is a quality problem is a clear indication that quality comes in first over production output. Keeping the line down until the problem is fixed shows determination and commitment to quality. Management support to quality should be unconditional, providing a sufficient budget and the proper tools to do a first-class job. This type of commitment will pay in the long run, when products will sell because of an excellent quality reputation and customer satisfaction. It will also pay when savings are generated by reducing rework, rejects, and line downs.

A successful quality program should make every worker a champion and a team player. This is a goal that should be high on the list of accomplishments of every manager.

## 4.12 SUMMARY

Perfect quality is only achieved by people with a strong resolve to reach perfection. Perfect quality is job ownership. The most important factors that will influence the success of a quality program are worker commitment and training. Any quality system will fail if workers don't believe in it or are poorly trained. The second important factor in achieving success is management support. Once these two conditions are met, there is nothing but success ahead if the system sticks to the third rule: constant improvement. Quality is nothing but a continuous evolution toward perfection by taking small steps of improvement one at a time.

When a Just-in-Time quality system is implemented, it is very important that realistic goals are set so that the system won't be considered a failure if goals are not met. It is better to lower the initial goal expectations rather than change them midstream because they are too difficult to reach to begin with. This will discourage workers and will undermine the credibility of the system. In summary, perfection is never achieved in one quantum leap, but it is surely reached in rather small consecutive steps that always move forward.

# REFERENCES

CROSBY, LEON B. "The Just-in-Time Manufacturing Process: Control of Quality and Quantity." *Production and Inventory Management*, 25, no. 4 (1984): 21–33.

FEIGENBAUM, ARMAND V. *Total Quality Control*. New York: McGraw-Hill, 1983, pp. 737–805.

GOLDRATT, ELIYAHU M., and JEFF COX. *The Goal. A Process of Ongoing Improvement*. Croton-on-Hudson, N.Y.: North River Press, 1986.

HARTLEY, JOHN R. *Concurrent Engineering, Shortening Lead Times, Raising Quality, and Lowering Costs*. Cambridge, Mass.: Productivity Press, 1991.

HENDRICK, THOMAS E. "The Pre-JIT/TQC Audit: First Step of the Journey." *Production and Inventory Management*, 28, no. 2 (1987): 132–142.

ISHIWATA, JUNICHI. *IE for the Shop Floor: Productivity Through Process Analysis*. Cambridge, Mass.: Productivity Press, 1991.

OHNO, TAICHI. *Toyota Production System: Beyond Large-Scale Production*. Cambridge, Mass.: Productivity Press, 1988.

SHIMBUN, NIKKAN KOGYO. *Poka-Yoke: Improving Product Quality by Preventing Defects*. Cambridge, Mass.: Productivity Press, 1989.

SHINGO, SHIGEO. *Zero Quality Control: Source Inspection and the Poka-Yoke System*. Cambridge, Mass.: Productivity Press, 1986.

SHINGO, SHIGEO. *A Revolution in Manufacturing: The SMED System*. Cambridge, Mass.: Productivity Press, 1985.

SHINGO, SHIGEO. *A Study of "TOYOTA" Production System: From Industrial Engineering Viewpoint*. Tokyo: Japan Management Association, 1981.

# 5★

# *Quality and Process Control: Build It Right*

In the business of manufacturing, nothing can be taken for granted. Once a process is defined, workers properly trained, and suppliers have begun shipping quality parts, it would be naive to assume that perfect-quality products will always pour out at the end of the process. There are so many things that can go wrong that something eventually *will* go wrong. Changes can happen in small increments, so that by the time workers—or even worse, customers—realize that something is wrong, there will be thousands of nonconforming products already shipped into the market.

The best way to keep a process under control is to assume it can go wrong at any moment. Manufacturing needs a system to track, analyze, and take corrective action should the process signal any deviation. A process control system is nothing but a positive feedback system where process data are collected and analyzed. If the data are within certain limits, nothing happens. If the data are out of limits, or heading in that direction, then a corrective action is applied to the process. Sometimes this corrective action is minor, amounting only to a simple tweaking. In other cases the corrective action required is major and should be applied quickly. The stability of a process will depend on the sensitivity of the monitoring system and the time it takes to implement corrective actions that bring things back to normal.

The concept of positive feedback is simple to use, but the methods of data collection, analysis, and feedback actions are critical to the process they monitor. This chapter will present some of these techniques used to ensure product quality and their tradeoffs.

A process control system is not very different from a life-support system. Both systems monitor the vital signs of the patient and create a series of stimuli to keep the patient within the limits established by the doctors. The health of a process relates to the quality of the product it produces.

## 5.1 PROCESS CAPABILITY

The capabilities of a process must be tailored to the requirements of the product it builds. It makes no sense to manufacture a product with tight tolerances with a process that is not capable of meeting them. Process capabilities must match the product's requirements with regard to accuracy and repeatability.

The first step in understanding the capabilities required for a process is to understand the tolerances associated with the product. Design engineers normally specify the tolerances of a product. These tolerances ensure the performance of a product within the operational range for which it was designed. Operating ranges for a product are not easy to ascertain, because they are difficult to gauge. The difficulty is to predict accurately the buildup of worst-case tolerances that can occur in volume production runs. Figure 5.1 shows the operating range of a typical product. The range is normally specified by a set of variables that plot the envelope of a curve showing the operation of the product. The type of variable will depend on the type of product. For example, a set of variables for an electronic product will be temperature, voltage, and speed of the devices used. For an electromechanical product, the variables will be temperature, voltage, and mechanical tolerances.

A process designed to build a product should consistently produce products that have an operating range within its limits. Figure 5.2 shows the relationship between a process curve and a product's operational curve. In real life, however, a process will produce products that fall within a range of operating ranges as they are determined by a variability curve. This curve is plotted using the values of variances that can occur in a process.

Figure 5.3 shows a cross section of the variability of a process as it relates to a product's tolerances. The figure shows that the limits of a process capability distribution should match the product's requirements, so there is no wasted area between them. It is also important that the process performance be centered on the performance area of the product, so products conform to operational specs.

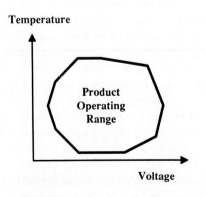

**Figure 5.1**  Product Operating Range

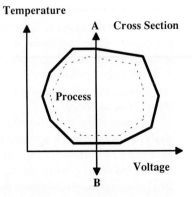

**Figure 5.2**  Relationship Between Process Capabilities and Product Operating Range

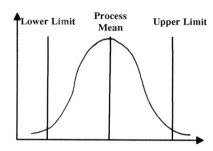

**Figure 5.3**  Variability of a Process Performance

## 5.2  PROCESS FLOW AND CONTROL

In a process material flows in a downstream fashion. Material always moves toward the end of the process, gathering labor and joining other material along the way. A work center in the middle of the process receives subassemblies from an upstream work center, performs some operation specified and perhaps adds more material, then sends the resulting subassembly to another work center downstream. This continuous flow of material and operations constitutes the process flow. Figure 5.4 shows the relationship between work centers in a process. Preceding process A, located at work center A, sends its output to work center B. The output of work center B is sent to work center C, which is the process subsequent to B. A work center could have many preceding processes or subsequent processes, depending on the flow of material and process steps.

A smooth process will run in a continuous flow of material and subassemblies with no wasted time on the part of the workers. The material traveling is always from preceding to subsequent processes. A system designed to monitor the quality of this flow should be dynamic enough to handle the volume of material moving from source to destination processes. Figure 5.5 shows an overview of the tasks that should occur in a work center for every operation step. Subassemblies and material arrive at the work center. The subassembly is first inspected for workmanship problems, per criteria set by the quality department. If the subassembly passes the criteria, the preceding work center performed the operation correctly. If the inspection fails, the subassembly is rejected and returned immediately to the preceding process. Just-in-Time calls for no inspection of material at a work center—the material should have been inspected at the source, the suppliers' production line. Rejected material is always returned to an MRB area. The ratio of passed subassemblies against the total arrived at the work center will determine the yield of the preceding work center.

The control criteria to pass or reject a subassembly should be clear and unambiguous to a worker. They should also be simple and easy to apply. If the criteria are complicated or require sophisticated measurements, the quality department should provide the proper tools to make the measurement simple and foolproof. A control criterion could be a measurement instrument with enough precision to meet process tolerances. It could also be a complicated test program that exercises the subassembly, to test its electronic parts. In any event, the criteria for passing or rejecting should be very clear; no parameters should be left to guessing.

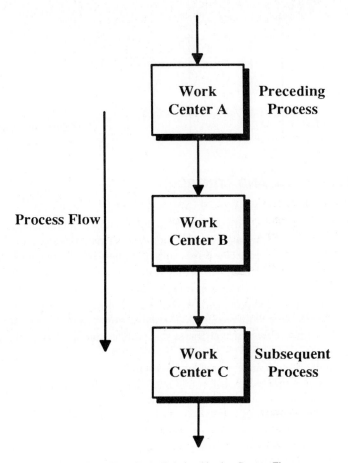

**Figure 5.4**   Work Center Relationships in a Process Flow

## 5.3 JUST-IN-TIME AND PROCESS DEFINITION

In a Just-in-Time system, anything that doesn't add value to a product is a waste; the only activity with value is one that builds a product. Activities that are considered a waste are material movement, material waiting, inspecting, and, of course, any rejection, rework, or idle worker time.

When manufacturing engineers design a process to build a product, they should clearly identify the *adding value time* of the process and the *nonproductive time* that decreases the productivity of the system. The engineers should spend considerable effort in eliminating the nonproductive time, or at least reducing it to a minimum.

Figure 5.6*a* shows a typical distribution of how a subassembly spends its time in a

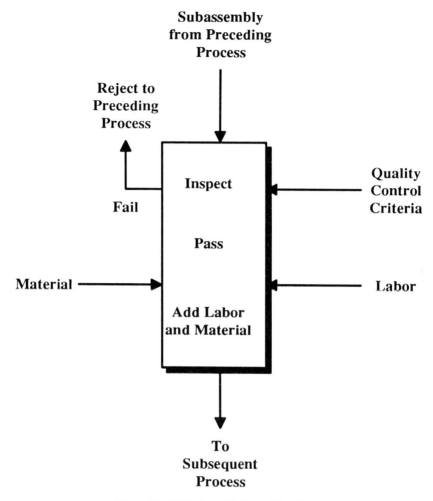

**Figure 5.5**    Work Center Division of Task Time

work center. A subassembly can be traveling, waiting, being tested or inspected, or having labor added by a worker. Just-in-Time considers assembly time the only activity that adds value to the subassembly. Figure 5.6*b* shows the overlapping of the subassembly's traveling time by providing a buffer of one at the work center. The worker will be working on assembly *N* while assembly *N*+1 is arriving. A further increase in productivity could be achieved by figuring out a way to test the just-arrived subassembly while the worker is still working on the previous one. This arrangement provides a 100 percent productivity output at the work center. Figure 5.6*c* shows this. It will require some kind of automatic testing at the work center to test the subassembly before work is added.

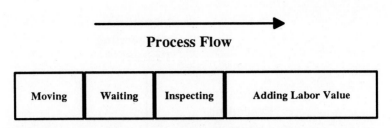

**Process Flow**

**Distribution of Time for Assembly N from Work Center 1 to Work Center 2**

*(a)*

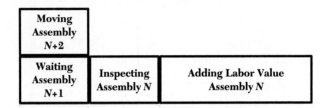

**Overlapping Assembly's Traveling Time**

*(b)*

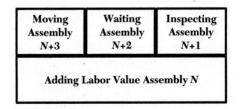

**Complete Overlap of Tasks**
**100% Productivity**

*(c)*

**Figure 5.6**   Breakdown of Process Tasks in a Just-in-Time System

## 5.4 PROCESS VARIATIONS DISTRIBUTION

A manufacturing process is statistical in nature. A process producing thousands of parts will never produce two exactly alike; there will be variations that will distinguish each part. As the process continues to produce parts, variations will repeat with a frequency of occurrence. This frequency of occurrence can be tallied in a frequency distribution table, indicating the distribution of the variances produced by the process. Figure 5.7 shows a simple way to obtain the frequency distribution for an operation in a process. Assume that a work center is machining small shafts, and that after the part is completed, the operator measures the diameter of the shaft and tallies this information on a table. The table will represent the frequency of distribution of the variations in diameter of the parts.

There are four important aspects of this table that need to be taken into consideration. They describe the value performance of the process at the work center. These four characteristics of the table will determine how well a process is performing.

1. The shape of the distribution table will show the probability distribution of the variances of the parts produced in the work center.
2. The width of the table will show the capability of the process to produce parts that only differentiate by small variances. A wide table shows the process is more out of control and has less capability to produce consistent parts. A narrow spread on the table will show that the process is under control, if the center of variances is centered around the value specified by the prints of the part.
3. The center of variances of the distribution table is calculated by the most occurrences of variances of the part. This center of variances represents the peak of the curve when the table is plotted in curve form.

| Diameter | Frequency Distribution |
|----------|------------------------|
| **1.335** | ///// |
| **1.336** | ///// / |
| **1.337** | ///// /// |
| **1.338** | ///// //// / |
| **1.339** | ///// ///// /// |
| **1.340** | ///// ///// // |
| **1.341** | ///// //// |
| **1.342** | ///// / |
| **1.343** | //// |

**Figure 5.7**  Tally of Frequency Distribution

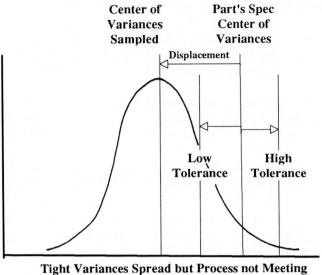

**Tight Variances Spread but Process not Meeting Specs**

*(a)*

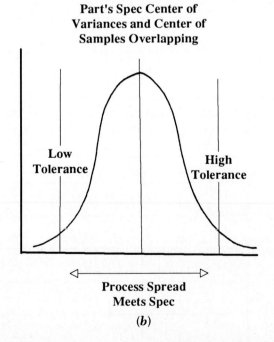

**Process Spread Meets Spec**

*(b)*

**Figure 5.8**  Representation of a Frequency Distribution in a Process

**4.** The difference between the center of variances and the value called on the specification of the part is very important. A process could be producing parts with a very
narrow distribution and a sharp center of variances peak, but still could be out of
control if its center of variances differs from the specification value on the print defining the part.

Figure 5.8*a* shows a curve representation of the frequency distribution table of Figure
5.7. The figure shows that the center of variances could be displaced from the actual center
of variances required by the part's spec. If this is the case, the process is not meeting the
requirements to produce the part to specifications. Figure 5.8*b* shows a process with a frequency distribution curve that meets the requirements of the part's specifications.

## 5.5 MEASUREMENT VALUES IN A FREQUENCY DISTRIBUTION OF VARIANCES

There are several measurement values that can be obtained from the frequency distribution
of variances in a series of readings. These values will play an important role in the distribution of values that defines the variances of a process. The most important measurement
values are as follows.

### Average Value

The *average* is nothing but the average value of all the readings obtained by adding them
and then dividing by the number of samples taken. The formula to calculate the average is
very simple. For a series of readings with values $x_1, x_2, x_3, ..., x_n$, the average $\bar{x}$ will be calculated as follows:

$$\bar{x} = \frac{x_1 + x_2 + x_3 + \cdots + x_n}{n}$$

For a large number of readings, the calculation of the average can be simplified by
calculating the average of groups of readings and then calculating the average of the aver-
ages. In this case $\bar{\bar{x}}$ is shown with a double bar at the top. The formula for calculating $\bar{\bar{x}}$ is:

$$\bar{\bar{x}} = \frac{\bar{x}_1 + \bar{x}_2 + \bar{x}_3 + \cdots + \bar{x}_n}{n}$$

For the readings listed in Figure 5.7, we can calculate the average of the variations:

$$\bar{x} = \frac{1.335 + 1.336 + 1.337 + \cdots + 1.343}{9} = 1.339$$

## Standard Deviation

The *standard deviation* measures the spread of variance readings of the sample measurements taken. The standard deviation has nothing to do with the size of the sample variable, only with its variances. The formula to calculate the standard deviation is

$$s = \sqrt{\frac{\sum\limits_{i=1}^{n}(x_i - \bar{x})^2}{(n-1)}}$$

The standard deviation for the samples shown in Figure 5.7 is calculated as follows:

$$s = \sqrt{\frac{(1.335 - 1.339)^2 + (1.336 - 1.339)^2 + (1.337 - 1.339)^2 + \cdots + (1.343 - 1.339)^2}{9-1}} = .0027386$$

## Average Standard Deviation

For a continuous process with large amounts of measurements, the *average standard deviation* can be calculated the same way as the average deviation. The calculation of the average standard deviation will simplify the system by allowing sets of standard deviation readings, and then averaging them into a single value:

$$\bar{s} = \frac{s_1 + s_2 + s_3 + \cdots + s_n}{n}$$

The average standard deviation provides a reliable measurement of the process variances spread throughout a series of measurements.

## Range

Another measurement that is important in a process is the *range*. The range is the biggest difference between two readings in a process. The value of the range is calculated by subtracting the lowest reading from the highest one. If we call $x_l$ and $x_h$ the lowest and the highest readings, the range value is as follows:

$$R = x_l - x_h$$

For Figure 5.7 the range is

$$R = 1.335 - 1.343 = 0.008$$

For cases where the measurements in the process are numerous and grouped, the average range can be calculated by the simple formula:

$$\bar{R} = \frac{R_1 + R_2 + R_3 + \cdots + R_n}{n}$$

The range provides a simple and quick way to see the trend of variations in a process. The standard deviation, however, provides a more accurate value for the actual trend of the process. For a small sample reading, the range is accurate and provides some value. The standard deviation is preferred to track variances in a process for large sample readings.

## 5.6 NORMAL DISTRIBUTION OF VARIANCES IN A PROCESS

Variations in a process are random in nature. If enough samples of variations are taken and plotted in a graph, the frequency distribution of the variances plotted against the parameter measured would have a bell shape called a *normal distribution*. The center of the normal distribution curve is the mean of the readings. There is a very important relationship between the mean and the standard deviation of the readings taken. The relationship provides the estimated probability where the variations will fall inside of the normal distribution curve. Figure 5.9 shows the relationship between the standard deviation $\sigma$ and the mean value $\bar{x}$ of the readings. The curve shows that:

- 68.27 percent of the variation readings will fall within $\bar{x} \pm 1\sigma$.
- 95.45 percent of the variation readings will fall within $\bar{x} \pm 2\sigma$.
- 99.73 percent of the variation readings will fall within $\bar{x} \pm 3\sigma$.

These percentages correspond to one, two, and three sigma values in a process. The variations in a process can be correlated to parts per million variations. For example, if a process has a three-sigma value, that means that all the population of variations from every million readings in the process will fall inside of the three-sigma area in the curve, with the exception of 2700 samples. Today processes are more tight than a three-sigma value and

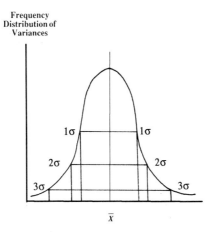

Variances

**Figure 5.9**   Relationship Between Standard Deviation and Mean

are measured in terms of *parts per million*, ppm. Most semiconductor processes operate well into the 100-ppm limits.

There is a relationship between the standard deviation calculated by doing a series of sample readings in the process and the standard deviation $\sigma$ shown in the normal distribution curve. Normally, a small sample population will not be accurate enough to calculate the standard deviation of a process. As the number of samples taken increases, the value of $s$ approaches the value of $\sigma$, and there is a corresponding value in the normal distribution curve. In Just-in-Time, taking samples for measuring the performance of a process should be reduced to a minimum. An efficient process should keep a proper balance between workers' productive time and time sampling. There are many tables in statistical control books that show the relationship between $s$ and $\sigma$. The entry point into these tables is the number of samples used to calculate $s$. The value of $\sigma$ can be obtained from the table, too.

## 5.7 DATA COLLECTION AND CONTROL CHARTS

The first step in setting up an SPC system is determining what types of data will accurately measure the quality performance of the process. Selecting the types of data and the frequency of their collection is not easy. Its influence on the overall opinion of the health of the process is extremely important. Another factor to consider is the people in charge of collecting the data and what tools are available to make the task accurate and simple.

Depending on the product and the process used, there are two types of data associated with them.

### Variable Data

*Variable data* are continuous in nature and are measurable on a sliding scale. These data can have a range of values and provide more information than attribute data. Variable data, however, are more difficult to measure because they require some kind of instrument and can be prone to error or misinterpretation. Workers taking variable data should be properly trained, and the instruments used to read the data should be calibrated frequently. Examples of variable data are voltage, weight, and dimension.

### Attribute Data

*Attribute data* are discrete in nature and can be binary. The system requires that workers clearly understand them, so there is no ambiguity when deciding the value of the data. One way to simplify the decision is to use a poka-yoke device to pass or fail a criterion. This technique not only saves time but will provide consistent measurements in the process. An example of attribute data is a pass/fail outcome of a test program for an electronic printed circuit module.

## Control Charts

Once the types of data samples are defined for a process, the next step is to plot a statistical chart that shows the trends of the process as it progresses to building products. *Control charts* show the performance of a process from two points of view. First, they show a snapshot of the process at the moment the data are collected. Second, they show the process trend as time advances. Process trends are important because they show the tendency to get out of control before it actually happens. Control charts help to detect variations in the process that are outside the normal operational limits. They also help to identify the causes of variations.

Figure 5.10 shows a basic configuration of a control chart. The $x$ axis will show the sequence in time of the variable's readings in the process. The $y$ axis shows the sample value of the readings. There are three horizontal lines that define the limits of the process. The center line represents the mean average of the readings. In the case of multiple readings, the center line is the average of the averages, $\bar{\bar{x}}$. The upper control limit, UCL, and the lower control limit, LCL, lines will determine when a process reading is out of control. Normally, most of the readings should fall between both lines. Any reading outside the limits implies the process is out of control and a corrective action has to take place.

Depending on the types of data measured in a process, there will be two distinct types of control charts. The following examples illustrate their use.

## Variable Data Charts

As the name indicates, these charts will use variable data sampled in a process. The variable data chart plots two statistical variable readings to give an idea of the tendency of the process. They are the frequency distribution of the variance readings and the spread of the readings. The chart is known as an $\bar{X}$ or $\bar{R}$ chart.

The formulas to calculate the UCL and the LCL for the $\bar{X}$ chart are

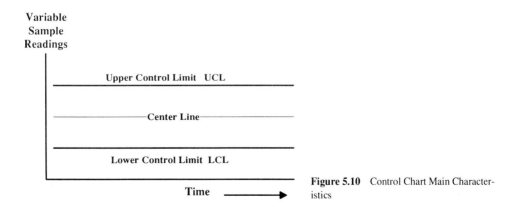

**Figure 5.10**    Control Chart Main Characteristics

$$\text{UCL} = \bar{\bar{x}} + A_2\bar{R}$$

$$\text{LCL} = \bar{\bar{x}} - A_2\bar{R}$$

The formulas to calculate the UCL and LCL for the $\bar{R}$ chart are

$$\text{UCL} = D_4\bar{R}$$

$$\text{LCL} = D_3\bar{R}$$

The values of $A_2$, $D_3$, and $D_4$ are constants that depend on the number of statistical samples taken in the process for a particular reading. These values can be found on tables in any statistical process control book.

For the example shown in Figure 5.7, we can now calculate the control limits for both charts.

The control limits for the $\bar{X}$ chart, using five readings per group, are

$$\text{UCL} = 1.339 + (0.58 \times 0.008) = 1.34364$$

$$\text{LCL} = 1.339 - (0.58 \times 0.008) = 1.33436$$

The control limits for the $\bar{R}$ chart, using five readings per group, are

$$\text{UCL} = 2.11 \times 0.008 = 0.01688$$

$$\text{LCL} = 0 \times 0.008 = 0$$

Figure 5.11 shows the limits plotted for both charts based on the data shown in Figure 5.7. The $\bar{X}$ chart shows the average performance of the process; the $\bar{R}$ chart shows the variability of the process. In general, the $\bar{X}$ chart behavior is process dependent. To improve the performance of this chart, it is necessary to make changes in the process itself. This means the equipment used in the process must be improved in order to improve the performance of the process. For example, if a machine tool producing shafts in a shop is changed for another one with more accuracy and repeatability, the $\bar{X}$ chart plotted on the second machine will have tighter control limits and better performance than the chart plotted for the first machine.

The $\bar{R}$ chart's performance is worker dependent. To improve the performance of this chart, it is necessary to improve the performance of the workers assigned to the process. Improving worker training will improve the performance of the chart. The quality of the material used will also affect the chart; an $\bar{R}$ chart out of control can indicate that bad material is being used in the process.

The criterion for a stable process is when all points on the plot fall inside the control limits. However, if the pattern of the plot is random and not repetitive, it indicates that the process is not stable, even if all the points fall inside the control limits. Some manufacturers have come up with a criteria list for defining an unstable process. The most common rules on the list refer to points outside the control limits:

# GEM SYSTEM

PN 500382

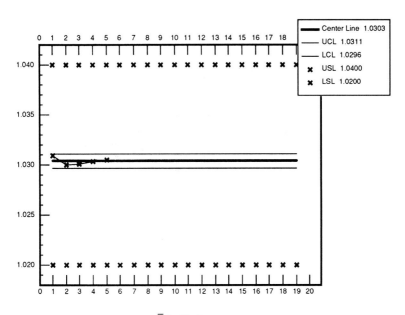

$\overline{X}$ Bar Chart

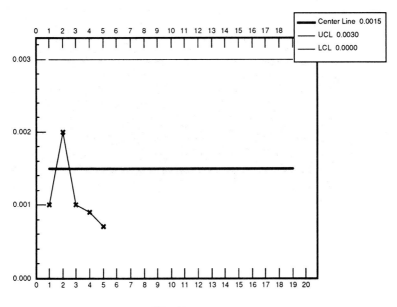

$\overline{R}$ Bar Chart

**Figure 5.11** $\overline{X}, \overline{R}$ Control Chart Plotting

1. Three consecutive points plotted inside the two-sigma limits.
2. Five consecutive points plotted beyond the one-sigma limits.
3. Eight or more successive points on one side of the central line.

Whatever criteria are used to define an unstable process, it is important that the procedure is always consistent and attention is paid immediately to out-of-control situations. Nothing frustrates workers more than to keep collecting process information for an SPC system, and then to realize that out-of-control situations are ignored by the people in charge of correcting them. When a process is out of control, there are nonconforming parts coming out—and that means bad quality.

## Attribute Data Charts

*Attribute data* are binary in nature and have different chart characteristics than variable data. The chart for attribute data shows those items that pass or fail requirements. Typical is a passed or failed inspection step based on process criteria: for example, a go/no-go test of electronic circuits that produces yield data or a number of percentage of some particular activity measured. Other examples would include a percentage of material shortages required to support a process and a percentage of errors made when material is kitted in the stockroom.

The attribute charts will have upper and lower control limits, but the formulas used to calculate them will be different from the variable data charts. The attribute charts can also use constant or variable sampling rates during a given period of time. For a variable sample rate, the number of samples taken is different for every period of time; in this case, the value of the upper and lower control limits will change for that particular interval.

Assume there are $m$ sample points in a process for a determined period of time, and that every particular instance has a constant number of $n$ readings. For example, 50 units are inspected in a high-volume production line every half hour. For an eight-hour period $m = 16$ and $n = 50$. Assume also that for every reading there are $N$ nonconformities to standards. For example, a worker testing electronic modules fails 2. $N = 2$ for that sample moment. The fraction $p$ of the process nonconforming for that reading is

$$p_i = \frac{N_i}{n} \qquad \text{where} \quad i = 1, 2, ..., m$$

For the previous example reading $p = \frac{2}{50} = 0.04$.

The average $\bar{p}$ of the sample readings in the period of time considered is calculated as follows:

$$\bar{p} = \sum_{\substack{i = 1 \\ m}}^{m} p$$

The value of $\bar{p}$ determines the center line of the chart. The control limits of the nonconforming readings in the process should be calculated. These control limits will determine the stability of the process at the time the *m* samples were taken. This criterion provides a snap picture of the process health at that particular time window. The formulas to calculate the limits are:

$$UCL = \bar{p} + 3\sqrt{\frac{\bar{p}(1-\bar{p})}{n}}$$

$$LCL = \bar{p} - 3\sqrt{\frac{\bar{p}(1-\bar{p})}{n}}$$

Table 5.1 shows data samples for an attribute data control chart during a period of 8 hours and 16 readings. The table shows the value of $\bar{p}$ and the values of the upper and lower control limits. Figure 5.12 shows the attribute control chart plotted for a three-sigma control limit. Points falling outside of the limits show that the process is not under control at that moment. A clue to predict the process behavior would be to study the data patterns of the chart before readings fall outside of the limits. Quality engineers can apply the same criteria for plot patterns and trends that were used on variable data charts.

## Attribute Data with Variable Sample Size

There is one further application used for cases where the size of the sample taken with attribute data is variable—variable flow processes where the sample size taken is a percent-

**TABLE 5.1**  ATTRIBUTE DATA SAMPLED IN A PROCESS AT A FIXED SAMPLE RATE

| Lot Sample | Pass | Fail |
|------------|------|------|
| 100 | 99 | 1 |
| 100 | 100 | 0 |
| 100 | 100 | 0 |
| 100 | 100 | 0 |
| 100 | 100 | 0 |
| 100 | 100 | 0 |
| 100 | 99 | 1 |
| 100 | 98 | 2 |
| 100 | 95 | 5 |
| 100 | 100 | 0 |
| 100 | 100 | 0 |
| 100 | 99 | 1 |
| 100 | 99 | 1 |
| 100 | 99 | 1 |
| 100 | 100 | 0 |
| 100 | 100 | 0 |
| 100 | 100 | 0 |
| 100 | 100 | 0 |
| 100 | 100 | 0 |
| 100 | 100 | 0 |

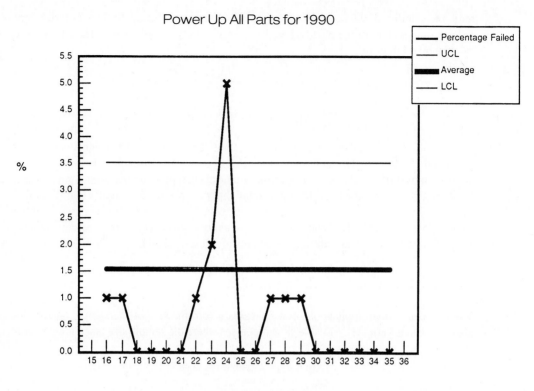

Power Up All Parts for 1990

Week Ending Sept. 7, 1990

*p* Chart Single Limits

**Figure 5.12**   Control Chart for Attribute Data with a Fixed Sample Rate

age of the number of units flowing through. This chart will have a unique upper and lower control limit for every sample window. Table 5.2 shows a process where sample sizes of the readings vary every time they are taken. Figure 5.13 shows the graphical representation of these data. Notice that the control limits are plotted for every sample instance and that they differ from the previous sample point.

In general, process characteristics will determine which type of data collection is required to monitor the process' performance. Once the data type for collection is defined, the implementation of an SPC control system is similar in most respects. Training workers to collect data accurately is one of the most critical aspects of the system. It is also important to select a good software system to convert data points into meaningful graphs without too much work. This part is tedious and there are many good packages on the market that can be implemented easily.

**TABLE 5.2**   ATTRIBUTE DATA
SAMPLED IN A PROCESS WITH A
VARIABLE SAMPLE RATE

| Lot Sample | Pass | Fail |
|---|---|---|
| 225 | 225 | 0 |
| 275 | 274 | 1 |
| 246 | 243 | 3 |
| 223 | 223 | 0 |
| 527 | 523 | 4 |
| 224 | 223 | 1 |
| 324 | 324 | 0 |
| 282 | 282 | 0 |
| 297 | 297 | 0 |
| 275 | 273 | 2 |
| 232 | 232 | 0 |
| 427 | 423 | 4 |
| 234 | 234 | 0 |
| 272 | 272 | 0 |
| 295 | 294 | 1 |
| 291 | 291 | 0 |
| 213 | 211 | 2 |
| 524 | 524 | 0 |
| 299 | 298 | 1 |

Once the system is implemented, care should be taken to take quick corrective action for cases in which the process is out of control. If workers see that nothing is done with the data, they will think they are wasting their time and the quality of the data readings will deteriorate.

## 5.8  SPC PROGRAM IMPLEMENTATION

The implementation of an SPC system should be carefully planned and executed. The system is not complex, but worker involvement affects its success. The purpose of an SPC system is to monitor the quality of a process, providing a warning signal when something is about to go wrong. Care must be taken not only to implement the system, but to set the rules and responsibilities when action needs to be taken. It is also important not to burden workers with more tasks than necessary to get the SPC system working. This is a good time to remember that collecting data is considered a waste in a Just-in-Time system.

The main steps to implementing an SPC system are:

**1.** For an ongoing process without SPC, do a complete quality and yield analysis and document all results before implementing the system. These data will help to monitor

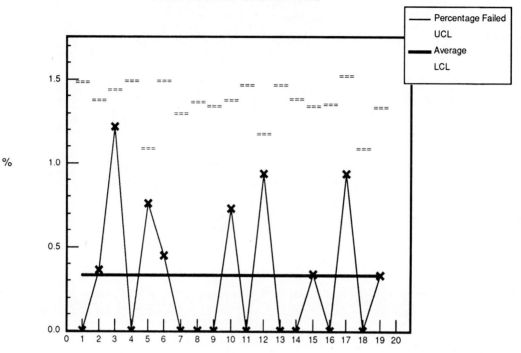

Figure 5.13   Chart for Attribute Data with a Variable Sample Rate

improvements introduced by the SPC. Use these old data as a benchmark to measure performance of the new system.

**2.** Start with a detailed flowchart of the process for the product being built, including the volume it will handle. Manufacturing and quality engineers should take over this task.

**3.** Select the types of data relevant to the process and to the product. Select the points in the process where data are going to be collected.

**4.** Define the system used to collect data and the amount of labor involved in doing this. For example, data could be collected manually on forms or by using bar code readers which will automatically feed them into a computer.

**5.** Procure a suitable software package to handle data conversion and chart plotting.

Ideally, this software system should have the capability to collect real-time data in the production line.

6. Document the data collection process and implement a pilot run to train workers on the task of collecting data.

7. Draft a set of rules that define the criteria for deciding when the process is going out of control. Train workers to understand and apply the criteria.

8. Set up a task force of quality and manufacturing engineers to take some corrective action when the SPC system signals that something is wrong.

9. Run the SPC system for a few days and do a complete evaluation involving workers and engineers who designed the system.

10. Carefully understand the amount of overhead introduced by the system. Reassess the entire system and its optimum use. A month later do this again, then six months later. Study the quality improvements and determine if the system is successful.

11. Compare the results produced by the system against the quality of the product before the system was implemented.

## 5.9 WORKER RESPONSIBILITY

The key to success in the implementation of an SPC is worker involvement. Workers in a production line should collect data for the SPC system and should own the system. However, care should be taken to avoid spending large amounts of time collecting data at the expense of productive time. A bar code system is an excellent way to increase productivity and to ensure the accuracy of the data sampled.

Before an SPC system is implemented, it is important that a good training program be put in place to make sure workers understand the key elements of the system and what it can do for them. The effectiveness of the system will depend on the accuracy of the data taken, which, in turn, depends on the quality of the job done by workers collecting them.

One very important aspect of an SPC system is the selection of the criteria used to determine when the system is out of control. Workers should understand these criteria clearly and should have access to SPC charts to determine when the process is heading in that direction. It is a good practice to display the charts in the manufacturing area, so workers can read them and monitor the performance of the process. When the charts show the process going out of control, it is critical that a team of technical people get involved immediately. Workers should also be involved in this process, so that they can see that the problem is addressed with a sense of urgency.

It is important to recognize that there is nothing workers can do to change the value of the upper and lower limits in a process. These values are process dependent. The only people who can change these values are management, by ordering some equipment change or improvement in the process. Improvements to the control limits of the process should always be a target task assigned to quality and manufacturing engineers. They are the ones who can change the process to improve overall quality performance and margins.

## 5.10 SUMMARY

Quality in the factory is the first step in improving the quality of a product, but not the only one. There is nothing a worker can do to improve the quality of a product if bad-quality parts are arriving at the beginning of the process. On the other hand, quality-perfect parts will not produce a quality-perfect product if there is not a first-class process putting the whole thing together.

Worker involvement is critical in implementing an SPC system. Training—and more training—is a key ingredient for success. There are many computer software packages on the market to automate SPC functions. A handoperated system is wasteful and will not produce accurate results.

The last factor to consider is that SPC should not burden worker productivity; it should, rather, become a tool to increase it. The time it takes to collect data should be small in relation to the productive time spent building a product. Collecting data should also take less time than the time it takes rebuilding products that get rejected at the end of the line. In other words, the productivity increase introduced by the SPC system should exceed the overhead necessary to run it.

A good SPC system is an invaluable tool in predicting process performance, but it should not be taken as the gospel to process control. Nothing can replace a judgment call based on common sense and experience to determine if a system is functioning at correct levels.

## REFERENCES

ASAKA, TETSUICHI, and KAZUO OZEKI. *Handbook of Quality Tools.* Cambridge, Mass.: Productivity Press, 1990.

BERGER, ROGER W., and THOMAS H. HART. *Statistical Process Control. A Guide for Implementation.* Milwaukee, Wis.: ASQC Quality Press, 1986.

CLEMENTS, R. *Handbook of Statistical Methods in Manufacturing.* Englewood Cliffs, N.J.: Prentice-Hall, 1991.

FEIGENBAUM, ARMAND V. *Total Quality Control.* New York: McGraw-Hill, 1983, pp. 394–463.

GRIFFITH, G. *Statistical Process Control Methods for Long and Short Runs.* Milwaukee, Wis.: ASQC Quality Press, 1989.

MONTGOMERY, DOUGLAS C. *Introduction to Statistical Quality Control.* New York: John Wiley & Sons, 1985.

ROSS, P. *Taguchi Techniques for Quality Engineering.* New York: McGraw-Hill, 1988.

# 6★

# Quality and Suppliers: A Partnership for Excellence

A supplier quality program is a vital part of a Just-in-Time system. Just-in-Time demands frequent deliveries of parts, at exactly the time they are needed in the process. The only way this system will work is for the supplier to deliver parts of perfect quality. The key to meeting this goal is developing a partnership with a supplier, with your process becoming an extension of the supplier's process, and both sharing the responsibility for quality. Equally important is the need to create an efficient information system to give quality and delivery feedback to the supplier. The system should be simple and precise, informing the supplier promptly when something goes wrong. Along with feedback, it is important to give technical support to correct problems that affect the quality of the supplier's process. This is a very important aspect of the quality program because, in most instances, a supplier will require changes in the part to increase its yields and quality.

In a Just-in-Time system, the makers of the parts are the people responsible for their quality. Suppliers must understand that they have the responsibility for producing quality-perfect parts, and that no inspection system provided by the customer is going to free them from that obligation. Just-in-Time also considers receiving inspection a waste; the quality of the parts shipped by suppliers should be good enough to make this task unnecessary.

If a supplier's quality performance requires some kind of inspection on the part of the customer, this inspection should occur at the end of the supplier's process. Source inspection is the most effective way to point out quality problems to a supplier, eliminating waste incurred by shipping parts that are not acceptable for a process.

A successful supplier's quality program is like a long-term marriage that requires commitment on the part of both parties to succeed. The program should be viewed as a partnership where members openly discuss problems and work together to solve them without assigning any blame. The supplier should be responsible for his or her problems and honestly try to solve them. The customer should have enough common sense to point out problems in a constructive way, offering help if it is required. Finally, the program should encompass more than improving quality—the supplier will need to improve his or her process to reduce lead times to support the Just-in-Time deliveries. All this effort will make the supplier leaner and more competitive in the marketplace.

## 6.1 QUALITY PROGRAM

A supplier quality program has four distinct phases. Before starting the program, it is important to understand the effort involved in getting the program off the ground and the resources required to implement it. It would be a mistake to outline an ambitious program without allocating the people and equipment necessary to implement tasks properly. Generally, the primary responsibility for the program rests on the shoulders of the quality department, but this requires close cooperation with the material organization, particularly purchasing and manufacturing engineering. These departments should share the responsibility for carrying out the program in a manner that ensures success.

### Phase One: Program Definition and Goals

Program definition and goal setting should cover quality areas needed to support a Just-in-Time system. The program should include: a goal to reduce the number of suppliers, quality goals to eliminate receiving inspection, lead-time reduction, elimination of buffer inventories, frequent shipments using a Kanban pull system for material scheduling, forecasting model, and information and support between supplier and customer.

The specific steps to define the program are:

1. Select product lines to be included in the suppliers' quality program. List suppliers that manufacture the raw material used in the process that manufactures the product. For a small company with a handful of products, you might select all the products. For a large company with many product lines, you could select a product line as a model for implementing the system. Then the program could be expanded to include other product lines as progress is achieved.

2. Rank suppliers by dollar value of shipments they contribute to the production line. For cases where there is more than one supplier shipping the same part, rank them as one, adding their individual dollar value as a single amount.

3. The group of suppliers should contribute to 80 percent of the dollars in material purchased.

4. Develop goals for the suppliers' program based on the suppliers included on the list, for example: number of suppliers certified for the program, reduction of the number

of suppliers, elimination of receiving inspection, and shipping in a Kanban pull mode based on the consumption of parts.

5. Articulate the suppliers' quality program on paper and make a summary presentation to introduce it to suppliers selected for the program.

## Phase Two: Supplier Selection and Program Launching

Once the suppliers' list has been completed, the next step is to set up a custom quality program for every one of them. This program should be based on their quality and delivery track record. The idea is to make a supplier's scorecard that covers the areas where the supplier is performing satisfactorily and the areas where performance needs improvement. This information should be shared with the supplier in a positive way, setting up a joint task force to correct problems. The scorecard can also be used as a reference to monitor the supplier's progress as the program advances.

The main steps in selecting the initial group of suppliers and launching the program are:

1. Select suppliers at the top of the list to be the group to start the program. The number of suppliers should match the resources available. Do not select more suppliers than resources.

2. For cases where there are several suppliers delivering the same part, rank them on their quality, delivery, and price performance (see Section 6.11 for ranking suppliers).

3. Develop a phaseover plan to eliminate redundant suppliers that supply common parts, based on the previous ranking. Include one supplier from every commodity group on the suppliers' list.

4. Prepare a Just-in-Time quality presentation and a supplier's Just-in-Time agreement to introduce the program. Appendix A shows a Just-in-Time supplier agreement used at Relevant Technologies. The presentation should cover the Just-in-Time basics and it should point out the benefits the program will produce under the new partnership.

5. Call for a suppliers' day meeting to launch the program. Invite all suppliers included in the first group. Make this event a privilege, and the beginning of the new partnership. Explain that you are going to work together as partners and the relationship will be exclusive and long term. In return, you expect suppliers to improve their quality, so there is no need for receiving inspection. Explain the importance of reducing lead times and the need to involve their own suppliers in the program, in order to ship products on demand. Finally, make sure suppliers understand that the exercise is going to make them more competitive in the marketplace.

6. At the end of the suppliers' day, explain that there will be a program implementation phase, and, if required, your technical people will help to implement the program at the suppliers' premises.

**Phase Three: Program Implementation**

This is the most involved of the three phases. It includes working with the group of suppliers to improve their quality to the point where there is no need for receiving inspection. Another key goal of this phase is for the supplier to start delivering parts based on consumption. In this phase, the supplier will be worried about there being no definite delivery schedule, but the Just-in-Time agreement should define the forecast and delivery rules that will protect the supplier. A Kanban system is a good tool to use to implement demand and pull deliveries.

The main steps of this phase are:

1. Make an appointment with each supplier and discuss the scorecard that you have kept on his or her company. This scorecard should show: (a) the supplier's quality track record, as well as his or her on-time delivery performance; (b) what the supplier is doing well and what needs improvement; (c) trends, if any; (d) the supplier's quality record supported by facts. Telling the supplier is not enough—the information must be substantiated.

2. Develop a plan of action with the supplier and a set of milestones to correct problems and to achieve specific goals. Be ready to go to any extreme to support the supplier in achieving the quality goals required—even redesigning the parts the supplier is manufacturing.

3. Get a commitment from the supplier to apply resources sufficient to correct problems in his or her process. As a way to improve communications, set up a source inspection program to provide quick feedback on quality, before the product is shipped.

4. Set up lines of communication with the supplier to report on quality as the parts are used in your process. Communication should be direct, not filtered through intermediate levels of nontechnical people. For example, your quality engineers should talk directly to suppliers' quality engineers. Your manufacturing engineers should talk directly to suppliers' manufacturing engineers. Keeping this communications line simple will speed up the transfer and accuracy of information.

5. Make achieving major milestones in the program a big event in the supplier's scorecard. Reward the supplier with recognition and status among other suppliers.

6. Mark the completion of the certification program by issuing a supplier's certification plaque. This is an important milestone. You can extend the certification to several suppliers at the same time and invite other certified suppliers to the event. Start Just-in-Time deliveries based on demand.

**Phase Four: Program Maintenance**

After certification, suppliers should be included in the supplier information system to keep them abreast of their performance as parts are delivered. This feedback system is very important in monitoring any early deviations from quality standards. Quick and accurate feedback is essential, so the supplier can take corrective actions before the quality or delivery track record gets below the limits called for in the program.

The main steps of this phase are:

1. Design a custom quality information report that reflects the supplier's process characteristics. Review this information with the supplier's technical people to make sure every bit of information is useful to them. Include the supplier in the distribution of the report and deliver the report religiously.

2. Establish quality and delivery goals to determine if a supplier is in or out of compliance with the program. Make sure the supplier agrees with these goals.

3. Conduct monthly reviews with the supplier. You can change the frequency of the reviews if something abnormal appears in the information. Point out the areas where the supplier is doing well, and those where the supplier needs improvement. Use the operating modes covered in the supplier information system (Section 6.6) to take action if something goes wrong.

4. Never accept quality goals with a supplier as something static or fixed. If the supplier is meeting goals regularly, work together to develop new goals beyond current performance. For example, if a supplier's quality performance is 99.5 percent conformance, set the next goal level at 99.9 percent. The same thing applies to on-time delivery: The goal here should be 100 percent. Also include in the goals a cost reduction program that calls for overall waste elimination and improvement of yields and productivity.

## 6.2 QUALITY IMPROVEMENT PROGRAM

A quality improvement program is necessary to improve a supplier's quality performance. The program should not be cluttered with requests for unnecessary information that distract the supplier from the main goal of improving process quality. Normally, there is a tendency on the part of suppliers to promise improvements in their inspecting system as a means of improving quality. This trap should be avoided. Quality improvements are not achieved by increasing product inspection in a process. There have to be improvements in the supplier's process to improve quality in a product.

A supplier's quality improvement program requires a high degree of cooperation between a supplier and a customer. This cooperation should be carried out in a friendly atmosphere and with a spirit of mutual benefit during the exercise. The main steps in a supplier's quality improvement program are:

1. Start with a clear understanding of the quality levels of the parts you are receiving from the supplier. A Pareto chart listing the key problems with the parts is a good start. Figure 6.1 shows a Pareto chart used at Relevant Technologies.

# Atlas Chassis Parts

### Sept. 1,1992 to Sept. 30,1992

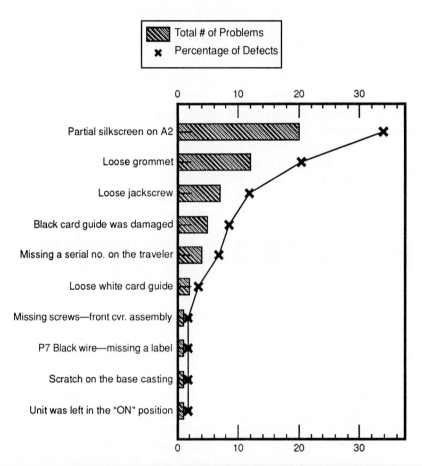

**Figure 6.1**   Pareto Chart Used at Relevant Technologies

2. Match the Pareto chart problems with the steps in the supplier's process where the problems originate. Use the supplier's process flow to identify the work centers involved in the problem. If the supplier doesn't have a process flowchart, ask him or her to make one.

3. After analyzing and correlating the problems shown on the Pareto chart with the process, work with the supplier's process engineers to classify problems into one of the following categories: process problems, machinery problems, raw material problems, worker training problems, or part design problems.

    **a.** Part design problems are yours. Work with the supplier's process engineers to redesign the part into a simple one that will produce higher quality yields in the process.

    **b.** Other problems are related to the supplier's process and should be solved by the supplier's technical people, helped by your technical people if necessary.

**4.** Set up a source inspection program to give the supplier instant feedback on quality issues as the program advances.

**5.** Work with the supplier to set clear goals for quality improvements within a reasonable time frame.

**6.** Encourage the supplier to use self-checking devices in the process—for example, poka-yoke devices to ensure quality parts without inspection. Worker training is also a very important aspect of the quality improvement program. Encourage the supplier to set up such a program.

**7.** When major quality goals are met, make this milestone a big and rewarding event for the supplier: Give the supplier additional releases or more business. Stop the source inspecting process and certify the supplier as a Just-in-Time quality supplier.

## 6.3  LEAD-TIME REDUCTION PROGRAM

Suppliers' lead-time reduction is a critical aspect in Just-in-Time. Just-in-Time calls for flexible schedules that pull material on demand and on short notice. This concept is often mistakenly taken by suppliers as a request for buffer inventories. Just-in-Time considers buffer inventories a waste. It would not be healthy for a customer/supplier relationship to shift the need for a buffer inventory from the customer to the supplier. In the long run, the supplier is going to resent it and will make the customer pay for it. Buffer inventories will also suffer the quality problems associated with keeping material built ahead of time and not using it immediately. Hidden quality problems will not show up until the parts are used in the product.

    For a supplier, the best approach is to reduce lead times. This will make the supplier lean and responsive and more competitive in the marketplace. But short lead times are not attained overnight. They require a commitment from the supplier to systematically eliminate time wasted in the process and to enroll its own suppliers in the effort.

    There are several critical steps that a supplier must take to reduce lead times. Below are some of them:

**1.** Using the process flowchart, measure the time it takes to execute every one of its tasks, including moving materials.

**2.** Classify these times into two categories: (a) Value-added time is the time that workers use to build the product. Every time that a worker uses this time, he or she is adding value to the product. (b) Overhead time is the time that adds no value to a product: for example, moving material, machine setup time, idle time, rework, inspecting, and so on.

**3.** Start a program to eliminate overhead time. In cases where it is not possible to eliminate it altogether (for example, machine setup), start a project to reduce it to a minimum. When overhead time is reduced to a minimum, try to overlap it with value added time.

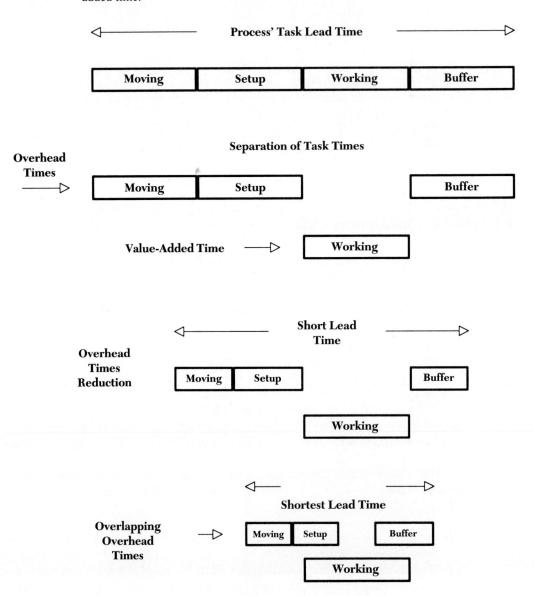

**Figure 6.2**    Lead-Time Reduction Program

   **4.** Start a program to reduce the value added time without affecting the quality of the product. Figure 6.2 shows the three steps used to reduce the lead time in a process.

The next step in reducing lead times is to work on the lead times of the raw material used to build the product. Without a program to reduce the lead times of this material, there will always be a need to stock buffer inventories to keep the process going. The steps to reduce raw material lead time are:

   **1.** Make a list of every supplier used in the process, ranking them by the longest lead time and volume. Make a list of the second-level supplier that supplies raw material to the first-level supplier.
   **2.** Ask a first-level supplier to work with his or her second-level suppliers to improve lead times. This effort should trickle down to several levels of suppliers.
   **3.** Make sure the first-level supplier clearly understands the lead-time requirement of his or her raw material before going to the second- and third-level suppliers.
   **4.** If design changes in the final product can improve the lead times of any of the multi-level suppliers, go ahead and implement them. Sometimes this effort is not obvious until a second- or third-level supplier is involved in the lead-time reduction process: For example, changing the type of raw material from one type of metal to another might speed up the manufacturing process of the first-level supplier, but only the second- or third-level supplier might be able to suggest the change.
   **5.** For cases where the first-level supplier still has a conflict with lead times and flexible, demand-driven schedules, create small buffer inventories to take care of the discrepancy. The goal should be to improve the multilevel chain of suppliers' lead times to eliminate the buffers.

## 6.4 PROCESS IMPROVEMENT

A supplier's process improvement program should concentrate on two fronts: to improve the overall quality of the process and to reduce the labor and lead times required to manufacture the part.

Process improvement is a tedious activity that is the responsibility of process and design engineers. This task should be shared equally between the designers and the builders of the part: Only their joint effort can produce substantial results. Process improvement might also require capital equipment investment to procure the right machinery for the process.

A training program for all line workers is essential to make sure the tasks involved in building the parts are correctly understood and executed.

Below are listed some of the key points in implementing a supplier's process improvement program:

1. Always start a process improvement program before the process is implemented. The best time to improve a process is during the part's design phase. This is the right time to introduce changes in the design that will make the process simple and foolproof.

2. Once the process flow diagram is completed, ask the supplier to execute a pilot run of the part to try the process. Provide feedback to designers in order to make the product design simple and the process foolproof.

3. Work with the supplier to reduce the number of steps it takes to build the part. Then try to reduce the time it takes to complete every step.

4. Ask the supplier to use automatic tools and machinery to make the workers more productive. Make sure workers feel ownership of the process once they have been trained. The supplier should include quality inspections as part of the workers' responsibilities.

5. The supplier should understand the overhead activities associated with the process and try to eliminate them to the extent possible.

6. The supplier should train workers to be consistent in their assigned tasks, and ask their opinions about possible improvements in the process

7. The process should be defined in simple steps that are clear to workers. The supplier should make sure workers are committed to quality first, and output second.

8. All data collection in the process should be minimal, automatic, and foolproof. Just-in-Time considers collecting data wasteful.

9. The process capacity should match the volume needs for the part. The supplier should never provide more capacity than needed or build more parts because there is excess capacity.

10. The process should have dynamic productivity goals. Once the current goals have been achieved, the supplier should set new goals and start the program all over again.

11. There is a difference between process improvements and a learning curve. Learning curve improvements are related to production volume and efficiency achieved by practice. Process improvements are attained by reducing the labor required in a process. A combination of learning curve and process efficiency should produce incremental improvements in results.

## 6.5 SOURCE INSPECTION

Just-in-Time considers inspection wasteful, and it should be eliminated or reduced to a minimum. The most common inspection in a factory is the inspection of parts that arrive at the receiving dock. The system for receiving parts in a factory is simple: Parts are received by entering them into the company's computer inventory system, and then they are inspected. Good parts are sent to the stockroom to join a part's kit later, or they are sent directly to the production floor, if there is a Just-in-Time program in place. Defective parts are sent to a reject shelf and later returned to the supplier, which wastes labor, paperwork, and transportation. Rejected parts also create a shortage of good parts to feed a process.

Rejections force the material organization to reorder more parts in a hurry to cover for the shortage or to plan for unwanted buffers to cover for them.

Normally, receiving inspection is needed to ensure quality before parts are sent to a stockroom or a process. Sending bad parts to a production line will waste labor in replacing them once inspectors discover them, or even worse, result in a product with inferior quality, if they escape the quality system's scrutiny. Receiving inspection is supposed to cure this problem, but in reality it only causes a delay in correcting the part's problems and a lack of motivation for the supplier to correct them.

A source inspection program is intermediary between a receiving inspection and the elimination of all incoming inspections. The goal of a source inspection program is not only to ensure quality at the source but also to provide quick feedback to the manufacturer on problems, so they can be corrected and inspection eliminated.

The benefits of a source inspection program are:

1. Provides quick quality feedback to a manufacturer before parts are shipped.
2. Saves time and money by eliminating the return of rejected parts from the customer's receiving inspection process. It also eliminates unnecessary paperwork and buffer inventories that have no place in a production line.
3. Reduces workload in a production line—workers don't have to deal with bad parts.
4. Increases quality in the customer's products by eliminating the possibility that bad quality parts are being shipped.
5. Is very effective in uncovering quality problems at the source, rather than at the receiving end. Allows a supplier to see problems firsthand and to provide quick feedback to the process.
6. Provides an economical incentive for a supplier to correct quality problems, because bad parts rejected at the back door before they are shipped cannot be counted as a sale.

The main goal of source inspection is to provide quick quality feedback to allow a supplier to understand and correct problems at the source. Source inspection should only be a temporary step; then it should be eliminated. Source inspection should not shift the inspection burden from one place to another.

One of the problems encountered with source inspection is that the customer has to send someone to inspect parts at the supplier's premises. This effort is not great for suppliers close to the customer, but for distant suppliers it is very expensive unless the system is implemented properly.

For suppliers located far from the part's destination, the best way to implement source inspection is to hire a quality inspection service or a retired part-time inspector living in the area. This approach is economical and works very well, if the inspector is properly trained at the customer's location on inspection methods related to the part. With electronic mail and fax machines, it is very easy to keep track of source inspectors in other cities or countries. A well-implemented source inspection program can pay for itself quickly, and could solve a lot of quality issues before parts arrive at the receiving dock.

## 6.6 SUPPLIER INFORMATION SYSTEM

An effective supplier information system is the best vehicle to use to inform a supplier of the performance of parts in a process. In order to be effective, the system should operate in a bidirectional mode: Quality information should flow from the supplier's process to the customer, and then performance of the part in the customer's process should go back to the supplier.

Just-in-Time does not support receiving inspection. Once a supplier is certified, parts should travel freely from the supplier's shipping dock to the customer's process. This kind of arrangement will work only if the process of the supplier is good enough to consistently produce quality-perfect parts. Nevertheless, no such system should operate without safeguards to protect against possible problems. The information system should function like an early warning system capable of detecting quality problems with a supplier. The system should work early enough to allow corrective actions before line shutdowns occur.

Reports generated by the quality information system should be simple and effective. One way to accomplish this is to make sure they go directly to people who really need them, people who can take some action as a result of them. It is very important that the system not be burdened with layers of management or bureaucratic processes that delay or, even worse, prevent the reports from getting to the right people: For example, don't send quality reports through the purchasing department, when you can send them directly to the supplier's quality people. It is important that buyers be informed and involved in the quality performance of a supplier, but to avoid delays they should be eliminated from the direct path of information. Communication lines should be direct, short, and effective. Action taken as a result of the reports should be carried out effectively and by the people responsible.

Figure 6.3 shows a supplier quality report issued by Relevant Technologies. This report shows the supplier's quality performance in Relevant's process. This report is issued monthly by the quality department. Figure 6.4 shows a report from a supplier's quality department. This report could be issued with every shipment or at certain intervals, for example, weekly or monthly. It summarizes the quality performance of the process during the time it was manufacturing the parts shipped.

Below are the most important items to be reported in a quality information system:

### SUPPLIER'S REPORT TO THE CUSTOMER

1. Number of units inspected and number of units rejected. System used to inspect them. For example, 100 percent inspection, AQL level, poka-yoke device, and so on.
2. Ranking of problems that caused rejections, and corrective actions implemented.
3. Report on critical inspections per request of the customer's quality department. For example, report on critical dimensions that are to be checked on every part.
4. Report on any engineering change order (ECO) or rework implemented on the parts.
5. Report on any deviations agreed to by both quality departments.

## March 1, 1992  to  March 31, 1992

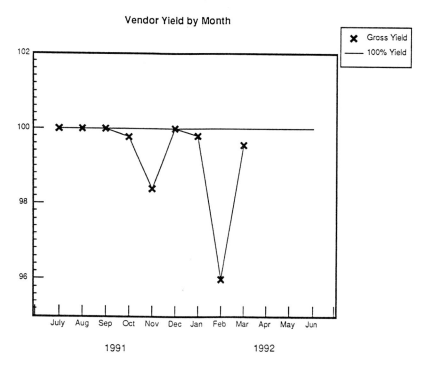

**Gross Monthly yield  99.56%**

**Gross YTD Yield = 97.53%**

**Total Pass        899**
**Total Failed      4**

| Date Received | Part # | Qty Rejected | DMR # | Comments |
|---|---|---|---|---|
| March 20, 1992 | 530–1468–03 | 4 | 10032 | Shorted between filter & P6 red wire. (Corrective Action implemented). |

Figure 6.3   Supplier's Quality Report from Relevant Technologies

# MILPITAS
## MATERIAL QUALITY REPORT
### FABRICATION

## RELEVANT
## ROLLING SUMMARY

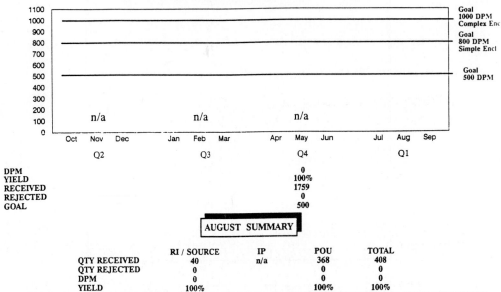

| DPM | 0 |
|---|---|
| YIELD | 100% |
| RECEIVED | 1759 |
| REJECTED | 0 |
| GOAL | 500 |

## AUGUST SUMMARY

|  | RI / SOURCE | IP | POU | TOTAL |
|---|---|---|---|---|
| QTY RECEIVED | 40 | n/a | 368 | 408 |
| QTY REJECTED | 0 |  | 0 | 0 |
| DPM | 0 |  | 0 | 0 |
| YIELD | 100% |  | 100% | 100% |

| PART NUMBER | QTY REC | QTY REJ | FAILURE DESCRIPTION | DPM |
|---|---|---|---|---|
| **RI/Source** |  |  |  |  |
| **530–1466–03 ＊** | 20 |  |  |  |
| **540–2029–01 ＊** | 20 |  |  |  |
|  |  |  |  |  |
| **POU** |  |  |  |  |
| **540–1831–01** | 60 |  |  |  |
| **540–1834–01** | 60 |  |  |  |
| **540–1894–03** | 60 |  |  |  |
| **599–1854–01** | 188 |  |  |  |

| COMMENTS | |
|---|---|
| **PART NUMBER** | **DESCRIPTION** |
|  | ＊ FRU/Spares |

**Figure 6.4**   Supplier's Quality Report to Relevant Technologies

82

**CUSTOMER'S REPORT TO THE SUPPLIER**

1.  Report on quality yields of the parts used in the customer's process. The report should include any critical requirements previously requested from the supplier.
2.  Priority list of problems that caused rejections. A Pareto chart will be sufficient in this case. The Pareto should clearly correlate defects to rejects, ranking them in order of occurrence.
3.  Criteria used to reject the parts.
4.  Performance of the parts once the product is shipped. This information should be supplied to the quality department by the field service people and in-house repair depot.
5.  Supplier's performance in technical support, on-time delivery, accuracy of lot count, and paperwork shipped with the product.

## 6.7  QUALITY SPECIFICATIONS AND QUALITY GOALS

One of the aspects most critical to a successful quality system is an understanding of the quality requirements of the parts used to build a product. Quality should not be specified by subjective opinion or loose specifications. Quality must be precisely defined and it must be clearly understood by the people in charge of judging it. The job of a quality specification is to provide the means to measure quality uniquely and without guessing.

For fabricated parts, the starting point in measuring quality is to meet the fabrication specifications within the tolerances the designer has specified on the blueprints. This should be accomplished with equipment precise enough to match the tolerances of the part. For a nonmeasurable quality criterion, specifications should be clear enough so there is no doubt whether a part meets the criterion or not. This is the most difficult part in the quality judgment process: Different workers could have different opinions regarding the achievement of the criterion if the measurement is subjective. It is the job of design and quality engineers to specify this criterion in the simplest and clearest way to make sure workers understand the differences between a good and a bad part. Examples of this are surface finishing, cosmetics, color matching, and so on.

In a Just-in-Time system, quality is the responsibility of the maker of the part. But it is also the responsibility of the part's designer to specify the quality requirements the part must meet. This effort should be jointly decided by designers and process and quality engineers, because the process capabilities have to match the quality requirements of the part. For example, it is not possible to manufacture a part with a machine that cannot meet the tolerances specified on the prints. Conversely, it is the responsibility of the maker of the part, the supplier, to make sure the quality requirements of the part are clearly understood. This implies the supplier should verify that the document is clear enough to build the part with consistent quality in a process capable of producing it at the right quality level .

The overall quality of a part should be associated with the overall quality performance of the process that builds it. This requirement should be put in writing as a quality specification for the process. Again, the supplier's process and quality engineers should work closely with the customer's design and quality people when defining goals. This might require changes in the part's design to allow the supplier to meet quality goals. Designers should be flexible enough to change the design, if that means improving the overall quality of the part.

In summary, the responsibility for the quality specification of a part should be shared between the designers and the makers of the part. The ultimate goal is to produce a part with consistent quality that conforms to the requirements of whichever product is going to use it.

## 6.8 TECHNICAL SUPPORT TO SUPPLIERS

The ideal relationship between a supplier and its customer should be one of partnership and cooperation. Just-in-Time calls for this partnership to include technical collaboration. The main goal of this cooperation is to produce quality-perfect parts with minimum waste, shipped in small, on-demand lots, and on time.

The best way to implement this cooperation system is to make sure that both sides share equally the overall responsibility for quality. There are, however, certain responsibilities that fall heavily on the customer's side. The customer's technical people should make sure the supplier clearly understands the quality requirements of a part. It is also the responsibility of the customer to help a supplier to fix quality problems, regardless of which side is responsible for producing the nonconforming part. This is the case where the supplier's process is out of control for reasons not associated with the design or tolerances of the part.

The best way to solve quality problems with a part is to have the designers of the part working together with the customer's quality and process people. Together, they should understand the issues associated with poor quality and should take corrective action to change either the process or the design of the part. No blaming should occur as a result of this activity—only positive cooperation and the spirit of teamwork will produce successful results.

## 6.9 ELIMINATION OF RECEIVING INSPECTION

Elimination of receiving inspection should be in place only after a supplier has demonstrated consistent deliveries with no quality defects. A source inspection program is commonly a preceding step before receiving inspection is eliminated.

Once a supplier has entered a Just-in-Time program, elimination of receiving inspection should be a milestone. This task, however, is not easy to achieve. A supplier doesn't build quality-perfect parts overnight. The steps to eliminating receiving inspection are simple but laborious, requiring a lot of attention to detail. Below are listed the most important steps in reaching this goal:

1. Prepare a scorecard of the supplier's receiving inspection quality performance. This report should include the supplier's track record on deliveries, because the quality of the parts should be measured not only according to how perfect they are, but also on how promptly they arrive.

2. The scorecard should include a Pareto analysis of the most common quality problems the parts have during receiving inspection.

3. Review the quality scorecard, the Pareto chart, and the quality specifications of the parts with the supplier to make sure there is a clear understanding of the problems encountered.

4. Survey the supplier's process to make sure it can build parts at the quality levels requested in the specifications. Make sure your specifications are realistic and do not demand unnecessary requirements that add costs and constraints to the process.

5. Understand the process lead time and work with the supplier to shorten it. Do this at the same time that the quality improvement program is being implemented.

6. Change receiving inspection to source inspection and agree with the supplier on the criteria necessary to eliminate the inspection process altogether.

7. Set up an early warning system to monitor the parts' quality in your process. The system should give the supplier quick feedback on quality once the source inspection is eliminated.

8. Once quality goals are met, stop inspecting parts and deliver them directly from your receiving dock to the process.

## 6.10 SUPPLIER QUALITY CERTIFICATION

A supplier is certified for Just-in-Time deliveries when he or she can consistently ship parts that require no receiving inspection at the customer site. The supplier has also embarked on process improvement and lead-time reduction programs that allow frequent shipments based on demand schedules, without the need for buffer inventories. The lead-time reduction program requires that suppliers of the supplier also implement Just-in-Time, so there is no need for storing raw material at the supplier's site.

Certifying a supplier should be a big event and should be recognized with a plaque the supplier can display at his or her premises. A certified supplier should also receive special treatment and be looked upon as a partner. For example, the supplier's paperwork should be given priority, and when problems occur, they should be resolved expeditiously. The supplier should also be connected with the customer through E-mail or an electronic data interchange (EDI) system.

The certification of a supplier takes three steps:

1. Qualification of the overall supplier's operation. This should include systems and procedures, plus resources available.

**2.** Quality certification of the process that is going to build the parts. The qualification should include process improvement recommendations, lead-time reduction goals, and quality goals required to eliminate receiving inspection. The certification should also include the supplier's suppliers that provide critical secondary options to the supplier's process, for example, planting and painting.

**3.** Supplier's quality and delivery performance for a period of time before the certification is granted.

The certification of a supplier is not a static award—the supplier has to earn it with every shipment. Parts should arrive at the receiving dock with perfect quality *every* time and *on* time. If a supplier degrades its quality performance below the level required by the certification, a recovery program should be put in place immediately. This recovery program requires that the supplier show good will in correcting the problems expeditiously. If the supplier doesn't recover fast enough, this can lead to revocation of the certification and the program will have to start all over again.

In return for achieving certified status, a supplier receives preferential partnership standing. This entitles the supplier to privileged business information, special financial arrangements, preferential consideration for new purchases and programs, and, more importantly, single-source commitment.

## 6.11 SUPPLIER RANKING

One of the key activities in the early phases of a Just-in-Time program is a reduction in the number of suppliers supporting process material needs. Just-in-Time considers the use of overlapping suppliers a waste. Furthermore, one of the benefits a supplier gets for becoming quality certified is the commitment to becoming a single-source supplier. It is important to develop a procedure for ranking suppliers that is fair and equitable. This procedure will be the performance yardstick used to come up with an initial list of supplier candidates. The process is simple, but it requires a careful analysis of the capabilities of similar suppliers to make sure there is no mistake in selecting the single-source supplier.

The old method of ranking suppliers was primarily driven by price, delivery, and quality. Just-in-Time requires the order to be reversed. Companies use different ways to rank suppliers, but the principles are similar and produce comparable results. The method used in this section is simple, requiring only three parameters to establish the ranking.

First, suppliers' operations are audited to rate their capabilities as they relate to the parts they are manufacturing. This activity is similar to the one required to approve a new supplier. Assume three suppliers are shipping the same part, and only one supplier is required. If the audit proves the three suppliers have similar capabilities, then the next step is to rank them using their historical performance as a measurement.

The ranking is done in three areas with different weights:

1. Quality performance, *QP*, has a weight of 70 percent.
2. On-time delivery performance, *DP*, has a weight of 20 percent.
3. Price performance, *PP*, has a weight of 10 percent.

Suppose a supplier has a yield *Y* in the parts shipped during a three-month period. The formula to calculate the weighted value of the supplier's quality track record will be

$$QP = 70 - [(100 - Y) \times 3]$$

For example, the following yields *Y* will give three suppliers the weighted rating:

| Supplier | *Y* (%) | *QP* |
|----------|---------|------|
| Supplier A | 99.1 | 67.3 |
| Supplier B | 98.2 | 64.6 |
| Supplier C | 97.4 | 62.2 |

On-time delivery performance is calculated by taking the average number of days, early or late, of all deliveries in the last three months, weighting them in the following formula:

$$DP = 20 - (\text{Average days late/early} \times 2)$$

For example, the *DP* for the same suppliers listed above is as follows:

| Supplier | Average Days (late/early) | *DP* |
|----------|---------------------------|------|
| Supplier A | +3 | 14 |
| Supplier B | 0 | 20 |
| Supplier C | −5 | 10 |

Price performance is calculated by selecting the lowest price supplier as the base reference. Then the differences in price are calculated as a percentage against the base reference. The formula to calculate the *PP* will be

$$PP = 10 - \text{Percentage higher than reference}$$

For example, for the three suppliers listed above the *PP* can be calculated as:

| Supplier | Unit Price | Percentage Higher | *PP* |
|----------|-----------|-------------------|------|
| Supplier A | $75.45 | 1.6 | 8.4 |
| Supplier B | $77.25 | 4 | 6 |
| Supplier C | $74.25 | 0 | 10 |

The final ranking of the three suppliers will be

| Supplier | QP | DP | PP | Rank |
|----------|------|----|-----|------|
| Supplier B | 64.6 | 20 | 6 | 90.6 |
| Supplier A | 67.3 | 14 | 8.4 | 89.7 |
| Supplier C | 62.2 | 10 | 10 | 82.2 |

The table shows that Supplier C will be eliminated and the decision will be made between Suppliers A and B. Both suppliers have to work on their respective problems before either one is selected. Supplier B has to improve his or her quality record, and Supplier A has to improve his or her on-time delivery record.

## 6.12 MANAGEMENT INVOLVEMENT

A supplier's Just-in-Time quality program entails close management attention. Suppliers are required to ship small lots, on demand, and with perfect quality every time. They are also required to reduce lead times and to enroll their own suppliers into the program. All this effort requires a great deal of work on the part of a supplier, including a drastic change in operating mode. Such changes will not occur smoothly unless the supplier's management team gets involved, providing the necessary commitment and support.

High-level attention to a Just-in-Time quality program should be given by the management of both companies involved in the process. The support should be real, not just lip service. People responsible for carrying out the program will need resources; management should allocate the support necessary to carry out the program successfully.

The best way to obtain management support is to start the education process with the managers responsible for allocating the resources. This education process should extend all the way up to the president of the company. Commitment to the program, the returns it will bring to the company, and the effort it will take to implement it are key factors that require management's understanding before the program starts.

## 6.13 SUMMARY

Supplier quality is one of the most important components of the success of Just-in-Time. But consistent part quality arriving at the receiving dock is also one of the most difficult tasks to accomplish. The effort affects many different suppliers' operating environments that are not necessarily prepared to make changes to meet requirements. The program also requires an investment that will not show a return until later in its implementation.

Once the program starts and the list of suppliers is drafted, it is important to assume that not all the suppliers on the list are going to go along with it. At this stage, it will be necessary to have some backup suppliers to cover for dropouts.

The quality program should be implemented in a friendly atmosphere, with a spirit of partnership and with infinite patience. As long as a supplier is genuinely trying to improve, the supplier should be given the benefit of the doubt and full support. In the long run, the supplier will improve and will be grateful for the help provided. This process will improve the relationship between both partners, providing the base for more ambitious programs in the future.

Finally, a supplier's quality program is a process that should have no completion date. Suppliers should always try to improve quality levels, even when they are consistently reaching the goals assigned. Static quality programs that always meet their goals but do nothing to challenge the system will become routine. In addition, routine things will always degrade, drifting into trouble.

## REFERENCES

AKAO, YOJI. *Quality Function Deployment: Integrating Customer Requirements into Product Design*. Cambridge, Mass.. Productivity Press, 1990.

HERNANDEZ, ARNALDO. *Just-in-Time Manufacturing: A Practical Approach*. Englewood Cliffs, N.J.: Prentice-Hall, 1989, pp. 95–109.

ISHIKAWA, KAORU. *What Is Total Quality Control? The Japanese Way*. Englewood Cliffs, N.J.: Prentice-Hall, 1985, pp. 155–170.

LAFORD, RICHARD J. *Ship-to-Stock. An Alternative to Incoming Inspection*. Milwaukee, Wis.: ASQC Quality Press, 1986.

LASCELLES, D. H., and B. G. DALE. "The Buyer-Supplier Relationship in Total Quality Management," *Journal of Purchasing and Materials Management* (Summer 1989).

The Manufacturing Institute. *JIT Partnerships: Teaming with Your Suppliers to Get the Most From JIT*. Audio Cassettes. New York: Institute for International Research, 1991.

MASKELL, BRIAN H. *Performance Measurement for World Class Manufacturing. A Model for American Companies*. Cambridge, Mass.: Productivity Press, 1991.

MERLI, GIORGIO. *Co-makership: The New Supply Strategy for Manufacturers*. Cambridge, Mass.: Productivity Press, 1991.

SANG, M. LEE, and A. ANSARI. "Comparative Analysis of Japanese Just-in-Time Purchasing and Traditional U.S. Purchasing Systems." *International Journal of Production Management*, 5, no. 4 (1986).

SHINGO, SHIGEO. *A Revolution in Manufacturing: The SMED System*. Cambridge, Mass.: Productivity Press, 1985.

# 7★

# *Quality and Customers: The Perception Factor*

To survive in today's competitive environment, companies must monitor the quality performance of their products once they are delivered to customers. The very survival of a company depends on this. The quality of a product is usually defined by its working condition when it arrives at the customer's site. It is also measured by the reliability the product shows during its expected useful life. But very few companies define quality by the level of customer satisfaction achieved when the product is used.

Customer satisfaction as an index of a product's quality should cover two important areas:

1. The actual performance of a product compared against the expectation fostered in a customer's mind during the selling process.
2. The level of customer support provided after the delivery of the product.

A failure of the first quality index is common and very difficult to measure. A failure of the second one is rarely considered to be a quality issue.

This chapter addresses the methodology necessary to measure quality from the point of view of the customer. It will also address the point that customer satisfaction is the ultimate measurement of the quality of a product. It doesn't matter how many inspections and tests are implemented—if a product doesn't meet customer expectations, it is of poor quality and something must be done about it.

Measuring quality at the customer site is not a simple task. It requires that someone contact customers to learn how the product is being used and if it has met their expectations. It also requires tracking the product's performance over time. Normally, a field service organization has this task. For companies with no field support, the way to solve this problem is to design a simple system that monitors customer satisfaction by mail or by phone. This type of system is not burdensome and will pay for itself many times over by finding out the real value of a product in the field.

## 7.1  THE ULTIMATE INSPECTOR: THE CUSTOMER

The ultimate measurement of a product's value is the service it provides to its user. A product is delivered to do a job that has been described to a potential customer in several different ways, for example, through a set of specifications, brochures, verbal description provided by the salesperson, demos at the manufacturer's site, and training. All this information has built a model in the mind of the customer describing the capabilities of the product. When the customer receives the product, most likely he or she is going to compare it against the opinion he or she formed during the sales cycle. If the product fails to satisfy this image, the company has delivered poor quality.

It is important to emphasize the notion of delivering quality, because a product delivered might be executing the tasks for which it was designed, but if the company has misrepresented the product during the sales cycle, it may fail to deliver quality.

*The ultimate inspector of a product is the customer.* The criteria that a customer uses to inspect a product are not only the result of reading specifications but also absorbing the information passed on during the sales cycle. If a customer is satisfied, then the product has quality. If a customer is not satisfied, the company needs to understand why and take the necessary corrective actions. It is important to realize that sometimes the customer's level of expectation has been raised beyond capabilities. In this case the problem is the misrepresentation of the product and it should be corrected immediately.

Most of the time problems encountered in a product after delivery are related to defects; it is important to understand why the quality system passed the product without detecting them. Immediate corrective actions should be put in place to correct these problems. The last place we want to find a defect is at the customer's site.

For OEM companies delivering Just-in-Time products on demand, the need to deliver quality is even greater. The customer is taking products in small quantities, without buffers, and at the very last possible moment. In this case a poor-quality product will have a very serious impact on the customer.

Just-in-Time doesn't call for receiving inspection at the receiving dock. Actual inspection occurs when the product is used for whatever application it was bought. The final criterion for quality is actually using the product. To ensure proper quality, the product's manufacturer should clearly understand the use of the product and try to replicate a final test that mimics its use. This test will be the final inspection before shipping.

## 7.2  QUALITY EXPECTATIONS

One of the problems related to product quality is an understanding of the performance it is supposed to deliver. It is a manufacturer's responsibility to cover this item carefully. When a customer buys a product, he or she expects the quality and performance to match the level of expectation set during the selling process. If a manufacturer fails to meet this goal when a product is delivered, then the manufacturer has shipped a product of poor quality. Normally, companies assume that a quality problem is related to defects in manufacturing and that it has nothing to do with performance. A product will fail the perfect-quality qualification if it doesn't deliver the performance the manufacturer has represented to the customer.

Shaping the quality expectations of a customer is an important aspect of selling a product. Very few companies address this subject, other than by saying a product has excellent quality and that it never breaks. In a competitive environment, a manufacturer has to deliver a product that matches the customer's expectations.

The solution to this problem is to set the customer's expectations right, so there is no misunderstanding about the product's performance, quality, and reliability. Product documentation is the primary source of this information and it should be clear and precise. Training classes and performance representation through sales activities also contribute to customer expectations. The quality of this service will determine the final quality of a product.

## 7.3  CUSTOMER SATISFACTION

Measuring customer satisfaction accurately is more of an art than a science. Successful companies have satisfied customers. Failing companies have unsatisfied ex-customers that went someplace else to get their needs met.

There are two aspects required to measure customer satisfaction. The first one is simple and empirical—sections 7.7 to 7.10 will show how to. The other aspect is subjective, difficult to measure, and usually badly done. It has to do with the degree of satisfaction with a product and to what extent a customer will purchase the next product when there is a need to replace the one just bought.

Many manufacturers include a satisfaction survey form with the product they ship. This method of measuring customer satisfaction is difficult and usually doesn't reflect the true feelings of the customer. Questions in the form are too standard to fit all customer profiles. The majority of customers generally fail to return the form, or return them too early to really know how they feel about the product.

Another alternative to find out how a customer feels about a product is to use the sales force as a sounding board. This method, however, could lead to a biased conclusion, colored by the interest of the people doing the survey.

The best method to gauge customer satisfaction is to have management responsible for the product talk directly with customers to find out how they feel about it. Managers should evaluate the response honestly and should correct things that make the customer unhappy. In the long run, companies that succeed in this process will have nothing but satisfied customers and great products.


## 7.4 THE ROLE OF FINAL INSPECTION

Final inspection is the last chance to stop a defective product before it reaches a customer. Just-in-Time considers inspection wasteful, but in a manufacturing environment it is very important to keep a system of checks and balances to protect the customer when something goes wrong.

The job of a final inspector is to represent the customer by accepting the product as good before it is shipped. The series of checks a final inspector does on a product should be similar to what a customer will do when he or she receives the product. A common practice in many companies is to base final inspection only on the looks of the product, rather than testing its functioning. This cosmetic inspection is wasteful, adding no value to the product.

Depending on the complexity of a product, final inspection should be precise enough to prove functionality. Any defect encountered should be reported immediately and investigated, because there is something wrong with the process that allowed it to happen. A final inspection program should be complemented by an out-of-box audit system. This system selects random boxes ready to ship and does a complete tear-down audit and test of the product. The out-of-box audit is a more complex process that includes not only functionality but also workmanship and process analysis. The audit should also include packaging, documentation, and paperwork. Defects found should be brought up immediately to process engineers, so that causes are investigated and corrected with workers in the production line.

Finding process defects at shipping time is a serious problem that should be dealt with immediately. Defects encountered late in the process are more serious because the system has passed them along without safeguards to detect them. Defects found in final inspection or during out-of-box audits are the worst offenders. These defects require exhaustive analysis and immediate feedback to the process to avoid repetition.


## 7.5 FIELD QUALITY FEEDBACK SYSTEM

The responsibility for tracking customer satisfaction and field quality falls to field support. Field organizations have a direct, firsthand input on the quality of a product during installation and then during the life of the product. The best way to channel that information back to the company is to create a feedback system that reports quality status during installation and thereafter. Field organizations are slow in reporting problems because paperwork usually takes a back seat to other activities.

A good feedback system is an important tool for supporting customers because it helps to improve quality by cutting down defect rates in future shipments. A feedback system should be precise and timely, detailing problems encountered with a product. The information should be sent to the company's quality department and then distributed to people who can do something to fix the problems reported. As a rule, this information should be distributed to manufacturing and design engineering and management.

The best way to improve customer satisfaction is to respond quickly to quality problems reported by the field organization. If some of the problems are design related, they should be promptly addressed by giving them top priority over other tasks in the department.

Another important benefit of analyzing field information is to study the trends as time develops. The quality department is responsible for tracking field quality trends.

For companies with no field organizations, the best way to track field performance is to follow the activity of the repair centers that repair the product. A high level of activity repairing products too early in their life cycles spells problems for the product. The quality department should also track this activity. The information should be distributed to manufacturing and design engineering.

A quality feedback system should have a companion problem correction system implemented with it; feeding back problems without a system to correct them would be a waste of time. Just-in-Time requires this information to be precise and minimally burdened with overhead. Just-in-Time also requires the information to be sent first to people in charge of solving the problems, issuing corrective actions. The feedback system should not be designed to tell management how great a product is. It should be designed to expect problems and to correct them efficiently. After all, behind every defective product there is an unsatisfied customer.

## 7.6 QUALITY SATISFACTION MEASUREMENTS

The main goal of a quality system is to produce products that fully satisfy the needs of customers. A quality system in a company is not a system designed to inspect quality in products. In a Just-in-Time system, a quality system is a series of foolproof process steps designed to build products with perfect quality consistently.

The quality of a product is measured by the level of customer satisfaction. A product that has good quality but doesn't satisfy the customer's needs from a performance point of view is a product bound for failure. The level of functionality of a product should also measure its overall quality. This aspect of quality is the most difficult to gauge because it is subjective. Also, there is no product that can offer a level of functionality that fully satisfies the needs of all customers.

Two key aspects used to measure quality in a product are hardware performance and actual level of functionality compared against specs. Both measurements are equally important because a product will not survive in the market if it doesn't meet both requirements.

Hardware performance relates to the working condition of a product when it arrives at the customer's site. It also relates to how long it works without breaking or excessive maintenance. The following sections will address different measurements used to determine a product's quality performance from a hardware point of view.

Customer satisfaction based on product performance is more difficult to measure because it involves the customer's (subjective) opinion of the product. Several methods are used to measure this aspect of quality. Customer surveys using questionnaire mailings, monitoring key installations, user group meetings, and management visits to large user installations are among the methods used. The problem with most of these methods is that they have to be interpreted by another layer of people, who, in turn, might see the information in a different light from its original intent. This distortion could change the product's perception factor from a customer point of view, misleading management into a different strategic direction.

## 7.7 DEAD ON ARRIVAL (DOA)

The DOA rate tracks the percentage of products shipped that don't work when they arrive at customer sites. The rate is related to the concept of plug-and-play. The customer receives a product and it gets installed, or plugged, and it doesn't work.

Many companies have a narrow definition of a DOA product. For example, if the product works electrically, but the power cord or manual is missing, it is not a DOA. Just-in-Time calls DOA anything that makes the product different from what the customer expected when it was ordered. A missing manual or piece of software would be counted as DOA.

DOA rates reflect a direct measurement of customer satisfaction. Nothing will make a customer more dissatisfied than receiving a product that either doesn't work or has incomplete documentation or software. A company with a perfect-quality program should have a zero DOA rate. Management should monitor this rate very carefully because it reflects the quality of the process that builds the product. DOA also measures handling and shipping damages after the product is shipped.

Reporting DOAs correctly is the responsibility of the field service organization or the responsibility of repair centers, if they receive DOA products for repair. It is important that the causes of DOAs are clearly listed in categories that can be traced and fixed. For example, *Product Doesn't Work* is not a clear description of a problem.

One of the first goals of a Just-in-Time quality program is to understand the DOA rate of the products. Then a program should be put in place to solve the most common DOA problems reported by the system. This task may require a redesign effort on the part of the development groups. Goals to reduce DOA rates should be implemented and executed. The quality department should be responsible for spearheading this effort, but the effort should involve manufacturing and design engineering, including quality and field engineering. If the problem is paperwork, then the people responsible for this task should be involved. Cutting DOA rates is the most urgent effort of any quality program, because this is the single most common cause of customer dissatisfaction.

## 7.8 INFANT MORTALITY

Infant mortality is defined as a malfunction of the product within a short period of time after installation and initial usage. This time frame should be short, but not so short that it misses product failures right after the end of the window. For example, any failure in the first 30 days of usage could be a window for infant mortality.

Infant mortality is usually a measurement of the quality of the components used to build the product. It could also mean poor workmanship in the process that built the product. When infant mortality is analyzed, the cause of the failure should be determined clearly and a corrective action should follow. Common causes of infant mortality are component failures that require replacement or redesign.

A problem analysis program is key to understanding the causes of infant mortality. A product with a high rate of infant mortality is a product bound for failure; it will fall out of grace with customers rapidly. It will also cause costly repairs and customer damage recovery.

Most companies don't track infant mortality, considering a failure after installation just a field failure. Infant mortality is difficult to track because of the time sensitivities associated with it. Customers sometimes don't report and return a failed product promptly, within the time frame required to call it an infant mortality failure.

Companies sensitive to customer satisfaction should have an infant mortality program. This monitors the rate of failure returns and the time frame when they occurred. The company should also have an active program to reduce infant mortality to zero. This program requires improvements in the process and an engineering effort to fix individual component failures that caused the early failure. Infant mortality programs should be coupled with a program to reduce DOA rates.

## 7.9 MEAN TIME BETWEEN FAILURES

Mean time between failure, MTBF, is the average number of hours a product will operate before a failure occurs. MTBF is a direct measurement of the reliability of the product, which depends on the individual reliability of every component used to build it. Every product should have a goal MTBF when it is designed. The selection of the components used to build the product should be directly related to this goal. MTBF is a design feature; it should be included in the original product spec, after functionality.

There are two ways to calculate the MTBF of a product. The first is theoretical, used by reliability engineers who develop the reliability model of the product components using the statistical failure rate of each one. The theoretical MTBF is usually calculated at design time, and it should influence design changes to improve the reliability of a product.

The second way to calculate the MTBF of a product is a practical one. The manufacturer adds the working hours of products in the field and divides by the number of failures that occurred during the time period. If the population of products in the field is large enough, the empirical MTBF should closely track the theoretical number calculated. If this number is smaller, it will be an indication that some component is failing earlier than antic-ipated and an engineering analysis is required to fix the problem.

## 7.10  MEAN TIME BETWEEN SERVICE CALLS

For complex products that have a combination of hardware and software, the MTBF is not an accurate measure of the product performance once it is installed. Customer satisfaction is better measured by tracking the mean time between service calls, the MTBSC. This index will also track problems with a system that are not hardware related—for example, soft-ware problems, poor customer training, errors in documentation, or excessive maintenance visits. The MTBSC will be a better measurement of customer satisfaction than MTBF.

Practical experience shows that MTBSC runs about half the number of hours as the MTBF. For example, a complex computer system with an MTBF of 10,000 hours will have an MTBSC of approximately 5,000 hours.

Once tracked, MTBSC should be improved by reducing the number of service calls required to keep the product working. The best way to accomplish this goal is to work on key problems that caused the service calls. Many companies overlook this index and think they have a great product because MTBFs are high. However, the customer's satisfaction is not high because field people are constantly visiting them to solve documentation inconsis-tencies or software problems.

A Just-in-Time quality system considers service calls in excess of the equipment's normal wear and tear wasteful. A good index to measure this is to compare the actual MTBF of the installed equipment to the empirical MTBF. Then MTBSC should closely track MTBF hours. Any difference between these indexes is considered a waste and should be minimized.

## 7.11  QUALITY OF SERVICE

When there is a problem with a product, servicing a customer is of utmost importance. Any customer can accept a product failure because he or she understands the sheer probability that a malfunction could occur. The same customer will not accept slow or incomplete support once a problem is reported. Quality of service plays a very critical role in shaping customer satisfaction.

There are several important factors used to measure quality of service: speed, quality, and cost of service.

*Speed of service* measures the time that it takes to service a customer after a problem has been reported. For complex systems that require a field service person to travel, speed of service should include the time it took to get the repair engineer to the customer site. If a product was sent to a repair depot, then speed of service will measure the time that it took to fix and return the product to the customer.

For complex computer systems, a customer expects speed of service in the neighborhood of hours. A customer also expects full twenty-four-hour, seven-day-a-week support. The time to repair index, TTR, measures the speed of service for a product. TTRs are affected by the design of the product and the ease of failure diagnostics. Field replaceable units, FRUs, are the smallest replaceable units in a complex product that will be replaced in the field upon a failure. These units should be defined at design time, so a product can be easily repaired on the field.

*Quality of repair* has to do with the working condition of the product after it is repaired. Nothing could be more annoying to a customer than a product that fails again after it has been repaired. The goal of a field service organization is to complete repairs with zero defects.

Just-in-Time quality considers speed of service and quality of repair to be important indexes that measure customer satisfaction. Just-in-Time also calls for the elimination of waste in a service organization. For example, in the case of speed of service, the time a field engineer travels adds no value to the customer and is considered waste. All activities classified as waste should be minimized, so field engineers can concentrate on activities that really provide value added—fixing customers' problems.

*Cost of service* relates to the inventory level of spare parts required to support customers. Just-in-Time provides valuable assistance in the management of the spare parts used to support a field repair organization. Maintaining a large buffer inventory of spare parts is against Just-in-Time principles. Distribution of spares should be based on actual consumption of spares, not on the forecast of their use. Actual field consumption rates should be used to plan and execute a Kanban system to pull spares into repair depots. This operational arrangement will minimize the use of spares, increase their quality, and minimize the logistics to manage spares traffic in the system. The goal of such a system is to improve the quality of service, which, in turn, will increase customer satisfaction.

## 7.12 SUMMARY

Achieving customer satisfaction is not easy. Any company can focus on a particular aspect of customer service and keep some customers satisfied at the expense of others. But to achieve customer satisfaction across the board requires dedication, attention to detail, and unconditional commitment at all levels of the organization.

A company with satisfied customers is a successful company. From the quality point of view, a customer's opinion should always be the final opinion of a product's quality. A quality system should always be sensitive to this fact and respond quickly when something goes wrong. The Just-in-Time quality system should view itself as a representative of the customer inside of the company. To the extent that a quality system achieves this goal, the company will be successful.

Customer satisfaction should be the driving force behind a quality organization. Measuring the level of customer satisfaction correctly is an important part of a feedback system—and correcting problems when they are discovered is even more important. Once a product is delivered, the only way for a customer to be satisfied is for the product to perform to his or her expectations. It is the job of the company to make sure this expectation is fully met.

# REFERENCES

BLAISDELL, MIKAEL. *When it Comes to Support, the Customer is King. Info World*, 14, no. 25, 22 June 1992, 60–65.

D'EGIDIO, FRANCO. *The Service Era: Leadership in a Global Environment*. Cambridge, Mass.: Productivity Press, 1990.

FEIGINBAUM, ARMAND V. *Total Quality Control*. New York: McGraw-Hill, 1983, pp. 570–612.

HARRINGTON, H. JAMES. *Poor-Quality Cost*. Quality and Reliability/11. New York: ASQC Quality Press, 1987, pp. 123–148.

HOROVITZ, JACQUES. *Winning Ways: Achieving Zero-Defect Service*. Cambridge, Mass.: Productivity Press, 1990.

JURAN, J. M. *Juran on Planning for Quality*. New York: The Free Press, 1988.

# 8★

# Problem Detection and Correction: Observe, Detect, and Correct

Achieving perfect quality in a product is a job that never ends. Even when we have a perfect product shipped off of a production line, there is always room for improvement. This is the most important concept for excellence in quality. Another possibility is that something goes wrong, the recipe for quality is lost, and the product comes out of a process defective.

Companies that consistently produce quality products have a first-class quality system in place. They also pay careful attention to details discovering problems before they happen. Problem detection and correction are very important aspects of a quality system. Problem prevention is even more important in guaranteeing a consistent level of quality in a product.

To achieve consistent quality, it is important to assume that the job of a quality system never ends, even when quality goals are achieved. It is also necessary to remember that deterioration of the quality never happens suddenly with a change that is immediately noticed. Quality usually deteriorates in small increments that tend to hide until their sum is so obvious that they hit the manufacturer right in the face. A first-rate quality prevention system should be able to detect these small changes, so the system can take corrective actions before small problems are compounded into a major one.

Another factor that affects the quality of a product once it reaches acceptable levels is resources priority. Normally, companies assign a lot of resources to solve problems with products in trouble. This effort siphons support from other products that are going through a process with perfect quality. The result is that a poor-quality product gets fixed and a good product turns bad. It is very important to balance properly the resource allocation of a quality system to avoid poor quality switchover. Safeguards should be put in place to raise a warning as soon as the system starts to behave that way. Management should also be wary

**100**

of this problem because management is the first to cause resource imbalances when under pressure to solve the hottest problem on hand.


## 8.1 QUALITY SYSTEM OPERATING MODES

A Just-in-Time quality system should operate in two different modes: information and correction. The modes are not exclusive and are responsible for monitoring, detecting, and solving quality problems in a process.

An effective Just-in-Time quality system must pay attention to details and have a strong resolve to fix problems. A problem with a part causes an immediate impact on the process, because there is no replacement for a defective one. Therefore, the quality system has to be very attentive to details, so it can anticipate problems before they happen.

Any quality program designed to address problem prevention rather than correction should focus on the front end of a process, including raw materials. This system emphasizes the Just-in-Time concept that quality starts at the source: the makers of the parts.

To implement a Just-in-Time quality system successfully, it is important to understand the conditions that trigger a switch from one mode to the other. The following sections will present a detailed description of the modes, including implementation suggestions. Figure 8.1 shows the relationship between the information and correction modes as they interface with a process. Notice that the correction mode should send corrective actions to sections of the process preceding the place that triggered the switch. The information mode is always present in a process and will not stop working during a problem-solv-

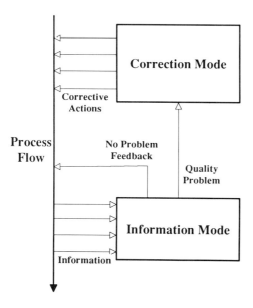

**Figure 8.1**  Quality Control Operating Modes

ing phase. Section 8.3 will show the role of the information mode changing when the system turns a correction mode on. The correction mode is used to correct problems when they are detected or, if the system is properly set, to prevent the occurrence of problems.

## 8.2 INFORMATION MODE

In a normal production environment, there is always the possibility that something will go wrong when it is least expected. The job of the information mode is to monitor the process and be able to detect a problem before it becomes a defect. The mode should analyze critical data that allow for quick detection of problems.

The information mode should be effective and nonbureaucratic, with a minimum of paperwork requirements. The main priority of the system is to inform workers promptly that *something is about to go wrong*. The information should pinpoint precisely where the problem is, helping workers to take corrective actions to fix the problem immediately.

Information modes differ in scope and implementation, depending on the process and the people involved with the product. In general, the system should not only monitor a process but also monitor suppliers contributing raw material. The main goal of the system

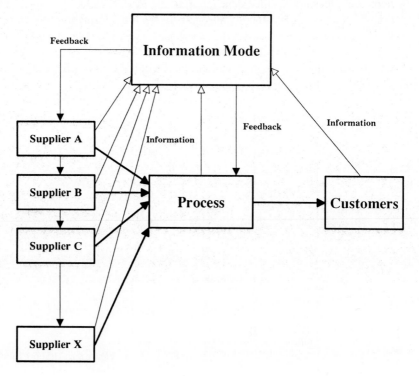

**Figure 8.2**  Information Mode Areas of Application

should be proactive rather than reactive. The information mode will be working effectively when it can prevent a problem before it happens, rather than correcting a problem after it has affected quality. Figure 8.2 shows the information mode key areas of operation. Quality information is collected from suppliers, the process, and the installed base. Then it is sent to the processing information center. The analysis of the information is then sent back to the makers of the parts, including a warning if something is about to go wrong.

Effective information modes are not burdened by bureaucratic layers of paperwork and people. This could delay the quality feedback in reaching the makers of the parts. The simplest and most effective feedback mechanism is to implement small information/correction cells that provide immediate feedback to workers. This is the concept used in the poka-yoke system, where a process operation is monitored and stopped immediately if something goes beyond the limits established by the poka-yoke device. Figure 8.3 shows the concept of a single cell of an information/correction mode. This system provides immediate feedback to people doing the work. The cell is not burdened by a bureaucratic layer that could delay the interpretation and action necessary to correct a defect. A combination of many information/correction cells placed along critical places in the process is the best way to monitor and protect the quality integrity of a product. This arrangement will also avoid the propagation of a defect beyond the point where it originated.

The main characteristics of an efficient information mode system are:

1. Avoid layers of paperwork that will delay quality feedback to the place where the data came from.
2. Implement a system where there is a short path between the data collection activity and the place in the process where the feedback mechanism takes corrective actions.
3. Carefully select the critical points required to monitor quality in a process. Implement a 100 percent sampling if possible. For example, use poka-yoke devices.
4. Set up a system that places the authority to correct a process at the lowest possible level.
5. Implement a simple feedback system to inform suppliers about the quality performance of their parts. Agree with them on the critical parameters the quality system is

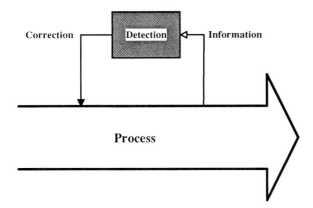

**Figure 8.3**  Single Cell of Information/ Correction Mode

going to monitor. Get commitments from suppliers on the turnaround time to fix problems once they are reported.

6. Implement a system to collect data on the quality of products once delivered to customers.

7. For design-related problems, implement an engineering feedback system to correct problems promptly.

8. Define the process' minimal set of quality criteria that the information system is going to monitor in order to judge overall quality.

9. Implement a statistical process control (SPC) system to monitor the overall performance of the process from a global point of view.

10. Never keep the quality criteria of the monitored points in a process static. When quality targets are achieved consistently, tighten the goals and start all over again.

## 8.3 CORRECTION MODE

The correction mode is a mode of action. Something is wrong and needs to be fixed. A good correction mode is measured not only by its ability to solve problems but also by how quick and permanent the fixes are. A manufacturing process producing defective parts should be stopped immediately; that is the time when the correction mode takes over and fixes the problem.

The first task of a correction mode is not to fix a problem but to find out the cause of a problem. The execution of this task should be carried out by a team rather than a particular person. In a Just-in-Time system, the team assigned to solving problems in a process should be composed of quality and manufacturing engineers. Once the solution is found, the system will require a corrective action to be implemented immediately, so the process can continue production.

A three-step procedure provides a simple way to correct a problem in a process. Figure 8.4 shows the interrelationship of steps with a process and the sequence required to solve a problem. First, the problem is investigated by collecting all the data related to pos-

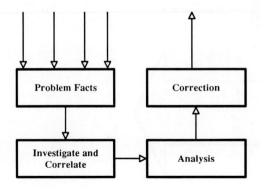

**Figure 8.4** Problem-Solving Process

sible causes. This is the most important phase of the problem-solving process because the information will be the basis for the analysis that will follow.

The second step is the analysis of the problem based on the causes and effects produced. This step should also consider different solutions to the problem, selecting the one that fixes the problem permanently.

The final step is the implementation of the fix required to solve the problem. The fix should be permanent.

The three-step problem-solving procedure is summarized below:

1. Don't stop investigating until all possible causes of the problem are explored and clearly understood.
2. Analyze thoroughly all the effects produced by the causes. These effects show up in a product in the form of a quality nonconformance. Model fixes to prevent the causes. Make sure the effects disappear completely when all the causes are eliminated. Don't compromise the overall quality of the process at the time of selecting a final fix.
3. Implement the fix permanently and return to the information mode.

## 8.4 THE ROLE OF WORKERS IN PROBLEM DETECTION AND CORRECTION

In a Just-in-Time system, the workers building a part have the responsibility for the quality of the part. Many companies' quality systems don't follow this rule and insert quality inspectors in a process to inspect quality in a product. In general, quality inspectors look for defects by following a criterion that separates a good part from a bad part. Inspectors are not trained to work in a process and most of the time cannot assemble a product. The role of inspectors is to detect and inform when something doesn't match the quality criteria. A properly trained worker knows how to build a product and understands the steps necessary to do the job correctly. It is very easy to upgrade a worker to become his or her own inspector, as well as the inspector of the previous worker in the line. This additional responsibility puts the burden for quality on the makers of the part. This system also provides immediate feedback about what is causing a quality problem in the process. A worker trained in assembling a product has a better chance of knowing what is wrong than a quality inspector only inspecting a part.

Workers should play an important role in problem detection and correction. After all, they are responsible for causing problems, in most cases. For cases where a machine is producing a defective part, there is still a worker responsible for monitoring the machine. Workers also have a good insight as to what has to be done to correct a problem.

Many companies make the mistake of not consulting workers whenever there is a quality problem. They assume that manufacturing engineers know it all and don't bother to consult the people building the product. Worker feedback is of utmost importance in fixing a problem. It also gives quality and manufacturing engineers immediate feedback when a fix implemented in a process doesn't work. A worker who participates in the investigation and solution of a problem will take personal responsibility to avoid a repetition of the problem.

There are a few simple rules we can use to make a worker's quality system effective and responsive.

1. Train workers to be alert and responsive to changes in a process that will lead to poor quality output.
2. Simplify workers' inspection roles by introducing self-checking devices that will immediately detect any variations in the process. Use poka-yoke devices for this task.
3. Involve workers in the investigation of problems.
4. Make workers part of the solution to a problem by consulting them on possible solutions. Test fixes with workers first.

## 8.5  DATA COLLECTION

An important job of a Just-in-Time quality system is to set up a simple system for collecting and analyzing quality data in a process. It is important to remember that this activity does not add any value to the product and therefore should be minimized.

Normally, there is a close correlation between data collection and data analysis. The effectiveness of the analysis will depend on the type and accuracy of the data collected. Proper correlation will also indicate trends in a process even when there are still no defects reported.

Many times manufacturing organizations are buried under a mountain of data, making it almost impossible to see trends or to spot trouble until the problem is so obvious that no data collection is needed to point it out. The main job of a data collection system is to detect early symptoms of trouble before it actually happens. This brings up the concept of problem prevention versus problem correction.

Many manufacturing companies working in assembly processes collect quality data manually. Other companies with financial and technical resources use a computer data collection system. No matter what the level of automation used, the quality system will be as effective as the quality of the data collected. In general, the system should not be burdened with unnecessary, wasteful information that hides problems until it is too late to prevent them.

Below are a few rules to use in order to assure the quality of the data collection process:

1. Select process measurement points that will provide information for the prevention of quality problems rather than detection of defects.
2. Avoid duplicity by selecting a minimum set of data points that cover all measurements you want to make in the process. This minimum set is called the critical set of measurements.

3. Safeguard the data collection process with a set of poka-yoke devices installed along the process. Make sure they don't duplicate the data collection effort.

4. Analyze the effectiveness of the data collected to prevent quality problems. Always try to reduce the number of data collection points, investigating the impact on quality output of the process.

5. Categorize the data collection process to make the data interpretation and analysis easier. Change categories as you learn the critical characteristics of the process.

6. Minimize the amount of worker involvement in collecting data. Whenever possible, automate the process.

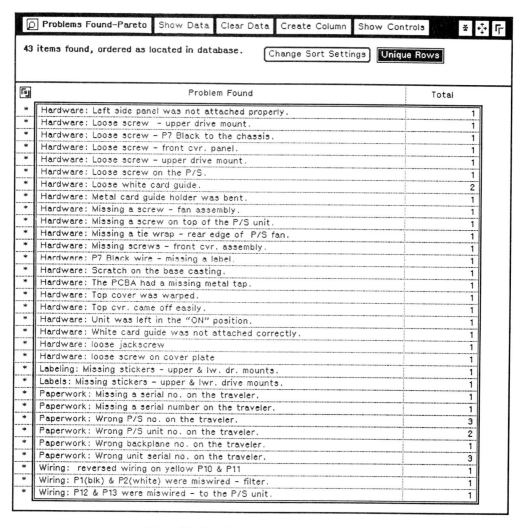

| Problem Found | Total |
|---|---|
| Hardware: Left side panel was not attached properly. | 1 |
| Hardware: Loose screw  – upper drive mount. | 1 |
| Hardware: Loose screw – P7 Black to the chassis. | 1 |
| Hardware: Loose screw – front cvr. panel. | 1 |
| Hardware: Loose screw – upper drive mount. | 1 |
| Hardware: Loose screw on the P/S. | 1 |
| Hardware: Loose white card guide. | 2 |
| Hardware: Metal card guide holder was bent. | 1 |
| Hardware: Missing a screw – fan assembly. | 1 |
| Hardware: Missing a screw on top of the P/S unit. | 1 |
| Hardware: Missing a tie wrap – rear edge of  P/S fan. | 1 |
| Hardware: Missing screws – front cvr. assembly. | 1 |
| Hardware: P7 Black wire – missing a label. | 1 |
| Hardware: Scratch on the base casting. | 1 |
| Hardware: The PCBA had a missing metal tap. | 1 |
| Hardware: Top cover was warped. | 1 |
| Hardware: Top cvr. came off easily. | 1 |
| Hardware: Unit was left in the "ON" position. | 1 |
| Hardware: White card guide was not attached correctly. | 1 |
| Hardware: loose jackscrew | 1 |
| Hardware: loose screw on cover plate | 1 |
| Labeling: Missing stickers – upper & lw. dr. mounts. | 1 |
| Labels: Missing stickers – upper & lwr. drive mounts. | 1 |
| Paperwork: Missing a serial no. on the traveler. | 1 |
| Paperwork: Missing a serial number on the traveler. | 1 |
| Paperwork: Wrong P/S no. on the traveler. | 3 |
| Paperwork: Wrong P/S unit no. on the traveler. | 2 |
| Paperwork: Wrong backplane no. on the traveler. | 1 |
| Paperwork: Wrong unit serial no. on the traveler. | 3 |
| Wiring:  reversed wiring on yellow P10 & P11 | 1 |
| Wiring: P1(blk) & P2(white) were miswired – filter. | 1 |
| Wiring: P12 & P13 were miswired – to the P/S unit. | 1 |

**Figure 8.5**   Data Collection Systems Used at Relevant Technologies

Figure 8.5 shows a set of data collected in a process to monitor quality performance. These data were collected at different points in the process and were organized into categories to make the analysis simple and effective.

## 8.6 PROBLEM ANALYSIS

Once data are collected and tabulated into categories, several methods can be used to analyze the meaning of the information. The most common is to chart the data into visual trends and relationships. Charts organize information in such a way that they can lead to the detection of defects before they happen. Charts also provide information about the occurrences of different defects and possible interactions among them. The main goal of charts is to provide a systematic analysis of problems and a path to prioritize changes in a process.

In general, any methodology that leads to analysis of problems and their causes is the first step in solving a quality problem. Two of the most common charts used by quality engineers are the Pareto chart and the cause-and-effect diagram (also known as the Ishikawa diagram, in honor of its inventor, Kaoru Ishikawa). The Ishikawa diagram is also known as the fishbone diagram.

Figure 6.1 shows a typical Pareto chart. The chart shows a list of problems in a process and their relative priority based on their rate of occurrence. The chart is very useful in organizing the efforts of quality teams to solve the most common problems first. The chart can also be used to list the problems that cause a single defect, and then the correction effort can be focused on solving first those problems that most influence the defect under investigation.

Figure 8.6 shows Ishikawa's cause-and-effect diagram. Ishikawa classifies the cause factors into five categories: material, machine, measurement, man, and method. He calls these the *cause factors* in a process. The effects of these cause factors are the quality characteristics of a product. The diagram resembles a fishbone and is commonly called that.

Besides the two previous charts, there are other types of diagrams that are commonly used to formalize the systematic analysis of problems and solutions. Among them are histograms, feedback charts, and scatter diagrams.

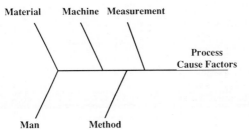

**Figure 8.6**   Ishikawa Cause-and-Effect Diagram

## 8.7 CORRECTIVE ACTION

Once the solution to a quality problem is identified, the next step is to come up with a plan to address all the issues associated with a corrective action. Corrective actions should address three important factors associated with a process: effectivity, disposition, and cost.

*Effectivity* determines the timing to implement a corrective action. The effectivity criterion is based on the complexity of the problem and the nature of the fix. In general, there are well-defined boundaries in the natural flow of building a product that can point to where to implement a corrective action:

1. Raw material not used yet.
2. Work in progress, WIP.
3. Finished products not delivered to customers yet.
4. Products already delivered to customers.

A typical corrective action to fix quality problems on products already delivered to customers is automobile recalls to fix design flaws. A corrective action might be just to fix raw material that has not been used in a process.

*Disposition* of material is a cost-related factor that affects the implementation of a corrective action. Parts can be so defective that the best solution is to scrap them and reorder new ones. Many manufacturers don't take this decision lightly because of the cost implications. Then they risk reworking costs or costly field retrofits that cause customer dissatisfaction. The *cost* of disposition should take second place to the commitment for quality in a product. The main goal of the system is to correct a quality problem no matter what the cost. Any policy that compromises this activity will push back a manufacturer to being a second-rate producer of products.

Once the decision is made, a corrective action should be speedily implemented, so quality is brought back to the perfect level. Another aspect of effectively implemented corrective actions is the message sent to workers, showing the company's commitment to keeping quality a first priority. Nothing would be more devastating to worker morale than delaying a corrective action because of costs implications or lack of resolve on the part of management.

A proper feedback mechanism to track corrective actions is important in assessing their effectiveness. After implementing a corrective action, the next step is to gather fresh quality data to track the effects of the change. This effort should use the same procedures and charts that warned about the problem initially. The system should also monitor actual costs incurred against estimated costs. The team in charge of implementing a corrective action should be composed of the people who found the solution to the problem; this allows them to see the results of their work. This approach to solving problems reinforces the resolve of management to keeping quality a first priority.

## 8.8 PROBLEM PREVENTION

A Just-in-Time quality system strongly supports the concept of problem prevention rather than problem correction. A problem prevented is a problem that caused no waste; a problem corrected is a problem that caused a waste of labor, material, and customer satisfaction. Problem prevention requires a clear understanding of the criteria needed to detect problems before they happen. The correct approach to this methodology will depend on the type of products and processes and the type of problems that are preventable.

The principles of problem prevention cover three specific areas:

1. Careful *observation* of early signs of trouble.
2. Intensive *worker training*.
3. *Preventive maintenance* of the equipment used to build products.

Early observation of signs of trouble is the most difficult part of problem prevention. In general, trained workers, doing their jobs over and over again, develop an extra sense that tells them when something is about to go wrong in a process. The workers' intuitive sense that detects something about to go wrong should be encouraged and rewarded. Conversely, workers should never be punished when they apply judgment erroneously. Policies that encourage workers not to say that something is wrong until it is obviously wrong should be avoided—workers will be afraid of making a mistake, of stopping a line for nothing. A quality-conscious manufacturer should encourage workers to err on the safe side rather than to ignore early signs of trouble and then stop the line after defective products have already been built.

Intuitive feelings about problems threatening a process can be fostered by carefully monitoring process performance charts on a real-time basis. Some manufacturers have sophisticated process charting systems to track process performance, but they update those charts once a day, not often enough to detect sudden problems that could be prevented. The frequency of updating process charts should be related to the throughput rate of the process. For high-output processes, a real-time chart should watch trends almost up to the minute. The chart should provide a sufficient early warning to stop the process as soon as the first symptoms of trouble appear.

The second step in preventing problems in a process is to concentrate on worker training. Most of the defects in a process are caused by untrained or overconfident workers. Training programs should be an ongoing activity for a quality-conscious manufacturer. Assuming that once trained, workers will continue doing their jobs right forever is a dangerous mistake. Train your workers over and over, making sure they develop a preventive approach to solving problems as the best way to prevent defects.

Another thing that can go wrong in a process is equipment. A properly implemented preventive maintenance and calibration program is the key ingredient in a first-class quality system. Equipment should be restored to its initial condition after it reaches the hours of use limit specified by the manufacturer. Then when the equipment reaches the end of its useful life, it should be replaced with a new piece of equipment. Many manufacturers don't follow this approach, thinking that a maintenance program is enough to keep equipment operational forever. In practice, all equipment has a definite limit to its useful life. It is up to the manufacturer to know the length of this life and to make sure new equipment replaces old when that time comes.

To develop a prevention-minded organization:

1. Collect process quality data in the real-time mode. Make sure the data show trends in the process as time passes.

2. Clearly define the criteria used to determine when a process is about to go wrong. Then use these criteria to take corrective action against the conditions that are causing the trend to change.

3. Train and encourage workers to look for things that are about to go wrong. Reward them when they discover something that is nearly bad rather than unsalvageable.

4. Retrain workers every six months, or sooner, if the work is complicated.

5. Train workers to stop a process when the first defect is found, rather than waiting to see if the next part will be good.

6. Don't punish workers if they pulled a line stop mistakenly because they believed that something was about to go wrong.

7. When possible, install poka-yoke devices to stop a process as soon as the first defect is detected.

8. Implement a first-class maintenance program on the equipment used in the process. The program should include calibration and maintenance.

9. Ascertain the manufacturer's recommended useful life for all equipment used in the process. Replace equipment as it reaches the end of its life.

## 8.9 SOLVING MULTIPLE PROBLEMS

Poor quality is not like lightning—it strikes more than once. Quality problems generally show up in groups at the most critical times in a process. Quality teams monitoring a process need to prioritize resources carefully to solve the most critical problems first.

Fortunately, quality problems also follow the 20/80 percent rule, where 20 percent of defects cause 80 percent of problems. The question presented to quality teams is how to analyze which ones belong to the 20 percent and which ones do not.

There is a simple four-step procedure used to solve multiple quality problems. This procedure is important for cases where there are not enough resources to solve all problems at once. If the resources are capable of handling more than the top three problems, then the number of problems should be increased to match the resources.

1. Itemize problems on a problem list, putting the most urgent ones at the top.

2. Analyze the top three and develop corrective plans to solve them.

3. Implement the corrective actions.

**4.** Start the process again with the next set of problems. Don't stop the loop until all problems are solved.

One trap to avoid in using this procedure is rushing solutions that will not solve problems permanently. The problem will be back on the list shortly, affecting the morale of the team and the need for more resources.

## 8.10 QUALITY TEAMS IN THE FACTORY

It is usually assumed that quality teams are composed only of quality engineers. This assumption is wrong. Quality teams should gather the technical people who can best solve quality problems regardless of their jobs within the organization. Management should encourage a variety of participation, so the best expertise is used to solve problems quickly and effectively.

Another responsibility of quality teams is to carry out successive improvements in a process even when there are no quality problems causing delays. Normally, quality engineers and process engineers are the key members in quality teams. Workers should also participate because they are the ones who have experience building the product.

The goals of quality teams are to increase yields and eliminate defects. The first goal should be an ongoing activity aimed at increasing productivity; the second focuses on problem detection and correction. Whenever there is a problem, quality teams should take over to discover the cause of the problem and its optimum correction. If the correction requires interface with a supplier, the team should become involved with the supplier's operational people. Quality teams are also responsible for defect prevention programs and for training workers assigned to them.

A factory may have several quality teams operating in different processes or in different sections of the same process. Quality teams should cooperate and share information with other quality teams. They should also have methods and training procedures in common, so workers don't get confused when transferred from one team to another. Quality teams should have a sense of urgency. They should also document changes and corrective actions properly. In essence, they are factory doctors who go around practicing preventive medicine on the health of a process, before it gets sick.

## 8.11 THE ROLE OF DESIGN ENGINEERING

Quality teams usually don't require the direct involvement of design engineers. In some instances, however, quality problems are related to poor, marginal design practices. In those cases, design engineers should be assigned to quality teams, allowing them to participate in the solution of the problem.

Quality problems are usually related to process problems, caused by defective raw material or worker involvement. Furthermore, there are cases where a quality problem is clearly assignable to a design flaw or a part that has been wrongly designed into the product. These design-related quality problems are easy to detect. The ones that are difficult to handle are the marginal ones disguised as process dependent. In this case, a design task force should take the job of redesigning the problem out of the product, so margins can be restored. A sense of urgency is of extreme importance in this case, because the marginal design will certainly produce low yields, material waste, and poor quality.

Management should become aware of these situations, making sure that design engineers are properly focused on solving the problem. Design changes in a released product should always take precedence over design efforts on new products.

## 8.12  FEEDBACK TO SUPPLIERS

No quality system can operate efficiently without a first-rate feedback system to suppliers. There should be no difference between communicating problems to workers in a process and communicating problems to suppliers that feed material to the factory. Quality feedback to a supplier should be timely and directed at people in charge of monitoring the quality of the supplier's process. The supplier's role is not to be defensive and to take immediate action to correct problems pointed out by the feedback information.

Here are a few important points with regard to a supplier's quality feedback system:

1. Quality feedback to suppliers should be an ongoing process rather than only when there is a problem with a part.
2. Information should go directly to the supplier's people responsible for monitoring the quality of the process.
3. Feedback information should be precise, containing only pertinent data related to the supplier's parts. The supplier and the customer should agree on the format of the information.
4. Quality information should be presented in a positive framework. It should also tell the supplier what he or she is doing right.
5. Once the information tracks a problem, the system should not stop reporting until the supplier has corrected it and there are enough data to prove the problem has been solved.
6. The reporting process should be simple and should include historical performance. Excess paperwork that produces unnecessary work and waste should be avoided.

## 8.13  SUMMARY

Quality degradation in a process rarely shows up all of a sudden. A process is still producing quality parts when the first signs of trouble appear. A first-class quality system needs a mechanism to detect the smallest quality deviation before the product actually goes bad.

This capability is more important in Just-in-Time than in any other manufacturing environment, because the process will have no excess parts to cover for the defective ones.

Just-in-Time calls for waste elimination, and defective parts are certainly one of the most expensive forms of waste. A good quality feedback system, with an efficient problem detection and correction system, should monitor and control process quality as soon as the system deviates from the established norm.

Companies that are successful in producing quality-perfect products are good not only at controlling quality but also at solving problems when something goes wrong. The challenge of good quality is not only to produce good parts consistently, but to be able to detect bad ones before they appear. A system with this kind of capability will be efficient and cost effective and will never fail to meet customers' expectations.

# REFERENCES

AKIYAMA, KANEO. *Function Analysis. Systematic Improvement of Quality Performance.* Cambridge, Mass.: Productivity Press, 1991.

FUKUDA, RYUJI. *CEDAC: A Tool for Continuous Systematic Improvement.* Cambridge, Mass.: Productivity Press, 1990.

ISHIWATA, JUNICHI. *IE for the Shop Floor: Productivity Through Process Analysis.* Cambridge, Mass.: Productivity Press, 1991.

JUSE Problem Solving Research Group. *TQC Solutions: The 14-Step Process.* Cambridge, Mass.: Productivity Press, 1991.

KANE, V. *Defect Prevention: Use of Simple Statistical Tools.* New York: Marcel Dekker, 1989.

LEHRER, ROBERT N. *Participative Productivity and Quality of Work Life.* Englewood Cliffs, N.J.: Prentice-Hall, 1982.

ROBINSON, ALAN, ed. *Continuous Improvement in Operations: A Systematic Approach to Waste Reduction.* Cambridge, Mass.: Productivity Press, 1991.

SHINGO, SHIGEO. *The Shingo Production Management System: Improving Process Functions.* Cambridge, Mass.: Productivity Press, 1992.

# 9★

# Quality Information System: Inform Promptly

A key ingredient to quality in a product is information. Workers involved in a production line need to know where they stand with regard to quality every step along the way. They need as much advance notice as possible when something is about to go wrong. They also need a red flag as soon as something *does* go wrong. Many quality information systems are complex in nature and burdened by layers of paperwork that slow the flow of information to workers.

In a Just-in-Time system, paperwork is wasteful and it should be kept to a minimum. Just-in-Time demands first-rate quality; there is no better way to achieve this than to maintain a quality information system to monitor a process. The need to minimize paperwork should be accomplished by a system that is not bureaucratic and reaches only people who can do something about quality problems.

In general, quality information should be precise, simple, and timely. It should also reach people who are experienced and have the authority to do something about correcting deviations in a process.

The key to a first-rate quality information system is the accurate collection of critical process data and formatting these data before they are presented to workers. The biggest challenge to any quality information system is to minimize paperwork and overhead without affecting the quality of the information provided.

## 9.1 THE ROLE OF A QUALITY INFORMATION SYSTEM (QIS)

Many companies have an elaborate quality department with many inspectors and quality engineers, but fail to use them effectively because their quality information system is inefficient and bureaucratic. The role of a quality information system is to transform process data into information that accurately measures the quality of the product being built.

Transforming process data into information for analysis at first seems easy. But the effectiveness of the information system will depend on data selection and transformation. The productivity of the system will depend on the methods used to collect data, because any activity associated with this task is nonproductive and doesn't add any value to the product.

Companies should view the role of a quality information system as necessary to ob-

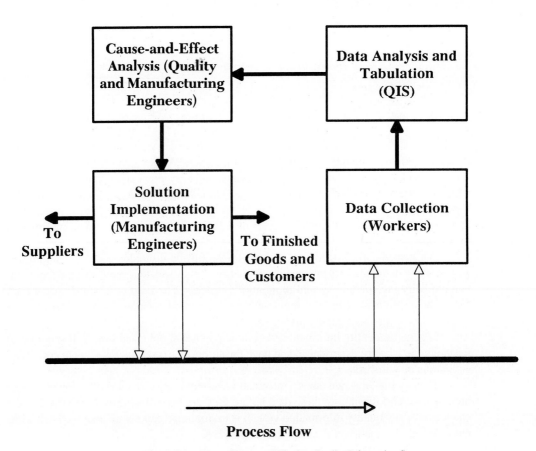

**Figure 9.1**   Areas of Responsibility in a Quality Information System

tain perfect quality in their products. A poorly implemented quality information system will never support a perfect-quality product. The system will only be as effective as the quality of the data collected.

The responsibility for implementing an effective quality information system falls to the quality department. The responsibility for collecting data, analyzing them, and taking corrective action falls to the people using the system—production workers and quality, manufacturing, and design engineers. Quality is everybody's responsibility, and a first-rate quality information system requires cooperation and commitment from everybody using it.

Figure 9.1 shows a closed-loop information system. This system samples a flow of data that triggers a chain reaction that produces actions to correct, or prevent, quality deviations. Notice that corrective actions should be implemented upstream, ahead of the place in the process where the data were sampled, so there is a positive correction feedback to the system. Depending on the type of problem and the time it takes to detect, there is a possibility that the corrective action needs to reach finished goods inventory and customers. The system might also trigger corrective actions to suppliers, if the problem is related to the quality of a part sourced outside the process.

## 9.2 QIS DATA SELECTION

Selection of the data to be sampled is a critical task necessary to assure an effective quality information system. Quality engineers sometimes don't give enough thought to selecting the best set of data samples that minimize information collection yet ensures complete coverage of a process. This data set is not cast in concrete; it can change as more knowledge about the process behavior is gathered with time. Any further changes in data sampling points should be motivated by the need to optimize the coverage of information, so quality trends are properly monitored. Below are some considerations in selecting an optimum data set:

1. Draw a quality flow of the process, understanding the quality requirements of the system in every work center.
2. Select sample points in them that monitor critical parameters which most affect quality.
3. Define the type of data to be collected in those points and tabulate the information they provide, making sure they don't overlap with other readings.
4. Carefully select the criteria defining data as good, marginal, or bad. Define the proper type of statistical charts to use to track the data.
5. Eliminate data collection points that could automatically be checked using poka-yoke devices. These devices will save data collection and analysis, because they will have an embedded criterion for stopping the process when something goes wrong.
6. Review the data collection process with workers to make sure they find the task easy to implement.

7. Overlay areas covered by the data points against all process activities to ensure that a full quality picture is covered by the set.

## 9.3 DATA COLLECTION

Data collection is a menial task that needs careful attention. It easily turns into routine work for workers, affecting the quality of the information collected. A solution is to automate the data collection process as far as possible, so that it will not depend on workers' skills and moods.

Another important aspect of data collection relates to waste and worker productivity. In a Just-in-Time system, there are no quality control inspectors monitoring a process' quality and collecting data. This task is assigned to workers building the product. But a worker collecting quality data is not producing, therefore engaging in wasteful activity. The solution to this is to automate data collection as much as possible. Bar code reading or computerized visual inspection systems are examples of automatic data collection activities.

There are a few important steps to the implementation of a data collection system, influencing the accuracy of the data and the productivity of the workers assigned to the job:

1. Select the data range of values as objectively as possible. Make sure there is no subjective opinion on the part of workers. Cosmetic inspections, for example, are always very subjective and workers should be properly instructed on what to look for in the inspection.

2. Use instruments with the proper range to measure the data tolerances required by the process.

3. Make the data collection as simple as possible and write down the method used to execute it.

4. Minimize paperwork. Enter data directly into a computer. Menu-driven data type selection, entered by bar code readings, is a good example of this.

5. Train workers in the method used to collect data. Retrain them periodically, so they can eliminate any bad habits acquired doing the job.

6. Validate data collected through random audits of the system and methods.

7. Look for duplicate data readings along the process that contribute nothing to quality but burden worker productivity.

8. Periodically review the effectiveness of the data set collected and its influence on the product's quality. Try to find a new, smaller set of data points that produces better results.

9. Don't burden the system with excess data that hide the source of problems and mislead workers.

10. Use the data collected to monitor and control quality in the process. Show results to workers, so they don't feel they are wasting their time.

## 9.4 DATA TRANSFORMATION AND ANALYSIS

There are many software packages on the market that can do an excellent job of transforming sampled data into meaningful quality information. This task used to be tedious, was done manually, and was composed mainly of tables and primitive charts. Today, there are three-dimensional color charts that clearly show quality trends, facilitating problem analysis. Data transformation counts as overhead and should be completed with a minimum of labor. It should also convert data into practical charts and tables that show a snapshot of the process' quality at the time the data were sampled. The charts should also show trends.

The main purpose of data translation is facilitating data analysis, making it simple and easy to understand. To make data translation a success:

1. Use computers to automate the data translation function. Make the system real-time, so information is updated as it is collected.
2. Whenever possible, use charts to plot information. Charts show trends in data samples.
3. Make sure charts show clearly what constitutes good, bad, and marginal data (about to go bad).
4. Don't overcrowd charts with too many data types; this will confuse the people studying the charts.
5. Clearly identify the spots in the process where data are collected. Also, show relationships with other data samples downstream in the process. This correlation will help to analyze process trends as data change.
6. Always try to minimize the number of data items in a chart. There is always an optimum set of data points that gives a good picture of the quality of the process at any particular time.
7. When there are several quality readings in a chart, show their relative importance, so proper priorities can be set.
8. Make sure charts track revisions in the process and product, so they can track a history of changes and the effect these changes have had.
9. Display charts in working areas, teaching all workers how to read and understand them.

## 9.5 EARLY WARNING

Companies that succeed in producing perfect-quality products excel in preventing quality defects before they happen. Conversely, companies that are always correcting quality defects operate in a reactionary mode. The purpose of a quality information system is to produce a sufficiently early warning so that quality problems can be corrected before they happen. This task cannot be accomplished without translating quality status into charts that provide an early warning system to avoid problems.

There are a few important features that an effective warning system needs to have. The first is the time relationship between charts and process data. Real-time updates are the best way to feed data into charts. There is no time lag between data values and the pictorial representation of their effect on the process.

Another important feature is data trends. Data trends provide a continuous view of the process' behavior over time. When data are still within legal quality limits, but the readings trend moves the chart into a danger zone, this is the time to raise a warning.

The last important ingredient is the selection of danger zones that define a process as still good, but about to produce poor quality if nothing is done about it.

Critical zones define quality about to go bad. Every control chart should have them defined and tracked. Engineers and workers should watch for quality drifting into those zones rather than looking for defects that have already happened. This is the basis of preventive quality programs. Preventive correction actions should take place immediately, before the problem produces a line stop or a rework condition.

## 9.6 DISTRIBUTION OF INFORMATION

The waste generated by paperwork can be avoided by transmitting information electronically to workers who need to use it. This system, however, could become overburdened if it is assumed that electronic distribution is not paperwork—excess information distributed electronically is also waste.

There are a few rules necessary to improve the distribution of information to workers:

1. Send information only to people who can do something with it.
2. Distribute information on a need-to-know basis. For example, workers will need quality reports on the work they are doing and on the station that feeds their work centers. There is no way workers can correct a quality problem originating in a work center downstream to theirs.
3. Display in common work areas quality trends that show all of the process. The objective is to remind workers that they are a team and the process is their responsibility.
4. Provide summary information to management that shows trends and critical goals. The higher the management level the report reaches, the simpler it should be.
5. Distribute quality information to all levels of management in the company, including the president.
6. Train workers and management in the interpretation of charts and the information they convey. Set clear rules that define what actions to take when the chart reaches warning zones. Retrain workers periodically on chart interpretation. You will be surprised how quickly people start to interpret charts their own way.

## 9.7 JUST-IN-TIME AND QUALITY INFORMATION SYSTEMS

Just-in-Time views a quality information system as overhead that adds no value to a product. However, the complex nature of manufacturing cannot ignore the fact that when something can go wrong, it will. The best compromise with Just-in-Time's principles is to minimize the overhead required to support a quality information system by reducing the labor wasted in sampling, collecting, and distributing information.

Just-in-Time demands perfect quality in a process, so the system can function with a minimum of inventory and waste. A quality information system provides the necessary checks and balances to Just-in-Time to assure good quality once inventories are reduced. This role is even more important when a company is going through the transition from the traditional batch-oriented manufacturing to a waste-conscious Just-in-Time system. The prudent thing to do during this transitional phase is to lean on the side of more information, rather than less. Once Just-in-Time and the quality system are working correctly, the quality information system can start reducing information and simplifying reports to minimize the overhead associated with them.

## 9.8 SUPPLIER QUALITY FEEDBACK UNDER A QUALITY INFORMATION SYSTEM

Suppliers are an integral part of a quality system in a company; they should participate in the design and implementation of a quality information system. Suppliers will have different needs for quality information, depending on the type of part they are shipping to a customer's process.

Timely quality information to suppliers should be one of the main goals of a quality information system. Suppliers are physically remote and are often mailed reports that take days to bring news about quality. A simple system that most companies can afford today uses fax machines. Faxed reports should be precise, directed to the people who can do something about problems when they occur. It is important to eliminate middle people from the distribution loop. There might be a summary distribution on a need-to-know basis, so that management is informed.

Better than sending information by fax would be to distribute information electronically using an EDI system. An even better system is to allow suppliers to access their own reports on a real-time basis in the customer's computer.

Suppliers need training on the meaning of quality charts, and actions they should take when data fall into danger or problem zones. Quality engineers in charge of designing the quality information system should get together with key suppliers to understand what kinds of data are required to allow them to be preventive rather than reactive. This information should be incorporated in the charts and reviewed periodically to make sure there is still an understanding of the ground rules.

Other areas that might be included in a supplier's report are the accuracy of shipments and paperwork. The supplier's quality record should also include delivery and support performance when problems are present.

## 9.9 SUMMARY

There is a tendency in many companies to have a complicated quality information system that provides too much information, too late, and to the wrong people. The challenge to an efficient system is to find the combination that reduces the work required for data collection, paperwork, and distribution without compromising the quality of information.

With this kind of system, it is important to design a quality information system that is flexible enough to handle different product lines and processes with the same basic structure and types of reports. This approach should also be applied to suppliers, so there is no need for retraining when a new product is released to manufacturing.

The biggest challenge of all is to design a quality information system that is preventive in nature and flags poor quality about to happen. Once this system capability is achieved, a company has success waiting around the corner.

## REFERENCES

FEIGENBAUM, ARMAND V. *Total Quality Control*. New York: McGraw-Hill, 1983, pp. 677–736.

HALL, ROBERT W. *Attaining Manufacturing Excellence*. Homewood, Ill.: Dow Jones-Irwin, 1987.

HERNANDEZ, ARNALDO. *Just-in-Time Manufacturing: A Practical Approach*. Englewood Cliffs, N.J.: Prentice-Hall, 1989, pp. 95–109, 123–143.

LUBBEN, RICHARD T. *Just-in-Time Manufacturing: An Aggressive Manufacturing Strategy*. New York: McGraw-Hill, 1988, pp. 143–228.

# 10★

# *Design Quality into Your Products: Start Right*

Many manufacturing organizations faithfully follow the principle of building quality into their products. The concept is that perfect-quality products are not produced by inspecting: They are built one quality part at a time. Building quality rather than inspecting is very important, but there is no way a process can build quality if the design is faulty and the product is only marginally functional.

Design's influence over quality lies in the selection of parts used in a product. Normally, design engineering specifies the parts used in the process, including the level of reliability required for them. Unfortunately, many times this takes a back seat to cost goals and performance requirements. A regrettable example of this is the U.S. auto industry. For years U.S. car designers have released products where quality has not been at the top of their list, and the industry has paid the price by losing market share to Japan.

The primary responsibility of design engineers is to design quality into a product. They are also responsible for designing a product that can be built with quality in a manufacturing line. They should also produce quality documentation to specify a product for the people who need to build, use, and maintain it.

A well-designed product requires a proper balance between quality, performance, and cost. Quality, however, should have higher priority than the other two. No matter how high performance or how low cost, a product value to customers would be compromised by less than perfect quality.

## 10.1 ENGINEERING AND QUALITY DESIGN

Many prestigious engineering schools have design courses to teach future engineers how to design products that function to a specific set of requirements. Very few of these schools have a course dedicated to teaching how to design quality into a product. A product that is not designed with quality in mind is a product doomed to failure before the first unit is shipped. Designing quality products is an absolute requirement for the survival of a company in today's competitive market. Unfortunately, this message has not reached the many design engineers who prefer the challenges of technology to satisfaction from a perfect-quality product.

Managers running design groups are responsible for guiding engineering staffs to design quality into products. This task is by no means simple or easy to implement. Technology, market pressure, and costs are roadblocks to quality. One way to solve this quality/technology/cost conflict is to root the philosophy of quality deeply in the company, reaching all employees. This broad-based message will help design engineers understand and accept their roles as creators of quality products.

## 10.2 RELIABILITY AND PRODUCT DESIGN

Reliability relates to the number of hours a product will work without a failure. When a customer buys a product, he or she expects the product to perform without a malfunction during most of its useful life. Conversely, depending on the product's complexity, the customer assumes some failure will occur during its use. For example, most consumer electronic devices (a TV or a coffeemaker) are not expected to fail during their lifetime. No one, however, expects an automobile to have no failures during its life. Reliability is a measure of quality, but is not sufficient to ensure a quality product by itself.

Every product should have a reliability requirement to match its purpose. This requirement should balance cost and life expectancy. This balance needs to be considered at the design stage, and it primarily concerns the individual components used to build the product. Reliability, however, does not guarantee operational margins in a product; components can work reliably to a level that is not sufficient to meet the specifications originally created for the product.

Another factor that influences quality in a product is manufacturability. Engineers can select reliable components for their designs, but if the process is difficult and encourages worker mistakes, the quality of the product is not going to be consistent.

Engineers have more than one design choice that can affect the quality of a product. Once selected, these choices are very difficult and expensive to change because they imply product changes and, perhaps, retrofits. Among them, reliability is key to meeting customer expectations. But reliability alone is not sufficient to ensure success. Figure 10.1 shows the four quality keystones that provide a careful balance in design. Engineers need to consider them early in the design phase, so they have a good start toward a well-balanced product that meets customer expectations.

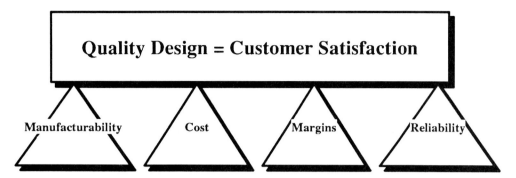

**Figure 10.1**    Product Design: Four Keystones of Quality Balance

## 10.3 QUALITY AND MANUFACTURING INVOLVEMENT AT DESIGN TIME

In general, products are designed only once; then, if successful, they are built many times over. The best time to involve quality and manufacturing people in the product development cycle is at design time. The concept of design for manufacturability is critical and it should be considered for any new product before it leaves the drafting table. This concept, however, is all too often ignored until it is too late to reverse the damage inflicted on the product.

Quality and manufacturing engineers should get involved in the design cycle early enough so that they can influence issues associated with assembly, testing, inspecting, servicing, and supplier selection. The right solution to every issue is based on experience, factory capabilities, supplier base, and mix of the workforce. Properly chosen, these will make the production process an easy and cost-effective one; mistakenly chosen, the design is not producible. Table 10.1 summarizes the areas that need attention during the design cycle, before specifications are cast in concrete. Many companies ignore this process or consider it too late in the design cycle, paying dearly. If started earlier, this process will affect design choices, leading to a cost-effective quality product that has nothing but customer satisfaction waiting for it.

## 10.4 PRODUCT VALIDATION AND ACCEPTANCE

A product's design verification normally starts with a few prototypes tested in an engineering lab. Then a pilot program builds a few units that are used for two purposes: alpha units to be tested internally in the company and beta units to be tested by prospective customers. Most of the effort invested during this process is directed at proving the product's performance; quality, manufacturability, and serviceability usually are secondary considerations. This order of priorities is reversed, a common mistake made by design teams. Another

**TABLE 10.1**   DESIGN FOR MANUFACTURABILITY CRITICAL FACTORS

| Quality | Manufacturing | Materials | Field Service |
|---|---|---|---|
| Quality process | Manufacturing process | Materials types by commodities | Reliability |
| Process control | Assembly procedures and work center layouts | Suppliers' qualification and selection | MTBF |
| Inspection procedures | Test procedures and tools | Suppliers' location | MTBR |
| Reliability | Capital equipment and line capacity | Material standard costs | Field replaceable units (FRUs) |
| Suppliers' quality | Material distribution | Finishing and coating | Repair centers |
| Quality cost | Labor cost | Fastening techniques | Support centers |
| Data collection and reporting system | Overhead support costs | Material cost as it relates to tolerances | Diagnostics tools |
| Control of tolerances | Packing methods and costs | B/M structures | User support |
| Suppliers' quality information | Shipping methods and costs | Just-in-Time deliveries | Product field testing |
| Documentation | Documentation | Documentation | Product feedback |
| Training | Training | Procurement cycles and protocols | Configuration control |

common mistake is to build prototypes in the engineering lab rather than in manufacturing. A product should be tested for manufacturability, and nobody can do that better than workers on a production line.

    Quality, manufacturing, and field service people should get involved in the alpha and beta test process. Their suggestions should be taken seriously and implemented before the product is released to manufacturing.

    Design validation must be completed before releasing a product: This verifies that the product meets the original design specs, including functionality and market testing. In today's competitive market, a company cannot afford to introduce a product that doesn't meet the goals for which it was designed. Design validation should be done by a group separate from design engineering, and it should also include quality and manufacturing verification—otherwise, a product cannot be manufactured efficiently and at the original level of quality for which it was intended.

## 10.5 PRODUCT DESIGN AND QUALITY

For many design communities, if the product works reliably and meets design goals, then it is of good quality: Adequate functionality means good quality. But if a product is difficult to assemble and test, then it will most likely be of poor quality. The point is that there are many factors that are not related to the quality of individual components that still can cause poor quality in a product, for example, the selection of a marginal supplier to manufacture a component, even if the component has been designed with good reliability. An engineer can specify a high-quality, tight-tolerance component, but if the supplier selected to manufacture the part can't produce it with consistent quality, then defective parts will be introduced into the process.

In general, designing quality into a product requires not only quality design but an uncompromising attitude toward quality choices in other areas related to the manufacture of the product. Unless engineers are directed to follow this principle, they can easily be seduced by technical choices that compromise the integrity of the product. Table 10.1 shows some of these considerations. Section 10.7 will list some of the most important rules for designing quality into a product.

## 10.6 PRODUCT DESIGN AND FIELD SERVICE SUPPORT

One of the last things in the minds of engineers at design time is the requirements for supporting a product in the field. Normally, the product is designed first and then thought is given to how it can be supported when it breaks. A product that is not designed for support is a product of inferior quality. This holds true no matter how many great features the product offers, because the customer will not be able to use any of them after the product breaks.

In general, no product is exempt from field service considerations. The nature of a product, however, determines the level and type of service it requires. For example, there is not much thought behind servicing a toaster. This appliance rarely breaks during its lifetime, and when it does, it can only be replaced. In this case, thought should be given to a warranty system to replace the toaster when a customer has a problem.

For complex computer systems, the servicing aspect is complex; it should be given as much consideration as the design itself. A quality system should work consistently, meeting the expectations of the customer. The repair history should be limited to the technical constraints of the product and the market it represents. It should also be properly supported by a service organization to minimize downtime (the time a customer is not using it because of a malfunction).

Another aspect of quality is the cost of support to the manufacturer and the customer. A product that can be repaired only at great expense to the customer is not a quality product. The cost of support should be included in the equation of quality, to determine the real value of a product. This factor is generally ignored, addressed only after a product design is completed.

## 10.7 RULES FOR DESIGNING QUALITY PRODUCTS

Below are some rules useful in designing quality products. These are by no means complete, but will guide design engineers on the path of designing quality products. These rules are also effective for designing products that will be suitable for manufacturing in a Just-in-Time system.

1. Make designs an evolutionary rather than a revolutionary process. Use experience to develop new designs. Engineers should apply knowledge gained with earlier generations of similar products to new ones. Assign engineers with previous product experience to teams designing the new product.

2. Always select the part of highest possible quality to be used in a product. Quality must have higher priority than cost.

3. The best way to increase reliability, manufacturability, and serviceability of a product is to reduce the number of parts used in a product. After the first phase of the design is completed, analyze every one of the parts, eliminating those that aren't necessary. Replace several parts with a smaller number of parts.

4. Select suppliers with a proven track record in quality and delivery. Price should take a back seat to the quality record of the supplier.

5. Design all the parts and subassemblies to be assembled in a unique, foolproof way. Avoid ambiguous assembly steps or inaccessible areas that make it difficult to manufacture and service the product. Consult manufacturing engineers on this matter.

6. Specify the product's reliability and operational margins before the design is started. Make sure they influence the design, rather than the design being influenced by them.

7. Develop a field service strategy before starting a design. Consult with the field service people in order to understand their capabilities and the type of support they can provide for a product. Define the level of downtime and cost the customer is going to incur when there is a malfunction. Don't compromise service for design features.

8. Tailor the product structure and documentation levels to the process used to build the product. Keep in mind that quality is first and manufacturability second.

9. Understand the requirements of the process used to build the product. Work with manufacturing engineers to plan the equipment needed and the poka-yoke devices required to set up a foolproof process. Know what equipment the company already has that can be used to build the new product.

10. Design for testability. Develop test procedures and test equipment during the design phase. Have the test requirements change the way the product is designed. Make the test procedures and equipment as simple as possible, so they can be learned and used by workers. Consider field test diagnostics and testability for functionality in your test design efforts.

11. Develop careful specifications for the parts needed to build the product. Review them with suppliers to understand cost tradeoffs and quality implications. Select suppliers with process capabilities to manufacture the parts; ask for feedback on how to improve the quality of the parts and reduce their cost. Review documentation with suppliers to make sure the parts' requirements are clearly specified.

12. Involve manufacturing, quality, purchasing, and finance in the selection of suppliers before you make a decision. Don't leave this process until the end, after you have tailored your part to the capabilities of a supplier not fitted to do the job. Select suppliers that are close to your plant, have Just-in-Time experience, and first-rate quality.

13. Set up a documentation control system as soon as the first prototype is built. Track

and document changes properly. Once the product is in pilot production, set up a formal change order procedure (ECO) to control the level of revisions implemented. Define the system configuration and date coding used for the product once it is released to manufacturing and shipped to customers. Keep paperwork current. Inform purchasing and manufacturing of changes promptly.

**14.** Follow the manufacturing process to understand yields, labor, and overhead. Investigate how the manufacturing learning curve and marginal design problems affect yields. Always assume the problem is with margins, until it is proven otherwise.

**15.** Follow the product's field performance and the level of customer satisfaction. Work with the quality department and the field service organization to collect proper information. Act promptly to correct problems before the product gets a bad name. This is the most critical aspect of a product's introduction—a dissatisfied customer will pass the word around, giving the product a bad reputation. Understand issues causing problems and address them properly. Take responsibility for them even if they are not design related.

**16.** Start a design improvement program as soon as there are enough data on the product's performance in the field. There is always room for quality improvement and cost reductions that will enhance the product.

## 10.8 THE PERFECT PICTURE: DOCUMENTATION

The final product of an engineering design group is not a few prototypes working to a set of specifications: It is the documentation package they send to manufacturing to release a product. Many engineering teams excel in design expertise, but fail miserably with the quality of documentation they release at the completion of a program. Documentation should be a high-priority task for any design team. Documentation should define a product, down to the smallest detail. Documentation is also a product by itself, used many times over the life of the program.

There are several issues related to quality in a documentation package. First, it should specify all components of a product without ambiguity. Then, it should define how the individual components fit together into subassemblies, and how subassemblies fit into higher level assemblies until the final product is completed.

Documentation should also specify tolerances, critical parameters, and quality requirements for every manufactured part. It should also supply special test conditions and anything special that is required to build the final product. Finally, it has to be up to date, incorporating all the latest revisions on the prototypes in the engineering lab.

With today's computer-aided design systems, the task of creating documentation is greatly simplified. The problem is still a burden placed on the engineer, for whom documentation may not be crucial given the pressure of deadlines and design problems. The key to producing quality documentation is to assign responsibility to someone who is not directly involved in the design effort. Appoint that person the documentation expert and make him or her part of the team developing the product.

Documentation quality should not be gauged according to the amount of information a package includes. It should be measured by how accurately and selectively the information is presented. One of the most common errors is to provide too much data that clutter and confuse, increasing the cost of parts because of extra tolerances and dimensions not critical to the process. The best documentation includes the minimum amount of information needed to specify a product completely.

## 10.9 DESIGN ENGINEERING SUPPORT TO SUPPLIERS

The support of suppliers selected to manufacture parts for the product under design is very important. The purpose of this support is to review the suppliers' manufacturing capabilities compared with the requirements of the part as specified by prints. The supplier feedback to the program should focus on how the part could be made simpler, more cost effective, and with perfect quality.

The best way to achieve this objective is to send engineers acting as consultants to the suppliers' premises. They should concentrate on reviewing suppliers' capabilities and the information suppliers need to be able to manufacture parts with the best quality and the lowest cost.

The consultant approach is a key to getting design engineers involved with suppliers. You will be surprised how much help suppliers will provide to improve their cost, quality, and manufacturability. It is in the suppliers' best interests to help at the beginning of the design cycle, so they can influence the product design to the capabilities of their production facilities.

Supplier consultation should not stop after documentation is released. Designers should visit suppliers regularly after the part is in production and the supplier has gained experience and can suggest changes that will lead to cost reductions and quality improvements.

To make the consultation approach successful, designers must avoid becoming defensive when suppliers suggest changes to their designs. Engineers should take suppliers' opinions seriously and understand that their only intent is to improve the product and the service provided.

## 10.10 DESIGN ENGINEERING AND QUALITY TRAINING

One common mistake that companies make is to assume that quality concerns only manufacturing. Nothing could be farther from the truth. Successful companies consider quality a discipline that involves all operational aspects of the company, including the design and development of products.

You would be surprised by how many design engineers have never had formal training in quality in their professional lives. The same engineers, however, spend innumerable hours increasing their technical skills in order to improve their designs. Training design engineers in all aspects of quality is an absolute necessity, if we want engineers to become quality conscious. Engineering quality should also apply to all aspects of the process of designing a product, including the documentation's quality at the end of the program.

Educating the technical staff about the principles of quality is very important and should be addressed by management. The curriculum of any training program should include all disciplines associated with quality, showing how they affect not only the quality output of a job, but the way the job is done. There is no quality output from any activity, if the process used to execute that activity is not implemented with quality. The point is that only a quality process can produce quality output. This involves all aspects of running a company.

## 10.11  BALANCING TECHNOLOGY WITH QUALITY AND COST

Designing new products is always a challenge for the people assigned to do the job. This challenge is normally viewed as one in technology, rather than in manufacturing and quality. Designers have a good idea of the market requirements and the latest technology available to make a product superior to the competition's. The cost of technology is also a well-understood variable that influences the design of a new product. Engineers can calculate it precisely and can relate it to the tradeoffs available to them.

The cost of quality and the choices available for the design of a product are often overlooked altogether. Quality usually gets associated with reliability, and a reliable product is erroneously assumed to be of good quality. Not taken into consideration are the hidden costs associated with marginal, poorly designed and documented products from a manufacturing point of view. These costs will not show up on the engineer's drafting board, but they will show up as wasted manufacturing costs with each unit built.

A first-class product is one that is equal parts technology, quality, and cost. This balance should be carefully evaluated at design time and it should be clearly uncompromised toward the quality side if there is a tradeoff to be made. Again, no matter how many great features a product offers and no matter how up-to-the-minute the technology used to design it, the product will not have any value for a customer if it doesn't have perfect quality performance.

## 10.12  SUMMARY

Quality must be planned and implemented the same way as any other feature of a product. Quality is not only related to the individual components of a product: It is influenced by the methods used to assemble and test individual components. Quality is related to documentation, field service support, marketing and selling, and training of people involved with any aspect of the product. Quality is how the customer sees the organization behind the product.

Design engineering has a great influence on quality and should be responsible for starting the process of producing a quality-perfect product. However, most of the time quality is not high enough a priority—it has less glamour than technology, and it is erroneously assumed that it will happen automatically.

The best way to bring quality concerns to designers is to get quality people involved early in the design cycle. It is equally important to get manufacturing people involved, so clear goals for manufacturability and quality are put in writing alongside the technical specifications of the product.

Finally, Just-in-Time requires that quality be first. It is important that engineering groups understand and adhere to this principle when designing products, by training them in the concepts of Just-in-Time and on the importance of quality.

## REFERENCES

ALLEN, C., ed. *Simultaneous Engineering: Integrating Manufacturing and Design*. Dearborn, Mich.: SME, 1990.

CHARNEY, C. *Time to Market: Reducing Product Lead Time*. Dearborn, Mich.: SME, 1991.

HARTLEY, JOHN R. *Concurrent Engineering: Shortening Lead Times, Raising Quality, and Lowering Costs*. Cambridge, Mass.: Productivity Press, 1991.

KECECIOGLU, DIMITRI. *Reliability Engineering Handbook, vols. 1–2*. Englewood Cliffs, N.J.: Prentice-Hall, 1991.

PHADKE, MADHAV S. *Quality Engineering Using Robust Design*. Englewood Cliffs, N.J.: Prentice-Hall, 1989.

WICK, C. and R. VEILLEUX, eds. *Quality Control and Assembly, vol. 4*. Dearborn, Mich.: SME, 1987.

# 11★

# Quality Is Not Free—But
# Good Quality Is Cheap

One of the most poorly understood and least-monitored areas in a manufacturing company is the cost associated with quality. Most companies honestly believe they keep track of their cost of quality accurately. They also believe that higher quality in a product means higher costs. Unfortunately, on both accounts they are wrong: Most companies don't have a clear picture of what their quality system is costing them. Furthermore, in most instances, high quality is associated with lower costs.

Tracking quality costs is generally the last priority of a quality department, because any problem in this area is not as immediately visible as it would be with a line-down situation because of a bad part. Good quality demands alertness and a fast response. When something goes wrong, it needs to be fixed immediately. When everything is all right, then something may be about to go wrong and quality should anticipate it, so it won't happen. Quality is always a reacting/preventing/reacting job. Like firefighters trying to put out a roaring fire, the last thing the personnel have on their minds is how much it is going to cost them to have the fire extinguished.

Knowing how much we do spend on quality, or how much we don't spend, is a very important measurement of the quality effort in a company. This information is not only important from the financial point of view, but also from the quality planning aspect. Managers need to know in detail how much money is being spent on quality. This information will help to direct efforts to the right areas of the quality process in order to obtain maximum return. The following sections cover the different aspects of cost in quality and suggest some of the methods necessary for proper tracking, planning, and maximizing of returns.

## 11.1 GOOD QUALITY IS NOT FREE

Assume that we have a perfect manufacturing company where the quality of the material that arrives at the receiving dock has no defects. The process and workers do a perfect job and the product is built with zero defects. The product arrives at the customer's site meeting 100 percent of expectations. This perfect company doesn't need a quality department, and the cost of quality should be zero, assuming that the company is not paying any premium for the perfect-quality parts and salaries of the skilled workers who never make mistakes. All of this is not realistic—certainly there is no such perfection in life; when something can go wrong, sooner or later it will.

Lack of investment in quality will not produce perfect-quality products: It produces poorly functioning products that cause customer dissatisfaction and costly repairs. Lack of quality causes waste in manufacturing before the product is shipped. It also forces companies to operate in a reactionary mode, band-aiding things in order to continue operating at bare minimum efficiency. Lack of quality is a disease that requires expensive medical treatment to prevent the death of a corporation.

Common sense dictates that there should be an investment in quality. This requirement is more critical in Just-in-Time because the system needs perfect-quality parts to avoid costly line stops. The question that most operational people face is how much they should spend on quality to meet Just-in-Time's requirements, and what the return on that investment should be. It is a typical question of how to invest wisely to obtain maximum return.

To set some guidelines on expenses and returns, a company should spend enough money on quality to assure that a product achieves total customer satisfaction. But there is not enough money to set up a quality system that makes a poorly designed product gain customer satisfaction. The system has to assume the product has met design requirements. Quality dollars should be invested in a support system that helps manufacturing to output perfect-quality products.

The first step in analyzing the cost of quality is to understand how the money is spent in the quality department. Figure 11.1 shows a typical organization chart for a quality department. This organization is not the same for every company, but the figure relates it to a fictional company "A." Assume the company has a budget of $3,000,000 for all expenses in the department. The next step is to understand the distribution of the expenses per department. Table 11.1 shows this distribution and the percentage of the total budget that has been dedicated to each department. The table shows how the money is spent.

The next step is to reorganize the table and the expenses by functions, seeing how much money is allocated to each one. Table 11.2 shows this new classification that will be used to understand the true allocation of costs as they relate to their activity in preventing or reacting to quality problems.

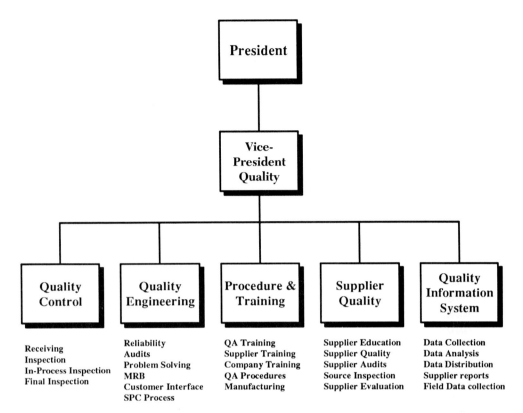

Receiving
Inspection
In-Process Inspection
Final Inspection

Reliability
Audits
Problem Solving
MRB
Customer Interface
SPC Process

QA Training
Supplier Training
Company Training
QA Procedures
Manufacturing

Supplier Education
Supplier Quality
Supplier Audits
Source Inspection
Supplier Evaluation

Data Collection
Data Analysis
Data Distribution
Supplier reports
Field Data collection

**Figure 11.1**   Typical Quality Department Organization Chart

**TABLE 11.1**   EXPENSES DISTRIBUTION PER DEPARTMENT

| Department | Expenses ($) | Expenses (%) |
|---|---|---|
| Management | 150,000 | 5 |
| Quality control | 1,350,000 | 45 |
| Quality information system | 150,000 | 5 |
| Quality engineering | 300,000 | 10 |
| Supplier quality | 900,000 | 30 |
| Quality training | 150,000 | 5 |
| Total | 3,000,000 | 100 |

**TABLE 11.2**  GROUPING THE QUALITY EXPENSES PER CATEGORY

| Category | Activity | Reactionary | Preventive |
|---|---|---|---|
| Overhead | Management | 75,000 | 75,000 |
| Passive quality | Quality control | 1,350,000 | |
| Inspecting, problem | Quality engineering | 200,000 | |
| solving, MRB, | Quality information | 100,000 | |
| audits, customer | | | |
| interface, rework | | | |
| Proactive quality | Supplier quality | | 900,000 |
| Supplier quality, | Training | | 150,000 |
| training, reliability, | Quality engineering | | 100,000 |
| SPC process | Quality information | | 50,000 |
| | Total expenses ($) | 1,725,000 | 1,275,000 |
| | Total expenses (%) | 57.5 | 42.5 |

## 11.2  JUST-IN-TIME AND QUALITY COSTS: PASSIVE AND PROACTIVE QUALITY

Activities in any quality department fall into two specific types of functions. *Passive quality* includes those activities that react to problems or actually search for them. Inspecting is a reactive activity that assumes there are mistakes in a product and then searches for them as a way of eliminating them. We don't actually eliminate mistakes by inspecting a product. All we do is find errors and then ask workers to correct them. This kind of activity doesn't eliminate mistakes altogether, because there is also a human factor in inspecting—mistakes can pass through the system, reaching customers. No quality system can eliminate all mistakes in products through inspection. Passive quality is expensive; it does not reduce the cost of quality.

The next group of activities are those that are called *proactive*. Proactive quality is associated with prevention. Instead of looking for mistakes, this quality effort searches for the causes of mistakes and fixes them, so there are no mistakes produced in the next batch of products. Proactive quality reduces the defect rate of a product and reduces the cost of quality.

Quality departments should keep a good balance of resources allocated to both types of activities, because there is no simple way to eliminate inspection altogether. Normally, the smaller the amount of money spent on proactive quality activities, the larger is the amount of money spent on reactionary quality to maintain an acceptable quality level. Table 11.2 shows the grouping of the expenses for the department shown in the previous section. The table shows that 57.5 percent of the expenses is spent in reactionary activities, whereas 42.5 percent is spent in proactive tasks. An increase in preventive activities will most likely result in a decrease in reactionary expenses. An acceptable ratio of proactive/passive quality expenses should be 60/40; a very aggressive program that concentrates mainly on prevention might go as high as 80/20. This ratio will assure the highest quality at the end of the process with the smallest defect ratio through it.

## 11.3 THE DIRECT COST OF QUALITY

Another way to look at the cost of quality is to measure the *direct* cost of quality. This measurement derives from the concept of direct labor. Direct labor is associated with workers involved in building a product; the direct cost of quality is associated with workers involved in inspecting at the end of tasks that add value to a product.

There are four kinds of inspection tasks associated with a process:

1. Incoming inspections of parts arriving at the factory before they are sent either to the stockroom or to the process.
2. Quality control inspections associated with those activities of inspecting a product while it is being built.
3. Final inspections of activities after a product is built.
4. Audit inspections associated with detailed, usually tear-down, inspections that randomly inspect complete products.

Just-in-Time considers any of these inspections wasteful and calls for their elimination. Just-in-Time also calls for quality control inspections to be assigned to workers in charge of the process. In general, the direct cost of quality is comprised of those expenses associated with these activities and its value measures the level of inspecting activity. It also measures the level of investing a company is making in passive quality. A high direct cost of quality means a company is inspecting out defects rather than preventing them.

## 11.4 THE INDIRECT COST OF QUALITY

The indirect cost of quality is associated with prevention. These expenses are associated with an effort to understand and prevent the causes of defects in a product; the areas responsible for this are quality engineering and supplier engineering. The job of these two groups is not to inspect quality into a product, but to set up systems and procedures that will lead to the manufacturing of a perfect-quality product. Their efforts should be focused on understanding the critical issues that could cause quality defects and creating a system that will prevent their occurrence. The result of a good preventive quality program will not only show up in the improvement of the quality of the product but also in a reduction of the inspecting processes.

Normally, the areas of responsibility of these two groups are dissimilar, although they have some areas of cooperation. The supplier engineering group is responsible for selecting and interfacing with suppliers of the parts used in the product. The quality engineering group works with the internal departments in the company to assure that proper quality standards are met during the definition, design, manufacturing, testing, and shipping of a product.

There are important common areas of responsibilities to both groups that require close cooperation; for example, working together with suppliers to obtain a high quality level of parts. This is accomplished by interfacing with design engineering early in the design phase and by selecting the right suppliers. This activity will ensure that suppliers are selected with process capabilities that match the requirement of parts still on the drafting table.

Table 11.3 shows a list of quality activities that are required to set up a proactive quality system (the table is by no means complete and will vary depending on the type of product and services provided). Included in the table are groups responsible for implementing these tasks. These activities are proactive because they are designed to prevent defects rather than to detect them. One critical aspect of the system is to provide valuable field

**TABLE 11.3**   INDIRECT COSTS OF QUALITY

| Quality Activity | Quality Engineering | Supplier Engineering |
|---|---|---|
| Quality system planning | Yes | Yes |
| *Product development* | | |
| Design | Yes | Yes |
| Testing | Yes | Yes |
| Verification | Yes | |
| Reliability | Yes | Yes |
| Packing | Yes | |
| Supplier selection | Yes | Yes |
| Supplier feedback to design | Yes | Yes |
| Field support | Yes | |
| *Supplier support* | | |
| Quality planning | | Yes |
| Supplier's process | | |
| improvement and quality | Yes | Yes |
| Information system | | Yes |
| First article approval | | Yes |
| Receiving inspection | | Yes |
| Dock-to-WIP | | Yes |
| Factory process quality | | |
| feedback | Yes | Yes |
| Field quality feedback | Yes | Yes |
| *Factory process support* | | |
| Process control | Yes | |
| Worker training | Yes | |
| Quality worker training | Yes | Yes |
| Quality information system | Yes | Yes |
| Packing and shipping | Yes | |
| *Field product feedback* | | |
| Reliability | Yes | Yes |
| MTBF | Yes | Yes |
| MTBSC | Yes | |
| Failure modes | Yes | Yes |
| Product life | Yes | Yes |
| Audits | Yes | Yes |

quality feedback to a manufacturer and suppliers once customers start using a product. The feedback system has to be efficient and should reach the right people in charge of correcting problems detected by customers.

## 11.5 THE COST OF WASTE IN QUALITY

Most manufacturing organizations are well aware of the cost of waste in a classical manufacturing sense. Waste is incurred when something doesn't work and has to be fixed. Waste is also incurred when material is sent to the material review board (MRB) cage and sits there for days without any use—or worse, when it is scrapped. Most manufacturing companies track the cost of these wasteful activities and report them to management.

With the introduction of Just-in-Time, the concept of waste was extended to activities that add no value to the process of building a product. For example, moving material from one place to another or setting up a buffer inventory is wasteful in a Just-in-Time system.

Waste's cost is mostly related to defective material—defects that relate to poor quality, poor workmanship, rework, and faulty designs that require engineering changes. A

**TABLE 11.4**  CAUSES OF WASTE IN QUALITY

| Waste in Quality | Activities |
|---|---|
| Scrap | Obsolete material |
| | Faulty material |
| | Engineering changes, ECOs |
| | Bad workmanship |
| | Material in MRB |
| Rework | Faulty material |
| | Bad workmanship |
| | Engineering changes, ECOs |
| | Faulty paperwork |
| Moving | Wrong selection of carrier |
| | Poor packing of material |
| | Long-distance traveling |
| | Mishandling loading, unloading |
| | Defective material shipped |
| | Defective material moved to the process |
| Waiting | Defective material waiting in inventories |
| | Defective material waiting in the process |
| | Buffer inventories in front of machines waiting for setup activities |
| Labor | Inspecting |
| | Reworking |
| | Engineering changes, ECOs |
| | Moving material |
| | Counting material |
| | Line down because of faulty material |

cost-conscious manufacturing organization will track these costs not only to understand them from the financial point of view, but also to understand their causes and the steps necessary to eliminate them. Table 11.4 shows the types of waste in quality and their common causes. A quality system should track these costs and have specific goals toward correcting their causes, eliminating waste. Most of these causes will require some correcting activity. The best way to eliminate them is to assign ownership of the activities to a worker, or a group of workers, so they can take corrective action.

## 11.6 THE HIDDEN COSTS OF QUALITY

More treacherous costs in a quality system are hidden costs that nobody tracks. These are costs that are either associated with:

1. Activities buried under the bureaucracy of the system.
2. Activities that are assumed to be part of the normal way of doing things.

Activities that cause hidden costs are usually taken for granted, and there is no proactive effort to eliminate them.

Activities that belong to the first group do not necessarily occur in the quality or manufacturing departments. For example, expediting material deliveries in the purchasing department as a result of a batch of faulty components from a supplier is a wasteful activity. Another example is poor quality in paperwork, which causes accounts payable to delay payment of an invoice, with innumerable phone conversations with a supplier as a result of the mistake.

Buried activities that cause waste as a result of someone not doing his or her job can add up to expensive waste and loss of productivity. They can also affect the way business is conducted, resulting in a lack of sales to customers because of poor performance. These activities are hard to monitor and measure, but their impact can substantially affect a company's success.

Product warranty expenses and product services are normally considered part of the normal way of doing business, but warranty failures are usually a signal of poor quality. Most product-oriented companies allocate a small percentage of sales to cover warranty expenses; as long as these expenses are within guidelines, it is felt that there is nothing wrong with the product. In a Just-in-Time quality system, this is not acceptable—warranty expenses should be kept to a minimum by increasing the quality and reliability of the product. The level of warranty repairs is directly proportional to the level of customer dissatisfaction, affecting follow-on business. Allocation of expenses to correct potential problems with a product—such as warranty, service, field upgrades, recalls, or liability expenses—are considered a waste caused by poor quality. No company can be successful without a dedicated program to minimize all these expenses.

## 11.7 QUALITY COST AND SUPPLIERS

The quality of a manufactured product is only as good as the quality of every one of its individual components. We can visualize the quality of a product as a chain in which the quality of the individual links determines the quality of the total chain. Any weak, poor-quality link will cause the quality chain to break, resulting in a product malfunction.

No manufacturer produces 100 percent of all the raw material it uses in house. There is always some degree of dependence on outside suppliers. A cost-conscious quality system should monitor the cost of poor quality caused by suppliers. Although it seems easy to accomplish, this goal is commonly unattained, in great part because of the hidden costs of quality at the supplier's site.

High costs of bad quality in a supplier's base system include rejected parts, faulty components, rework, MRB, and challenged deliveries. These costs are normally easy to monitor and account for. The hidden costs of quality are those costs associated with the supplier's operational environment, which are invisible to the customer. Both costs the customer pays for unknowingly. For example, a supplier might deliver first-rate quality parts; the customer certainly would be very happy with the supplier. But if the supplier has

**TABLE 11.5**   SUPPLIER'S COST OF QUALITY

| Cost of Quality | Open | Hidden |
|---|---|---|
| Operational costs | Line inspecting | Over or under tolerances |
|  | Final inspecting | Over- or underinspecting |
|  | Line auditing | Faulty components passing |
|  | Rework | Poor controls |
|  | Engineering changes | Poor testing |
|  | Scrap | Reliability |
|  | Warranty | Down-level products |
|  | Repairs | Late deliveries |
|  | Maintenance | Early deliveries |
|  | Equipment calibration | Packaging |
|  |  | Process imbalances |
|  |  | Idle process |
| Administrative costs | Rescheduling | Paperwork errors |
|  | Cancellations | Frequent billings |
|  | Pull ahead | Excessive communications |
|  |  | Collecting faulty invoices |
| Worker training | Lack of training in quality | Not repeat training |
|  |  | Out of focus training |
| Information system | Incomplete reporting | Too much paperwork |
|  | Late reports | Faulty reports |
|  | Lack of system | Reports to wrong people |
|  |  | Lack of worker feedback |
|  |  | Too much data collection |
|  |  | Collecting irrelevant data |

to invest a great amount of effort in achieving the part's quality level due to inefficiencies, the additional cost will be passed onto the customer.

Another hidden cost of quality common in supplier-manufactured material is over-specification of tolerances requested by customers. These tight-tolerance parts will cost the supplier more to produce at acceptable quality levels, and the customer will pay for them.

Table 11.5 lists the most common causes of the supplier's hidden costs of quality. An efficient quality system should maintain a balance between the quality expected from a supplier and the effort and cost required to produce it.

## 11.8 SPEND QUALITY DOLLARS WISELY

Table 11.2 showed a distribution of expenses for a quality department. The expenses were grouped in three categories: overhead, passive, and proactive. The table showed that for a typical department the expenses for passive quality are larger than the expenses for proactive quality. This normally means that companies spend more money into reactionary activities which should not have been necessary.

Practice shows that a company focusing its efforts on proactive quality will prevent rather than correct quality problems before they happen. Preventing activities are always cheaper than correcting activities because *no damage has yet occurred.*

Figure 11.2 shows the effect of a budget increase for proactive activities. The net

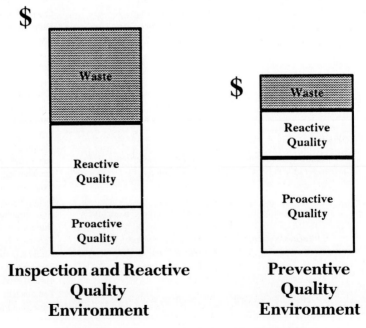

**Figure 11.2**   Impact on the Distribution of Quality Expenses

result of the change of activity's focus is the reduction of expenses for reactive activities. The sum of all expenses incurred in quality will decrease even after we have increased expenses in the proactive activities, because the change has avoided repair costs that burdened the system previously. The return on the investment will pay back many times over with the reduction of rework, scrap, and other associated problems that increased customer dissatisfaction.

## 11.9  COST ACCOUNTING AND QUALITY COSTS

Manufacturing companies' finances are structured by a cost accounting system. The job of cost accounting is to keep track of the overall product costs, including material, labor, and overhead. It also keeps track of inventories and other activities associated with purchasing and labor variances.

One of the activities that is neglected in most cost accounting systems is the monitoring of the actual cost of quality beyond budgetary expenses and inspection labor. A first-rate cost accounting system should track the actual costs of quality, informing people who are responsible for the results.

The process of tracking the actual cost of quality should be simple and not burdened by excessive paperwork. It should also include costs that are not normally considered as quality dependent. This information should be distributed on a regular basis, clearly tracking changes and trends of the normal quality operating mode developed. The best way to implement a quality cost tracking system is to assign the responsibility for its development to the quality, operations, and finance groups. After all, each one of these departments is responsible for one aspect or another of quality tracking and cost.

## 11.10  RESPONSIBILITIES FOR QUALITY COSTS

Perfect quality is the responsibility of every employee in a company. The same applies to costs associated with quality. Every department can affect in many ways the activities that save or waste costs associated with a quality product. It is important that this responsibility be rooted in the minds of people responsible for quality costs. The best way to achieve this is to measure costs as they relate to every department and distribute them to people who are responsible for them.

In most cases, the responsibilities for quality are accounted for by yields, rejections, and defects. This will be made more real if it can be associated with dollars wasted because of poor quality; a positive way to present it would be to estimate dollars saved because of good quality performance by a department.

The effort to measure quality performance in dollars should not eclipse the actual quality measurements, but it should be important enough that it encourages people to improve quality to attain savings. The distribution of actual costs of quality will help workers to understand their roles, not only as participants in building products, but also as being directly responsible for saving dollars by building the product right the first time.

The concept of quality costs and responsibilities should also be taken to suppliers as cost reduction programs. Cost reductions associated with quality problems are a way for a supplier to save money—savings that should be shared by both the supplier and the customer.

## 11.11  SUMMARY

The cost of quality is one of the most misunderstood variables in manufacturing. These costs are usually incomplete and don't accurately reflect the actual costs incurred in manufacturing a quality-perfect product.

Managers across all departments bare the responsibility of communicating and implementing a system for tracking the actual cost of quality. There is no way to reduce cost of quality if managers don't understand which areas are the ones incurring the greatest cost.

The worst error that could be made is to assume that the classical costs of quality, as described in most manufacturing operations, are the only ones affecting the cost of a product. People responsible for tracking costs should make a concerted effort to implement a system that also tracks all hidden costs. Once the system is implemented, it must not be burdened with too much paperwork and wasted labor, because this will also be a hidden cost in the system. This critical balance is a must in operating a successful organization that performs to goals with the least cost; the challenge is to achieve perfection, but at a reasonable cost.

## REFERENCES

CROSBY, PHILIP B. *Quality Is Free: The Art of Making Quality Certain.* New York: New American Library, 1980.

HUNT, V. DANIEL. *Quality in America: How to Implement a Competitive Quality Program.* Homewood, Ill.: Business One Irwin, 1991.

KANATSU, TAKASHI. *TQC for Accounting: A New Role in Companywide Improvement.* Cambridge, Mass.: Productivity Press, 1991.

MONDEN, YASUHIRO, ed. *Cost Management in The New Manufacturing Age: Innovations in the Japanese Automotive Industry.* Cambridge, Mass.: Productivity Press, 1992.

MONDEN, YASUHIRO, and MICHIHARU SAKURAI, eds. *Japanese Management Accounting: A World Class Approach to Profit Management.* Cambridge, Mass.: Productivity Press, 1990.

PERIGORD, MICHEL. *Achieving Total Quality Management: A Program for Action.* Cambridge, Mass.: Productivity Press, 1991.

# 12★

# Total Quality Control: The Company-Wide Approach

In a Just-in-Time system, there is a continual crusade against all kinds of waste, mostly in manufacturing activities. Waste is defined as any activity that produces no value in a task. In this case, waste is associated with any activity that adds no value to the operation of a department. In general, waste results from poor execution of manufacturing tasks.

Total quality control (TQC) is a company-wide approach to quality. It refers not only to the quality of a product from a production line, but also to the activities necessary to support its design and sale. In this case, quality means no productivity waste.

A total quality control program is difficult to implement because most people in an organization think the responsibility for quality belongs only to the quality department. The first step in a company-wide quality program is to educate everyone about his or her responsibility for doing a quality job, including a conscious effort to eliminate waste in all its forms.

A company-wide quality program should be strongly supported by management at all levels. It should also be endorsed wholeheartedly by the people doing the work. These people need clearly to understand the goals, requirements, and benefits of the program. This chapter presents the fundamental requirements for such a program, covering the factors critical to success. A total quality control program is slow to show progress, because it fixes problems that normally are buried in the bureaucracy of a company. The effort, however, will not be wasted. The savings from efficiencies obtained will add up to rewarding returns, including a population of satisfied customers.

## 12.1 QUALITY IS EVERYBODY'S BUSINESS

There is a simple test that will show how committed a company is to a total quality control program. In a company meeting, ask workers responsible for quality to raise their hands. If only the workers in the quality department or in manufacturing raise their hands, you are a long way from having a TQC program in place. After the test, it is time to ask all people, regardless of the department in which they work, to raise their hands—including the janitorial staff if they are available. Quality is everybody's responsibility—and this should be very clear to every employee attending the meeting.

Don't assume that telling workers they are responsible for quality is enough to make them believe it. You have to show them how their work can affect quality as it is perceived by the customer. The ultimate goal of quality is a product that satisfies the customer. This goal will not be met if the product is of perfect quality, but the rest of the support in other activities related to customers is not of perfect quality.

A total quality control program should engage the interest of all people working in a company. It should convince them that the responsibility for quality is as much theirs as it is the quality department's. The best way to instill this belief is to show them how a quality-minded company will perform and support customers' needs much better, providing complete satisfaction. It is important not to give the program lip service, covering walls with clichéd quality posters that are ignored. Avoid this by involving people in the program, passing ownership of its implementation onto them.

## 12.2 QUALITY IN OTHER DEPARTMENTS IN THE COMPANY

Quality is always associated with a product; in very few instances is quality associated with the work itself. Take, for example, the quality of paperwork associated with purchasing material in a purchasing department. You can ask a purchasing manager about the quality of his or her purchase orders. The purchasing manager will tell you that the orders are excellent without knowing exactly how many errors are in them, how much effort is wasted rewriting them, or how much material is coming, or not coming, as a result of mistakes.

Very few departments except manufacturing and quality have a quality measurement of the work they do. In addition, if you don't have a work quality measurement system, it is not possible to know how well, or how badly, you are doing in the completion of everyday tasks.

Figure 12.1 shows four areas of performance that determine the quality of work. Improvements in these areas will result in higher productivity and a sustained quality of work. The timely aspect of work relates not only to the time it takes to do a job, but to the completion date as it relates to the time needed for other activities in the company. Accuracy relates to the avoidance of mistakes. Simplicity concerns the simplification of activities required to do a job. Finally, efficiency relates to the elimination of waste—in this case, tasks that are not absolutely necessary to complete a job.

Consider the process of issuing a purchasing order. Table 12.1 shows a list of activi-

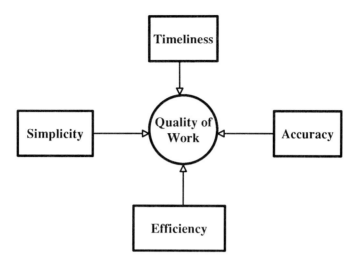

**Figure 12.1**  Factors That Influence Quality of Work

**TABLE 12.1**  TASK PERFORMANCE ASSOCIATED WITH A PURCHASING ORDER

| Purchasing Order Activities | Before TQC Program | After TQC Program |
|---|---|---|
| Purchase request from planner | Paper form delivered to buyer<br>File form after used with P.O. | Electronic transfer to buyer<br>Save request in electronic database |
| Send request for quote to suppliers | Prints and requests mailed or faxed to suppliers for quoting<br>Turnaround time 3–15 days | Reduce number of suppliers for quoting<br>Send information electronically<br>Preagree with key quality suppliers on volume/commodity purchases that eliminate quoting<br>Turnaround time 2–5 days |
| Agree on prices and place order | Verbal negotiation | Preagree prices on most commodity parts. Verbal negotiation only on special parts or new ones |
| Input purchase order | Three days' average time for completion<br>2% error rate on data input | One-day average time for completion<br>Zero error on data input |
| Send purchase order to supplier | Two days for mailing. Three days for mail transit to supplier | 0.5 days for electronic transfer and supplier arrival |
| Distribute purchase order copies | Three days for multiple copies, filing and distributing | 0.5 days for automatic electronic distribution and filing one hard copy |
| Supplier confirms order and deliveries | Five days for written confirmation | One-day electronic confirmation |

ties associated with this task and their performance criteria. Assume that in a company a typical purchasing order is placed 10 days from the time a planner sends a request for material authorization. A TQC program to improve the purchasing process will concentrate on three areas:

1. Improvement of communications to speed up the flow of information and its accuracy.
2. The identification of tasks that can be completed before the purchasing order is placed.
3. The simplification or elimination of activities that are not necessary to do the job, including paperwork.

This example can be applied to other departments that are heavily involved with paperwork, for example, the sales order department or the accounts payable department. The simplification process applies to any of them. The steps to this task are:

1. Make a chronological list of activities associated with the job, including a brief description of each.
2. Group the activities in three categories according to the type of work they accomplish:
   Paperwork activities—filing forms, data entry, etc.
   Verbal activities—phone calls, meetings, etc.
   Communications activities—mailing, distributing and receiving paperwork, traveling.
3. Group activities according to the timing of their execution:
   Activities that can be performed before the job is done—prequoting, prefiling forms, reduction of choices, etc.
   Critical activities that must be performed at the time the job is done—placing an order, sending information, paying a supplier or service, taking orders, etc.
   Activities that can be performed after the job is done—filing, mailing copies, etc.
4. Follow simplification rules for the activity groups listed in steps 2 and 3:
   Reduce paperwork activities to an absolute minimum.
   Replace paperwork with electronics as much as possible, for example, E-mail, electronic data interchange, EDI, electronic filing, etc.
   Replace verbal communication with as much electronic communication as possible. Make meetings more efficient and shorter by reducing the number of attendants and preinforming attendants, the followup on issues from previous meetings, etc.
   Replace mail and fax communications with electronic communication as much as possible. EDI is an example.
   Simplify and eliminate the number of tasks required to do a job.
   Move critical activities that must happen during the implementation of a task to the pretask time window. Figure 12.2 shows the rearrangement of tasks and their reductions.
   Reduce or eliminate tasks that are done after the job is done.

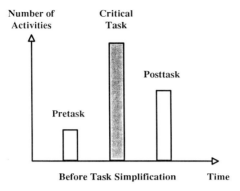

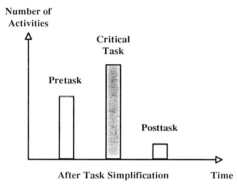

**Figure 12.2**   Task Reduction Before and After Simplification

## 12.3 QUALITY OF FIELD SERVICE

The most influential aspect of a product as it relates to customer satisfaction is the quality of the field service organization. When a product breaks or malfunctions, the customer is clearly disappointed. When a product breaks and is not serviced promptly, the customer is undoubtedly unsatisfied and probably will never buy another product from the supplier.

Any product can malfunction if the numbers out in the field are high enough; customers will understand that. What customers will fail to understand, and will have little patience for, is a careless manufacturer that does not act promptly to get a product fixed.

Many companies claim they have excellent customer support when in fact they are burdened by a huge bureaucracy that slows their service, making them insensitive to customer needs. Quality in customer service is as important as the quality of the product itself.

Quality of service is simple to measure. The four ingredients for quality of service can be related to Figure 12.1.

1. *Timeliness:* Customer service should be timely and promptly executed. A customer needing service is a customer not using the product because something is wrong with it.

2. *Accuracy:* The work required to fix a problem that requires service should be of a high quality.

3. *Simplicity:* The system used to deal with customers when something is wrong should be simple, not burdened by bureaucracy.

4. *Efficiency:* The actual service given to customers should not take more time than necessary.

The process of simplification listed at the end of the previous section can be used to increase the productivity of the service organization and to shorten the time it takes to service a customer. Other measurements like MTBF, MTBSC, and so on can be used to measure the performance of a product in the field, but they will not accurately measure the performance of the field organization supporting the needs of customers.

## 12.4 QUALITY IN DOCUMENTATION

Poor quality in documentation is one of the most common causes of poor quality in a product. Poor documentation leads to waste and costly mistakes in manufacturing. It misleads people purchasing material and inspecting, assembling, and delivering a product. Poor documentation is mostly created by employee neglect or by the use of the wrong standards. The problem may be lack of critical data. It can also be too much unnecessary data that confuse manufacturing with too many requirements that affect quality and costs.

Another aspect of documentation that affects quality is the lack of controls to update changes in the product as problems are found. Revision levels and cross-references to other documents are an absolute necessity if the documentation is to correctly reflect the actual product.

The last aspect, frequently missed, is the accurate correlation of the documentation with the database used to plan and purchase materials for the process that builds the product. A common problem is that the documentation is changed, but not properly updated into the database used to run MRP and other related materials planning needs.

Documentation control usually falls to engineering or manufacturing. The department assigned with the responsibility for documentation should make sure that documents are clear and follow a set of rules to control tolerances, revisions, cross-references, and distribution. The goal is to provide quality information to people who need it.

Setting up a first-class documentation system is the responsibility of all people needing the information. A committee of documentation users and producers should define the system, making sure there is agreement on the rules used to change and control documents. This is not always simple, for both groups have different needs. Where there is a conflict, users should get the last word because they are the ones who will be using the documentation long after it is released.

Below are some key points to remember when setting up a documentation system:

1. Avoid burdening documents with too much data that will clutter up the information they are supposed to convey.

2. Too little information is damaging as well. Information should be complete to specify the parts that it represents.

3. Make sure that tolerances used to specify a part match tolerances required of the whole product. Don't overburden parts with unnecessary tolerances: They cost money and cause quality problems.

4. Cross-reference document revision levels only to the levels high enough to need the change. Too much cross-referencing will cause changes to ripple throughout too many document levels, causing additional wasted work and an opportunity for errors. Insufficient cross-referencing will cause changes to go unnoticed on higher assemblies and will provide no control on the whole product when manufactured.

5. Only one department should be responsible for controlling documentation. This department should be on a neutral ground between design groups that specify documentation and users.

6. Always automate and simplify the documentation process as much as possible. Use electronic means for generation, distribution, changing, and storing of documents.

## 12.5 QUALITY IN MARKETING, SALES, AND FINANCE DEPARTMENTS

Quality in any of these departments is associated with the quality of work they produce. What is commonly missing is the association with the satisfaction of customers they service. For example, it is very difficult to associate customer satisfaction with the finance department. Finance is seen as servicing the internal needs of a company rather than the customers the company supports. This is a misconception because in any working environment the notion of customers doesn't necessarily have to relate to customers who buy a product. A customer is any person, or organization, that receives services from another department in the company. The customers of a finance department are other departments that receive its services, and there is an absolute need to include quality in the work it does. A simple example of this is payroll. Every worker is a customer of the payroll department and quality is a must, because no one will take a late, or smaller, paycheck.

Outside customers of the finance department are the customers of the company that receive invoices for services they have purchased. Other customers are suppliers that have sold material to the company and want to get paid. These are outside services the finance department must provide with first-rate quality. Finance is the department with the most customers—everyone who works in the company, plus stockholders, suppliers, and outside customers.

Marketing and sales are more traditional customer-oriented services. There is a population of customers that depends on them for product information, quotes, order entry, and managing delivery issues that affect the everyday operation of the business. Quality in those departments doesn't refer only to the quality of service, but also to the quality of information they provide. A misled customer is an unhappy one, and most likely will not remain a customer.

The principles described in previous sections can be applied to these departments to improve the quality of their services. The first step is to set up a system to measure their quality performance. Then techniques of analysis and improvement should be used to improve the quality of service. One risk in this process is that managers in these departments will fight any measurement system, claiming that their operations are in no need of improvement. These managers should be convinced that every system, no matter how efficient and perfect it is, will have room for improvements that can be systematically implemented. The process of improvement should never stop, or the department will drift back into inefficiencies that sooner or later will cause poor quality service.

## 12.6 CUSTOMER SATISFACTION

Customers are the ultimate judges of the quality of the service they receive. No matter how well a system is measuring itself, if customers are not happy with it, then something needs improvement.

A company-wide approach to customer satisfaction relates to the satisfaction of outside customers. It also relates to the satisfaction of those departments that are receiving services from other departments. A simple way to measure the level of satisfaction is to do a satisfaction survey. Another way is to implement a system that measures the quality of the service rendered.

The results of a survey should be shared with management and all workers in the department involved in producing a product. It should be honest and specific. It should also be followed up by corrective actions. All this requires management support and a mind open to accepting self-criticism without getting defensive.

A system is not capable of satisfying all the needs of all customers all the time. No system is perfect, no matter how hard one tries to improve it. But this should not stop management and workers from trying to improve and to correct problems that cause customer dissatisfaction—on a continuous basis no matter how improved the system is. Regardless of how well a system performs, there is always room for improvement.

## 12.7 MANAGEMENT COMMITMENT
## TO COMPANY-WIDE QUALITY

Management commitment to quality is not only the responsibility of top management, it is the responsibility of every manager regardless of the level on which the manager operates. Commitment to quality is a commitment to excellence in the work produced as well as to the quality of the product. Even more, a quality product requires a quality company behind it; otherwise, the product will not sustain its excellence.

Quality-wide awareness is a mentality that looks for small faults at all levels in the organization. Quality is never satisfied with the improvements achieved so far. Every work activity is imperfect and can be improved.

The quality mentality puts quality first. Quality strives to do the job right the first time and not to postpone until tomorrow what can be done right today. Quality is a true commitment, uncompromised, and never ending.

## 12.8 SUMMARY

A total quality control program needs to be embraced by every department in order to succeed. The initial effort should be driven by management, but it should be wholeheartedly supported by workers in order to make it a success. A TQC program should have clear goals, with specific guidelines for implementation in a reasonable time frame. It should not be a program that envisions a particular ending, because there is never going to be an end to it. When goals are reached, the program should move to a new set of more aggressive goals. Once a certain level of customer satisfaction is reached, a new goal should replace the old one. If this effort is not continued on an ongoing basis, the progress achieved will be lost. The system will drift back to its normal way of operation, accepting indifferently whatever level was operating before.

Management and workers should avoid the trap of self-gratification and accept that they are never going to finish a TQC program, that such an effort should be part of the everyday modus operandi in the company, and that it is as important as the product or services the company provides.

Commitment never to stop a TQC program is the first ingredient for success. The commitment should be company-wide, endorsed by every worker regardless of his or her responsibilities.

## REFERENCES

AKAO, YOJI, ed. *HOSHIN KANRI. Policy Deployment for Successful TQM.* Cambridge, Mass.: Productivity Press, 1991.

BLAISDELL, MIKAEL. *When It Comes to Support, the Customer Is King. Info World,* 14, no. 25, 22 June 1992, 60–65.

ERNST and YOUNG. Quality Improvement Consulting Group. *Total Quality: An Executive's Guide for the 1990s.* Homewood, Ill.: Business One Irwin, 1989.

ISHIKAWA, KAORU. *What is Total Quality Control? The Japanese Way.* Englewood Cliffs, N.J.: Prentice-Hall, 1985.

Japan Human Relations Association. *KAIZEN TEIAN 1. Developing Systems for Continuous Improvement Through Employee Suggestions.* Cambridge, Mass.: Productivity Press, 1992.

JUSE Problem Solving Research Group. *TQC Solutions: The 14-Step Process.* Cambridge, Mass.: Productivity Press, 1990.

# 13★

# *Teaching Quality to Everyone: Training Programs*

Critical to the success of any program in a company is the interest of the people participating in it. A program to improve quality is no different from any other as it relates to gaining the interest and commitment of the participants. Unfortunately, quality programs have gained a reputation as being implemented mostly for cosmetic reasons, or as a result of pressure from a major quality crisis that will fizzle as soon as the crisis is resolved. Quality programs are also associated with lip service programs on the part of managers. All these stigmas should be ignored by managers serious about improving quality performance.

The first phase of a quality program is to draw up a plan, clearly setting implementation goals and timetables. Key is the implementation of a training program to get the system off the ground.

It is a mistake to assume that training will stop once the quality system is in place. Manufacturing is a high-pressure environment that pushes workers to produce. This drive to output needs to be balanced by a continuous training program that focuses workers' minds on quality.

A good training program should also involve employees who are not normally associated with quality. Such broad training should introduce the concept of work excellence to everyone in the organization. In addition, a continuous training program will show that management is committed to improving worker skills on a long-term basis.

## 13.1  THE ROLE OF TRAINING

Workers don't have to be sold on the importance of perfect-quality products; every worker understands that good quality is good for the company and that bad quality causes dissatisfied customers. But workers cannot achieve perfection in quality without the help of the company. They need training programs to improve their working skills to achieve high quality standards. This training needs to be focused and consistent.

Training programs are the most important aspect of a quality system and should never be underestimated or shortchanged. A first-class training program should reach all employees in the company regardless of their functions and responsibilities. One mistake that many companies make is to create training programs that involve only workers in the production line, without considering all the other workers who are responsible for quality performance. Customers not only see the products they purchase, but the support and professional involvement of other departments when they deal with normal business issues. Quality performance from those departments is extremely important to maintaining quality service for customers.

Training programs need the support of all levels of management because training is usually looked on as an expense that can be reduced without affecting quality. Nothing is further from the truth. Training is awareness and the foundation for discipline in excellence. Training is teaching the basis for accepting responsibility. Training is the key to understanding the ways to do the job right the first time. Training is the first step down the long road that leads to a world of perfect quality.

## 13.2  RESPONSIBILITY FOR TRAINING PROGRAMS

The responsibility for training programs lies with senior management. Managers can set up task forces and budgets to implement training and to provide the drive necessary to get everybody involved. The best way for management to implement a training program is to assemble a team of quality-committed workers that become the driving force and organizers of the training.

The quality department should play a central role in this effort, but it should be clear that quality training will not be directed only at manufacturing and quality workers. The message is better transmitted to the organization by recruiting people from other departments in the company.

Once the team is selected, it will have to do its homework to come up with a quality curriculum that not only covers the operational departments, but all other departments. The purpose of training is to bring quality awareness to everybody and to make workers true believers in the program.

Members of the team don't need to be quality experts before their appointment. The most important requirement for belonging to the team is the enthusiasm and belief that quality is important and that it can be improved. For those members who have little experience in quality and training, it will be beneficial for them to attend quality seminars to become familiar with quality concepts they are going to disseminate throughout the corporation. The team's efforts should be synchronized with the operational needs of the company. For example, class schedules should be convenient for people attending training.

There are many quality training seminars available which will benefit the team before it embarks on designing training classes for co-workers. It is also possible to use the help of consultants who advise and provide materials to set up training.

The team's responsibility should also include the actual process of teaching classes, enrolling the help of different specialists in the company to act as invited lecturers. This approach will show workers that there are people with first-rate skills in the company who can be used to implement such a system. Some training classes might focus on the needs of customers who purchase products from the company. This will make workers more aware of the importance of quality and service as they relate to customers.

On a long-term basis, the team in charge of training might evolve into a permanent staff that does nothing but training. The money invested in this group would be recovered through improved quality and reduction of waste in the company. If the company is too small to justify a full-time training group, then it would be a good idea to rotate the members of the team, so the training effort could maintain the high level of interest and energy this activity requires. The key to success is to stay focused, making sure programs train the right people with the right tools.

## 13.3 MANAGEMENT TRAINING

Management support is critical to the success of any quality program. The best way to ensure success is to train managers on key concepts of the quality system and the importance of a well-implemented approach.

No manager will say "no" to a quality program. Many managers, however, will give it lip service and will avoid any substantial level of activity and commitment—"too expensive" or "we already have great quality." A training program for managers should include an outline of the Just-in-Time quality program execution phases. The presentation should list in detail the benefits the system will provide, but it should be carefully presented so it is not oversold as the solution to all the problems in the company. This approach might set managers' expectations too high, leading to cutbacks when results are not obtained quickly.

It is important to inform managers not only about the need for a quality system under Just-in-Time, but about the benefits that Just-in-Time will bring to the company.

Senior management involvement during training sessions with suppliers is of utmost importance. Management's presence in classes will show commitment at all levels of the organization, sending the message that the effort is serious.

Once managers attend training classes, they should be updated periodically on the progress of the program. Perhaps the best time to do this is when managers are updated on the results of the Just-in-Time program. Just-in-Time and quality are so closely related that it is better to present their progress at the same time. The information presented should be straightforward, covering issues that have handicapped the program and successes that have moved the program forward. This approach adds credibility to the program and will gain management support.

## 13.4 WORKER TRAINING

Providing training in quality to workers is not an easy task. A training program's main objective is to change workers' habits, so there is a conscious effort to produce quality every second they work on a product. It will be very easy to train quality-conscious workers because they already have a predisposition toward doing quality work. It can also be assumed that it will be very hard to change old working patterns in some other workers. Remember that no worker wants to do a bad job purposely; given a system with proper tools and a proper process with safeguards, workers will do a quality job.

The most important aspect of training programs is not the material the programs cover, but the frequency with which they occur. In most companies, training programs certify workers in quality and then never train them further. This almost guarantees that workers will return to old working patterns. A quality training program for workers should be repetitive, and it should continually review the fundamentals of quality.

Training programs should be simple and should cover lots of examples and working exercises. They should also include videotapes and visits to other companies with similar programs and excellent quality records. Nothing works better than teaching workers by example.

Worker feedback on training is important. Workers should be asked about ways to improve future programs. As a general rule, workers should be retrained every six months. If the quality program still has problems, then training sessions should be as frequent as needed. One way to avoid affecting the department's productivity is to offer training classes outside working hours.

Another crucial aspect of training is to teach workers both the importance of Just-in-Time and the importance of quality. They should become familiar with Just-in-Time's concepts and what they mean to the company. One effective way to show results of both programs is to bring satisfied customers to some classes, so they can tell workers firsthand how important it is that a quality product be delivered on time.

Finally, a training program should fill a dual role:

1. Bring worker skills to a level where they can do their jobs consistently with good quality.
2. Reinforce the belief that perfect quality is the only way to produce a product.

This second aspect is the most important because it will provide workers with the drive to search for perfection in the work they do.

## 13.5 ENGINEERING TRAINING FOR DESIGNING QUALITY PRODUCTS

Many companies offer training programs for engineers to improve technical and design skills. Some progressive companies also have business and managerial programs. Very few of them, however, have a program dedicated to designing quality into products. This lack of formal training in designing quality products has in many instances produced technologically advanced products that don't meet the quality standards required in a competitive market. In today's competitive world, designing quality is one of the most important tasks a design team must consider before implementation starts to take shape in a product.

If asked about the need for formal training in designing quality, design engineers will probably say they already know how to design quality and don't need any training. Even worse, managers of these engineers will probably say the same thing. This causes many poorly designed quality products to fail in the market.

There are four important areas to consider when designing quality in a product. These factors require careful analysis and proper weighing to produce a competitive quality product. Engineers should be trained to understand these compromises and not to be biased toward technological goals. Figure 13.1 shows the four areas of consideration that will guarantee a well-designed product. Technological goals should lead the product to a next generation that offers more performance for less cost. Material quality and the manufacturing process are areas that must be included at design time so that a product can be put together in a predictable way. Finally, customer support will ensure customer's satisfaction after the product is out in the field.

A proper balancing of these disciplines is not commonly found within the grasp of engineering design groups, because the technological star always shines brighter than the lesser stars of manufacturing, materials, and support. A good quality training program for design engineers should include basic training in these areas, helping engineers to understand design compromises.

By nature, engineers are aggressive about incorporating technology into their designs to have the latest feature that will put the product ahead of the competition. Engineers are also slow to accept quality compromises that lead to a lessening of technology and perfor-

**Figure 13.1**   Areas of Tradeoff for Quality in Design

mance. The only way to solve this conflict is to put engineers through a good training program that covers the basics of quality and addresses customer satisfaction from the point of view of reliability and ease of maintenance.

## 13.6 SUPPLIER TRAINING

A good supplier training program is critical to the success of a Just-in-Time quality program. Normally, suppliers will be wary of quality improvements beyond what they consider acceptable. The problem is compounded when Just-in-Time asks them to ship small lots, frequently, and with delivery schedules based on a demand pull system.

The job of a supplier training program is to make suppliers feel they are partners of the company in its quest for perfect quality. It is very important that the supplier understand the advantages of the new system. It is also important that they understand that the change will make them more competitive, not only with this particular customer but with *all* customers.

A training program for suppliers should also encourage them to engage their employees in quality training. One way to facilitate this training transfer is to share the basic training programs with the supplier, including training material, and by training the supplier's trainers.

Finally, a training program should include training classes offered by the supplier, teaching the supplier's process requirements for manufacturing a quality product.

## 13.7 DEVELOPING SYSTEMS AND PROCEDURES

A quality training program is generally the responsibility of the quality department and involves people from departments not associated with manufacturing. This broad training program requires careful planning and the involvement of management and employees.

The best way to sell management on the implementation of such a program is to put the scope of the program and the budget it will require into writing. The justification process should be simple and not burdened by paperwork. Remember, too much paperwork is a waste in the Just-in-Time system.

An important point to consider when planning training classes is to involve key people from other departments, so there is broad feedback on the needs of the training program. The result should be a program that is practical, flexible, and down to earth at the level of the people involved. The goal of training is to turn workers into believers in quality excellence, rather than to teach techniques that will be forgotten a week after the class.

A training program is not cast in concrete. Once it is started, it should be reviewed periodically and changed as feedback from people taking classes is received. This review process should never stop.

## 13.8 SUMMARY

Quality training is a very important part of any effort to improve quality. But training by itself will not cure quality problems; it is a bridge to the long road leading to the solution. The message given during training should turn into a working reality. This means "people involvement" at all levels of the organization, people doing their jobs as the training programs told them.

Providing tools to workers to do their jobs right is the best way to eliminate the lip-service problem. Many companies fall into this trap easily, preaching quality in training programs and then sending workers to the production line without proper support. Managers and workers should also have the latitude to make changes in the way they do their jobs to improve quality. Simplification is critical to improvement.

One final warning about training concerns the procurement of training programs from outside sources. There are many companies that specialize in quality training programs. These specialists provide a good start for training programs. But sending workers to such classes or using off-the-shelf class programs in house requires caution. The most effective training programs are those that are tailored to the needs of the company. The best way to start a program is to send people in charge of designing the training programs to outside classes, so they get a feeling of what is available and best fits their needs. Then the program should be tailored to match the requirements of the organization.

## REFERENCES

DYER, WILLIAM G. *Team Building: Issues and Alternatives*. Reading, Mass.: Addison-Wesley, 1977.

HALL, ROBERT W. *Attaining Manufacturing Excellence*. Homewood, Ill.: Dow Jones-Irwin, 1987.

JONES, KAREN, ed. *Best of TEI: Current Perspectives on Total Employee Involvement*. Cambridge, Mass.: Productivity Press, 1989.

MINARIK, ETIENNE. *Individual Motivation: Removing the Blocks to Creative Involvement*. Cambridge, Mass.: Productivity Press, 1992.

PYZDEK, T. *What Every Engineer Should Know About Quality Control*. Dearborn, Mich.: SME, 1989.

# 14★

# Implementing a Quality System: Practical Advice

You have been given an overview of the different components of a Just-in-Time quality system in the earlier chapters. The questions that are probably crossing your mind now are how to start such a program and how to ensure its success—you have studied all the pieces and you want to put it together and see if it "flies."

A first-class quality system is similar to an airplane in many ways. All its pieces have to fit together perfectly in order for the system to fly. Once in the air, it needs constant piloting to avoid a crash. The pilot's job, as well as the job of people involved in quality, does not end as long as the plane and the quality system keep flying.

Like an airplane, a quality system needs refueling with new ideas or it will crash. In addition, a quality crash can often be fatal for the people and company involved.

The following sections will show some of the requirements for starting a Just-in-Time quality program. A word of caution is necessary; not every company needs the same type of program. The secret to success is to understand the fundamental tasks required and then tailor the program to the specific needs of your company. This approach will increase the probability for success.

Quality improvement doesn't go forward with big leaps, but with small steps whose progress may not be visible until there are many of them. Persistence is the ability to keep working on the program even when there are no signs of success, to keep working when under pressure from both management and workers to stop a program that is apparently not producing results.

Quality is *persistence* and the *will* to improve. This combination will guarantee the program's success in spite of any temporary setbacks. The following sections will provide guidelines on how to assemble a quality "airplane" and how to get it off the ground. The piloting is up to you.

## 14.1 FRAMEWORK FOR A QUALITY SYSTEM

The first step in implementing a Just-in-Time quality system is to understand that the current system is not perfect and needs improvement. People in a company will fight the winds of change in many ways. Some will say that quality is not bad and the current system is working, but it could always be argued that no matter how good current quality is, there is always room for improvement.

A quality program should start from the top. Management should show an interest in improving the system. Even if the present system has a good track record, there should be management drive for a program that will take quality to the next level of perfection. The spark that lights the flame of change should come from management. This will add credibility to the effort and show the company cares.

The next step in keeping the flame alive is involvement. The concept of a new quality program should interest and involve middle management and workers as well. This effort should be engaged with a positive approach—even if there are pressing quality problems at the moment.

Middle management will be responsible for drafting and implementing the new quality plan. Worker involvement will provide the hands necessary to put the airplane together. Both groups will keep it flying after the plane has taken off.

The quality plan should be put together by a committee of people who represent all departments in the company. The plan should be reviewed by a sample of selected workers who can provide adequate feedback. The key to a successful plan is feedback and flexibility, a willingness to change. This a very important aspect because there will be changes necessary as implementation progresses and feedback is generated.

Figure 14.1 shows three steps in setting up a framework for change. First, start with top management drive and then involve middle management and workers. Finally, the new

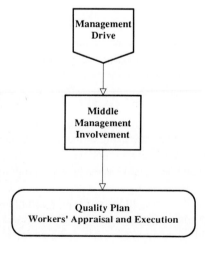

**Figure 14.1**  Framework for Change in Quality

quality plan is drafted, matching the company needs, including an implementation schedule. The next section will show the proper sequence for this process.

## 14.2 PLAN IMPLEMENTATION STEPS

A Just-in-Time quality program should follow steps that require careful ordering and company-wide coordination. If the company is embarked on a Just-in-Time program, it is important to synchronize both programs because they will need each other. You can use this outline as a framework that provides the backbone for your quality program. Details are not included in the structure because every company has different operating needs that will provide the flesh to fill it in.

The outline will be good enough to get the program's infrastructure in place, leaving the door open for individual customization. Figure 14.2 shows the implementation flow. A detailed description of the steps is listed below:

1.  Assemble a core team to drive the Just-in-Time quality program. This team should have company-wide representation, including employees not working in the quality and manufacturing departments—someone from purchasing or finance could be a member of the team. Recruit a quality champion to lead the team. This champion should have enough clout to be able to cross departmental boundaries to work with different managers.

2.  The first task is to search for comprehensive quality training programs offered outside the company and enroll in them. Training should cover all areas of quality and include Just-in-Time principles. This phase should last from one to three months, transforming the team into true believers in quality and Just-in-Time systems.

3.  Divide the quality effort into four areas. Figure 14.3 shows these areas and their interrelationships: suppliers, manufacturing, customers, and company-wide quality. Divide the quality plan into four sections that cover each one of these areas. Use the information from previous chapters to draft the plan and activities. The activities should cover: training employees on the concept of continuous quality improvement; statistical process control, SPC; data collection and analysis; cause-and-effect analysis; data information systems; prevention; and so on. The output of this step is a quality program with milestones and peoples' responsibilities assigned.

4.  The next step is to implement a quality assessment program. This should be carried out at the same time employee training programs are launched. The assessment will be used as a reference point to measure future improvement of the quality program. The assessment should be honest, and it should cover all four areas described earlier. This process is equivalent to a quality checkup. The three areas the checkup should measure are product quality levels, procedures, and cost of quality waste.

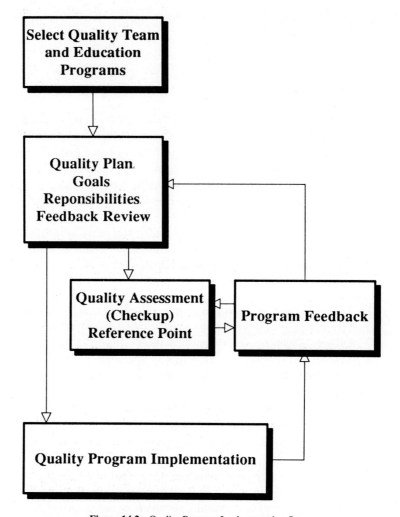

**Figure 14.2**   Quality Program Implementation Steps

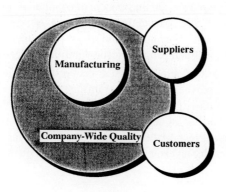

**Figure 14.3**   Quality Plan Areas of Activities

5. Implement the quality program following the milestones. Don't overburden the program with too much paperwork and reporting—the key is execution and commitment to change. The program should be implemented at a pace dictated by the resources available. Don't try to implement too much with limited resources. This will cause a lack of credibility in the program. For large companies with several product lines and divisions, start the program in a specific area and gain experience. Then share the experience with other groups producing other products. Don't implement the program with an easy product that will not test the resolve of the quality team.

6. Assess the program progress frequently. Benchmark the progress against the initial checkup data. Analyze those areas where there is little progress and change the plan to improve the system. Where there is good progress, analyze the reasons for this success and apply them to other areas. Never keep the plan static: Adjust it to increase efficiency.

## 14.3 MISTAKES TO AVOID

The three most common causes for the failure of a quality program are overcommitment, lack of progress, and worker apathy.

Overcommitment results from not using adequate resources. Management should analyze the scope of the program and then commit adequate resources. If insufficient resources are available because of the size of the company, then implementation should be done sequentially, by sections. It should start with the manufacturing department first, so the process is in order before going to suppliers. The recommended order is: manufacturing, suppliers, company-wide, then customers. Customers are left until last because they will benefit from each of the previous efforts as the overall quality of the company improves.

The second cause of possible failure is starting an ambitious program with plenty of resources. In this case, the risk is to lose the focus on key milestones because of the high level of activity involved. For large companies, it is recommended that the quality program start per product line, in order to achieve some degree of success that will encourage workers on other products to support it.

The last common cause of failure is lack of worker involvement. A quality program needs the support and the involvement of workers to succeed. The quality team should not force workers to get involved. Involvement comes through asking workers to become participants and by showing the benefits of the new system. Workers' quality training is a good start. Then workers should participate in drafting the quality plan. Workers will have ownership if they think they have participated in the program's definition and planning. It is also important to explain to workers the changes the program will bring and why they are necessary. Changes should not look arbitrary or forced by management. Remember, in some cases you are going to ask workers to do their jobs differently. For example, when quality inspectors in the manufacturing line are eliminated, this responsibility is transferred to line workers, and they should understand why it is happening.

## 14.4 THE QUALITY CHAMPION

The success of a quality program is very much dependent on the appointment of a quality champion. A quality program is a war against mediocrity. Like any other war, a leader should lead the troops to victory. However, there is a big difference between a quality war and a conventional war. A quality war never ends. The search for victory in quality is a never-ending process toward perfection.

The job of a quality champion is to lead the quality team. He or she should carry the banner high, no matter how difficult implementation is turning out to be. The champion should have enough clout to cross interdepartmental barriers. He or she should also be able to move mountains out of the way when the road to perfect quality is blocked.

The champion's appointment is critical and it should be made at the beginning of the program. The champion should participate in all training exercises with the quality team, even if he or she is already qualified for the job. The quality champion should be a manager at the directorial or vice-presidential level. The champion should also be a team player and a dedicated person, whose main role is to inspire and be the strategist and, most of all, a leader.

## 14.5 DEFINING QUALITY GOALS

One of the most common causes for the failure of quality improvement programs is related to setting quality goals. The team sets goals too high or too low. High goals will cause the program to miss, causing a loss of faith. Setting goals too low will not challenge the program, and eventually causes a loss of credibility due to lack of progress.

The best way to set goals is to distribute them to cover the four areas described in Figure 14.3. This grouping will allow a balanced set of goals that cover all critical areas. Table 14.1 list most goals that are common to these areas. The goals should be ranked in order of importance within their respective areas. Then the quality checkup should determine the current values when the quality program is about to be launched. A realistic appraisal of the improvement is then put into place, with a series of milestones for improving goals.

The trick is not to go from current values to final ones in one step: It is better to include several intermediate milestones that will show the rate of progress. For example, a quality yield is defined as a goal. A current value of the yield is 85 percent and the goal desired is 100 percent. Rather than setting a 100 percent goal as the next milestone in a year's time frame, it is easier to measure progress by setting an intermediate milestone of 95 percent for the next six months, and 100 percent six months later. This step-by-step approach to setting goals will also help to increase the team's morale when goals are met in a shorter period of time. In general, it is recommended that goals be set in increments of time spans of no more than one quarter, and in no increments smaller than one month.

**TABLE 14.1**  TYPICAL GOALS OF A JUST-IN-TIME QUALITY PROGRAM

| Quality Areas | Quality Goals |
|---|---|
| Suppliers | Quality yield improvements |
| | On-time delivery |
| | Process lead-time reductions |
| | Dock-to-WIP certification |
| | Just-in-Time pull shipments |
| | Reschedule flexibility |
| | Reduction of number of suppliers |
| | Suppliers' partnership programs |
| | Suppliers' training in quality and Just-in-Time |
| | Cost reduction and quality improvement programs |
| | Paperwork improvement programs, e.g., EDI |
| | Receiving inspection elimination |
| Manufacturing | Process yield improvements |
| | Rework reduction |
| | Quality control inspection elimination |
| | Worker training in quality |
| | Process output linearity |
| | Small lots quality and flexibility |
| | Buffer inventory reduction |
| | Absenteeism reduction |
| | Scrap and MRB reductions |
| | Lead-time reduction in process |
| | Poka-yoke implementations |
| | SPC implementation |
| | Down-time reduction |
| | Manufacturing instructions improvement |
| | Reduction of engineering changes |
| | Involvement with engineers at design time |
| | Product reviews and cost reductions and quality improvements |
| | Ship product on time |
| Company-wide | Engineering documentation improvement |
| | Foolproof design improvement |
| | Engineering cost reduction |
| | Design for assembly and testability |
| | Paperwork reduction and accuracy |
| | Travel reduction |
| | Employee training and communication |
| | Cost accounting tracking |
| | Finance reports on time |
| | Expediting shortages |
| | Short-time material planning |
| | Absenteeism reduction |
| | Cash management |
| | Accounts payable management and suppliers' problem-solving efficiency |
| | Accounts receivable management |
| Customers | Customer satisfaction |
| | Product on time to market |
| | MTBF and MTBSC measurement |
| | DOA measurement |
| | Customer training |
| | Customer documentation |
| | Sales brochures quality |
| | Order entry and customer support |
| | Responsiveness to solve customers' problems |
| | Ship products to commitments |
| | Invoicing accuracy and timeliness |

## 14.6 ASSESSMENT OF THE QUALITY SYSTEM

Assessing the effectiveness of a quality system is an exercise in self-analysis that should be honest and effective. Before a quality program is launched, it is very important that the company take a critical look at all the aspects of the quality system already in place. This information is very important in helping tailor the new quality program to those areas that need most work.

Companies in trouble with bad quality, bad manufacturing, bad suppliers, and irate customers are in more desperate need of a crash quality program to get things under control. The tendency in this case is to overreact and to change the system from scratch without too much thinking and planning.

The best advice is to take a close look at the quality system currently in place, then take a step back and prepare a comprehensive plan that prioritizes actions of the new plan in those areas that most need improvement. Get the house in order first before trying to improve suppliers' quality.

When the new program has been in place for a period of time, the company should analyze itself again to analyze the progress made and to compare results against initial values. The difference between new and old performance goals will indicate the plan's accomplishments.

For cases where good improvement has been achieved, it is important not to fall into the trap of thinking the program is no longer necessary, or that it should be relaxed. New goals need to be set challenging the program even more.

When there is not much progress and the new analysis shows the program is not working, the first reaction will be to scrap the program and start again. This would be a mistake because it gives everybody the impression that time has been wasted. It is recommended that after a careful analysis of the problems, new changes will redirect the effort without changing its overall scope—understand first what is causing the failure, then what corrective actions are necessary to eliminate the causes.

Success *or* failure should not cause a quality program to slow down or stop. The quality team should understand that the challenge of quality is not a passing one. There is always the possibility for improvement and better results, or the possibility that things will regress after efforts have been relaxed. Continue the program and do it in such a fashion that always challenges the team in charge of implementing it.

## 14.7 QUALITY AWARDS AND CERTIFICATION: AN EXERCISE FOR FITNESS

One effective way to improve the quality system in a company is to enroll in a quality award or a certification program. In the United States, the Malcolm Baldrige National Quality Award is the pinnacle of such awards. The Baldrige Award was created by the U.S. Commerce Department with the purpose of creating a blueprint for excellence in quality. The award grants points for performance in 32 criteria sections which cover management, suppliers, worker training, product quality, customer needs and satisfaction, and detailed quality measurement results, such as yields and cycle times. To apply for the award, a report on the company is filed. The report, not exceeding 75 pages, is reviewed by a panel of examiners selected from industry and academia. Companies that score high are visited by examiners, who make a recommendation to a panel of eight judges selected from the private sector. There are only two winners from manufacturing, small business, and service companies.

Winning a Baldrige Award is important for the winners as a marketing tool to advertise their excellence in quality. But the great return from winning, or just trying to win, is the series of improvements and self-assessments that are involved. Applying for a quality award, or for a quality certification from a credited organization, is an excellent way to get the company involved in the effort to improve the quality system. This type of effort usually requires a revision of the systems and procedures used to run quality. It will also force participants to make changes to improve areas of quality that are not performing at satisfactory levels. In other words, it will force the company to reach quality fitness.

Another certification program highly recommended for implementation in quality-conscious companies is the ISO 9000. The International Organization for Standardization (ISO) was formed in 1946 to develop a set of trade, manufacturing, and communication standards. In 1987, the ISO technical committee issued a Quality System Management Standard that consisted of five standard series: ISO 9000, 9001, 9002, 9003, and 9004.

The areas covered by the five standards are:

ISO 9000    Provides guidelines for the selection and implementation of quality management and quality assurance standards.

ISO 9001    Provides a model for quality assurance in design, development, production, installation, and servicing.

ISO 9002    Provides a model for quality assurance in production and installation.

ISO 9003    Provides a model for quality assurance in final inspection and testing.

ISO 9004    Provides a guideline for quality management and quality system modules.

Table 14.2 shows the basic requirements that compare the ISO 9001, 9002, and 9003 specifications. ISO 9000 and 9004 are advisory documents that provide guidance for the selection and use of the other three standards. ISO 9004 also includes guidance in marketing, quality costs, and product safety and liability. Read these two standards before reading the other three standards.

The ISO 9000 series is a flexible system that can be applied to all types and all sizes of companies. Basically, the series outlines the general structure of a quality system without specifying the level of quality that products should achieve. The system documents the quality system of a company, whatever this system is, and then makes sure that the company executes to the quality system it has documented. The standards provide a basic listing of the general topics a company should include when documenting its quality system.

The ISO 9000 has been adopted by many countries worldwide, and gained recognition when it was adopted by the European Economic Community as its quality certification

**TABLE 14.2**   ISO 9001, 9002, AND 9003 BASIC REQUIREMENTS

| Requirements | 9001 | 9002 | 9003 |
|---|---|---|---|
| 1. Statistical techniques | X | X | X |
| 2. Personnel and training | X | X | X |
| 3. Documentation and records control | X | X | X |
| 4. Handling, storage, packing, and delivering | X | X | X |
| 5. Nonconformity control | X | X | X |
| 6. Measuring and testing equipment | X | X | X |
| 7. Product verification | X | X | X |
| 8. Inspection and test status | X | X | X |
| 9. Material control and traceability | X | X | X |
| 10. Quality system | X | X | X |
| 11. Management responsibility | X | X | X |
| 12. Quality records and audits | X | X | X |
| 13. Purchaser supplied product | X | X | |
| 14. Corrective action | X | X | |
| 15. Process control | X | X | |
| 16. Purchasing | X | X | |
| 17. Contract review | X | X | |
| 18. Auditing internal | X | X | |
| 19. Design and R&D control | X | | |
| 20. Servicing | X | | |

program, starting in December 1992. A company complying with the ISO 9000 standards will benefit by establishing a benchmark reference in the 20 different areas in which the company operates, and will strengthen its worldwide position against the competition in those countries that have adopted the ISO standards.

One final word of caution when applying for an award or certification: Don't feel discouraged when the first results of the inspection produce a long list of problems. The solution for a long list of problems is to order problems by priority and then work on them one by one. You will be surprised when you reach the end of the list and your organization is producing a better product and has a clearer understanding of its responsibilities.

## 14.8 THE NEVER-ENDING PROCESS OF IMPROVING QUALITY

A quality improvement program is a never-ending search for perfection. Companies that take a realistic approach to quality, continuously working to improve processes and systems to reach higher quality levels, are companies that beat the competition. Companies that accept their quality levels as good and never try to improve the system are bound to fail. Quality improvement is always necessary, and is a learning experience, because there is always a better way to do a job no matter how well it is being done at the moment. In manufacturing, the process of learning and improving ways to do things never ends. Manufacturing is a discipline of skills, cleverness, and persistence. It is also a discipline of productivity and commitment to producing a better product no matter what level of perfection has been reached.

Like any other discipline, quality has a learning curve. This learning curve is repeated over and over again on every new product released to manufacturing. Each product has particular quality idiosyncrasies and needs, requiring a unique quality approach to make it manufacturable. Companies that succeed in introducing quality products have the skills for transferring the quality learning curve from one product to another. Key to this transfer is trained workers and quality systems and procedures that take care of new requirements. Every new product will test the quality system to its limits. A company should be prepared to meet the challenge and to change the system if necessary.

## 14.9 SUMMARY

Company-wide quality programs are the fuel for the quality engine that drives improvements within a company. In general, the great majority of these programs fizzle because they are too ambitious or inadequate resources have been allocated. Management causes most of these failures because it controls the resources. Workers and middle management cause most of the fizzles because they lose interest or think they have reached their goal. A quality team dedicated to succeeding should work closely with both groups to ensure the plan's survival. The best way to achieve this is persistence and honest self-assessment.

Progress can be elusive. Have periodic reviews with workers to solve problems quickly when they show up. This approach will encourage honesty and interest on the part of workers.

Management involvement is critical in keeping the program alive. But managers generally measure the program by leaps toward success and lose interest or cut back support when something doesn't look right. Management should be patient and supportive, even when not enough progress is being made. Managers tend to want immediate results, sometimes at the cost of cutting corners. It is important not to compromise the implementation of the quality system. In the long run, managers will be more satisfied with a solid system that performs consistently and will not evaporate once goals are reached.

Implement the Just-in-Time quality system in tandem with the Just-in-Time system. Each system will help the other, and each one cannot succeed without the other. Don't implement them one after the other because it will not work. You have to visualize both systems as the two rails of a railroad track. A train loaded with products will need both tracks.

## REFERENCES

BROCKA, BRUCE, and M. SUZANNE BROCKA. *Quality Management. Implementing the Best Ideas of the Masters.* Homewood, Ill.: Business One Irwin, 1992.

HUNT, V. DANIEL. *Quality in America: How to Implement a Competitive Quality Program.* Homewood, Ill.: Business One Irwin, 1991.

ISHIKAWA, KAORU. *What Is Total Quality Control? The Japanese Way.* Englewood Cliffs, N.J.: Prentice-Hall, 1985.

LEHRER, ROBERT N. *Participative Productivity and Quality of Work Life* . Englewood Cliffs, N.J.: Prentice-Hall, 1982.

MARQUARDT, DONALD, JACQUES CHOVE, K. E. JENSEN, KLAUS PETRICK, JAMES PYLE, and DONALD STRAHLE. "Vision 2000: The Strategy for the ISO 9000 Series Standards in the '90s." *Quality Progress* (May 1991): 25.

MAURER, RICK. *Caught in the Middle: A Leading Guide for Partnership in the Workplace.* Cambridge, Mass.: Productivity Press, 1992.

# 15★

# Responsibility for Quality: Management/Workers' Roles

Quality in a product just doesn't happen by accident or even by simple design. Quality products are the result of a complex and dedicated effort on the part of designers, workers, suppliers, and management to produce such a product. Quality is attention to detail and commitment to continuous improvement, even when it seems perfection has already been reached. Quality is the result of a team effort, rather than the effort of individuals. Quality is a management commitment to train and support workers to make sure manufacturing excellence is always applied.

One mistake many companies make is to assume that the responsibility for quality lies only within the quality department—yet the quality department is the only department that cannot *build* quality into a product. Many organizations mistakenly believe that a good inspection system can guarantee a quality product. Those companies have intense quality inspection teams that do nothing but reject wasted work. All that inspectors are doing is relieving the rest of the organization from the responsibility of producing a perfect-quality product the first time.

This chapter will define the responsibilities for quality in a progressive company that actually builds quality into its products. This company has no inspecting teams and produces few rejections in its products as a result of that. The responsibility for quality has been assigned to the people who are responsible for manufacturing the product—the workers.

## 15.1 DEFINING THE RESPONSIBILITY FOR QUALITY

In old-fashioned manufacturing, when a product showed some defects at the end of the line, or at the customer's site, management held the quality department's manager responsible. This is wrong. The product was not built by the quality department; the quality department only failed to realize that the product was bad. In the new system, the person to be held responsible for the problem is the manager of the manufacturing department that built the product.

Another old-fashioned concept is to blame suppliers when the quality of raw materials arriving at the production line is defective. No one ever held the purchasing department responsible for the poor quality of a supplier's product. The purchasing department is responsible for purchasing high-quality parts from suppliers.

Finally, the engineering department was never held responsible for designing a poor quality product, because quality was always associated with manufacturing and not with design. This lesson has been learned the hard way and finally today engineering is ultimately responsible for designing quality into a product. This couldn't be more visible than in the auto industry, where it took years to learn that a quality product is born at design time, not in the production line.

The first important step in producing a perfect-quality product is to assign the responsibilities for quality to people who actually influence the design, manufacturing, and procurement of material necessary to build the product. No amount of inspecting can produce quality in a product that is poorly designed, poorly assembled, or built with defective materials. Figure 15.1 shows the three keystones that support the production of quality in a product. All three should be met: The lack of one of them is enough to produce a defective product.

This change of philosophy should be the first step toward implementing a quality system in a company. It is critical that people involved in the program believe that the responsibility for quality belongs to them. The best way to achieve this is to train workers in the new concepts, then give them the tools and authority to exercise their new responsibility.

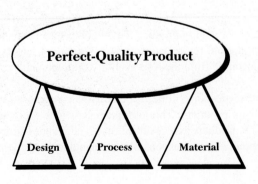

**Figure 15.1**   Major Keystones for the Support of Quality

## 15.2 WORKERS' RESPONSIBILITY

The manufacturing department is responsible for the quality of the product shipped to the customer. All workers who contributed to the process are responsible for the quality of the work they did. It is very important that workers understand this concept and take ownership of quality. The best way to accomplish this transfer of responsibility is to eliminate all in-process inspections and let workers be responsible.

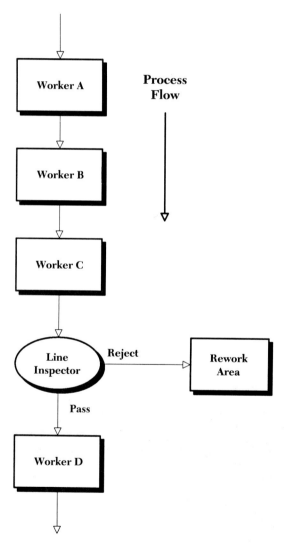

**Figure 15.2**   Old-Fashioned Line Inspecting System

In general, workers should not accept this new responsibility without proper quality training, including changes in the process that builds the product. Every worker is trained to become an inspector, as well as a worker, in the area for which he or she is responsible. The quality department will train workers to inspect key process steps before they proceed to complete the task assigned to them. This approach will provide immediate feedback on problems, because defective products will be returned to the source that is responsible for them.

Figure 15.2 shows the old way of using quality control inspectors in a process. Worker A completes his work and sends it to worker B. Worker B completes her task and sends it to worker C. Quality control inspectors inspect the work done by the three workers and pass the product through to the next step in the process, or reject it to a rework center. This method is cumbersome and tends to inspect quality rather than to build it. Besides having the propensity to cause bottlenecks at the inspecting stations, the system doesn't give the immediate feedback to workers A, B, and C that something is wrong. Even worse, when a defective product escapes inspection, the tendency is to blame the inspectors for the defect. The responsibility for quality is not correctly defined in this system.

Figure 15.3 shows the new system, where the first process step that a worker executes before adding any labor is to inspect key steps of the work done by the previous worker. If

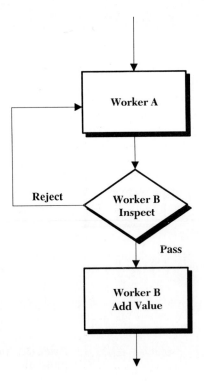

**Figure 15.3**  Dual Role for Workers and In-spectors in a Just-in-Time Quality System

a worker finds a defect, he or she will return the product immediately to the preceding worker for correction. This procedure immediately informs a worker that there is something wrong, forcing the worker to take corrective action to avoid future defects. The system also stops adding more labor to a defective product that needs repair.

Because there is no production value added during the time a worker is inspecting, process and quality engineers should balance the time a worker spends inspecting and the time spent working. Normally, this inspecting process should not be more than 5 percent of a worker's productive time. Inspecting procedures should be carefully selected to cover only critical items that can cause a reject. Work centers should also be equipped with automatic poka-yoke devices that eliminate the need for smaller inspection steps.

## 15.3 ELIMINATING INCOMING AND PROCESS INSPECTORS

There are many types of quality inspectors in a manufacturing company, whose jobs are posted along the flow of material in a process. Receiving inspectors are posted at the receiving door, watching the material that comes from suppliers. Quality control inspectors are sprinkled along a process to inspect the work in progress in the production line. Final inspectors are posted just before the shipping door, inspecting the final product before it is shipped to customers. Finally, source inspectors travel to suppliers, checking material at the source before it is shipped to the company. *All that these different inspectors are doing is relieving people doing the work of the responsibility for quality.*

A Just-in-Time quality system will start by removing process inspectors, assigning the responsibility for quality to workers. The second step is to gradually reduce the incoming inspection process by putting the burden for quality on the suppliers who build the material. This process requires a more extensive use of source inspectors than in a normal operation. But source inspectors are more effective than receiving inspectors. Source inspectors will reject defective material at the source of production. They can show a supplier immediately when something is defective and save shipping, handling, and return freight of defective material. Also, the supplier will have the burden of producing a good product before it can invoice the customer. This is a great incentive for a supplier to build quality before shipping.

The second step in reducing inspection overhead is to eliminate receiving inspection. The first priority of this effort is to work with quality-troubled suppliers to improve their quality.

Eliminating receiving and process inspections should be done carefully. It is best to do the conversion one step at a time. The risk incurred during this process is that faulty material reaches the process and then is used in the product. Inspection reductions have to take place with increases in the quality levels of the product being deinspected. New worker responsibility should be clearly established and assumed before the first reduction takes place. An intensive quality training program before the switch is extremely important. Inspection reductions don't take place just by removing the inspectors. Quality improvements need to be in place first, then a committed team must stand behind them.

## 15.4 FINAL INSPECTION

The final inspector's job is to be the customer's representative before the product is shipped. Final inspectors should look after customers and not favor the company for which they work. This is a conflict because the companies pay inspectors' salaries.

Final inspection reduction is the last step a Just-in-Time quality system should implement. This approach will keep the system honest, providing some checks and balances during the transition.

Once the new quality system is in place, the job of a final inspector becomes obsolete. Now, no defective product should reach the end of the line. Some people will say that no manufacturing system is so bulletproof that no bad product will ever reach the end of the line. But a system that considers failure as a norm has nothing but failure ahead. A manufacturing system with a perfect-quality commitment will reach this kind of perfection. Companies achieving this perfection will be ahead of the competition.

## 15.5 QUALITY CHECKS AND BALANCES: QUALITY AUDITS

A balanced quality system requires the implementation of some kind of system of checks and balances to detect deviations whenever they occur. A statistical process control system on a production line accomplishes this task on an ongoing basis. Source inspection audits of the supplier's process will also flag any deviation from the established norm. Inside the company, the system of audits will be implemented by the quality department and will consist of periodic process and final product audits.

It is recommended that workers and manufacturing engineers also participate in the audits. The purpose of the audits is to randomly select portions of the process and final products, tearing them down to see how they compare to the process and product specifications.

Audits should be properly documented, and most importantly, reviewed with the people in charge of doing the work so that they receive feedback on the problems encountered. Audits should also praise excellence when they find it. Some people think the only purpose of audits is to find something wrong. Audits should also point out what the system is doing well. This will inspire workers to continue doing a good job and prove they are on the right track.

The quality department should act as an independent party in the audits and should have the responsibility for them. It also includes supplier audits and customer feedback on the services the company is providing. Quality audits should be impartial and precise. They should conform to a set of rules that are clearly understood by everyone. Audits should be random and not preannounced, so the possibility of extra effort on the part of workers during the audit process is eliminated.


## 15.6 THE ROLE OF THE QUALITY DEPARTMENT


The quality department cannot directly build quality into a product, but it is responsible for setting quality standards workers should meet in the process. Quality should set standard levels of quality and inspecting procedures for workers while building a product. Quality should also provide training programs for manufacturing, engineering, and the rest of the people working in the company.

Quality is also responsible for monitoring the quality of parts received from suppliers. This doesn't mean parts should be inspected when they arrive at the receiving dock. Quality should monitor process yields as they relate to supplier quality and feed back the information to suppliers immediately for corrective action.

Interface with suppliers is one of the most important aspects of the quality system. The system requires closed-loop feedback on problems and solutions. When problems are reported, there should be a definite commitment on the part of the supplier to fix them. The communication is the responsibility of the quality department. If this task requires manufacturing engineering support, the quality department should work with its counterparts at the supplier's company to fix the problem. The key to a successful supplier's quality program is partnership and teamwork at the technical level. Management commitment from both sides is also needed to work out problems openly and in a positive way.

There are also two key roles for the quality department. One is training workers in quality principles and responsibilities. Training programs should cover other areas in the company not clearly related to the quality of the product. They should emphasize the quality of everyday tasks regardless of which department is responsible for their execution. The quality department has the responsibility for spreading the "religion" of quality to all employees in the company.

Another additional role of the quality department is to provide everyone with information about quality. The vehicle for disseminating quality information is the implementation of a quality information system, QIS. A QIS should provide quality information to workers, suppliers, and management. Care should be taken to avoid building a system that is burdened by paperwork and directed only at management. The main goal of a QIS is first to reach people on a need-to-know basis as it relates to quality. This includes people responsible for correcting problems that cause the system to have bad quality. Management should only get summary reports on a second-priority basis, after workers and suppliers.

The last responsibility of a quality department is to keep a hand on the pulse of the quality of the product shipped to customers. This information measures the level of customer satisfaction and the performance of the company as it relates to supporting customer needs. This information should also be distributed first to people directly responsible for correcting problems when they are reported.

## 15.7 COMPANY-WIDE QUALITY RESPONSIBILITIES

Very few companies have a company-wide quality program that includes all its employees. Today's market competition demands this kind of program. The performance of a company as it is seen by customers will not only depend on the quality of the product, but on all other business aspects associated with purchasing, servicing, and training. The main responsibility of a quality system is to eliminate all waste in activities that produce no value to a customer. This principle can also be applied to all job aspects in a company.

Company-wide quality programs tend to fail after a few months because people assume the responsibility for quality belongs only to the quality department. The message that a quality program should send to workers is that there is quality in everything they do, and their contribution will influence the way customers see the company. A successful quality program is like a puzzle where every worker is a piece that needs to fit properly with the rest of the organization.

The next subject is the "religion" of quality. Successful companies must be religious about doing the job right no matter what job is being done and how it relates to the rest of the organization. The assumption is that all jobs are equally important for reaching the goal of customer satisfaction.

## 15.8 SUPPLIER'S QUALITY RESPONSIBILITIES

Implementing a first-rate supplier quality program is critical to the success of a Just-in-Time quality program. It is also the most difficult to accomplish because the number of suppliers supporting a product is large and every one of them has different operational and quality needs.

The best way to implement this task is first to group suppliers by commodities, designing a flexible program that suits their needs. It is also important to rank suppliers by current quality performance, so the most troubled ones are given immediate attention. Adequate resources to implement such a program are important, because suppliers will get discouraged or lose faith in the effort if they are not supported properly. The responsibility for such a program lies with the quality department. The quality department by itself, however, will not be able to implement such a program without the help of manufacturing engineering, design engineering, and purchasing and materials. Quality should be the catalyst that draws support from other departments in the company to implement the supplier's program. Quality should also drive the effort with the supplier, channeling all communication to the right people on a need-to-know basis. Quality should not be an obstacle to the program, but the avenue for communication and cooperation.

If a supplier drags its feet and doesn't want to cooperate or change its ways of doing business, then the economical realities of this attitude should be clearly pointed out by the purchasing department. The supplier should realize the effort will make it a better manufacturer and a more competitive enterprise. The return on the investment will come later, when business increases as a result of improving services.

The department responsible for hiring or firing a supplier is the purchasing department. This authority makes purchasing responsible for the performance of the supplier. Quality is one of those measurements; therefore, purchasing is responsible for supplier quality.

Most purchasing people will object to accepting responsibility for supplier quality, but they are the ones who make the final decision on whether or not to do business with a supplier, and quality should be a critical factor to consider. The most common excuse used is that purchasing doesn't have expertise in that area. This excuse, however, is unacceptable because one of the key roles of the quality department is to support purchasing as it relates to the quality performance of suppliers.

## 15.9  MANAGEMENT COMMITMENT AND SUPPORT

The role of management is critical to the success of a quality program. Management should back the program with adequate resources and training to ensure that quality takes priority over any other activity in the company. Many quality programs fail because they only receive lip service—all talk and no action. This is always evident to workers and causes morale problems that render the quality program nothing more than a wasted effort. Managers should be the driving force behind quality programs to assure success.

Managers should show their commitment by example rather than by words. This resolve will be tested when they face decisions involving quality that may compromise quality in a product. When faced with this situation, managers should not compromise the quality resolve. This will send a strong message to workers that management is serious about quality. The point is not to send mixed signals to the organization, because they could be most disruptive. Management's message should be one of consistency, commitment, and an uncompromising stand for quality excellence.

## 15.10  SUMMARY

Understanding and accepting responsibility for quality is key to achieving quality excellence. This task is not easily accomplished, because there will always be skeptics who will complain they already do their job with quality and don't need to change their work habits.

Resistance to change has always been one of the most difficult barriers to new programs. Accepting company-wide responsibility for quality is one of those concepts that will meet resistance. The best way to win this battle is to gradually implement the new system by training and involving all workers. Most people don't do bad work purposely, and many think they are doing the best possible job and need not change. Quality training programs and the reassignment of responsibilities need to be supported by success stories that will convince nonbelievers that there is a better way.

If failures occur during implementation, it will give nonbelievers grounds for believing they are right and change is not needed. The program team in charge of implementation should learn from its mistakes and try to avoid them. Members of the team should also be honest and accept failure without being defensive. Implementation should continue uninterrupted, but it should be changed to avoid the mistakes that caused the failure. In the end, the company will win the battle against poor quality and make workers very proud of the new system.

# REFERENCES

BIRKHOLZ, CHARLES R., and JIM VILLELLA. *The Battle to Stay Competitive: Changing the Traditional Workplace.* Cambridge, Mass.: Productivity Press, 1991.

DYER, CONSTANCE E., ed. Compiled by the Japan Management Association. *Canon Production System.* Cambridge, Mass.: Productivity Press, 1987.

HALL, ROBERT W. *Attaining Manufacturing Excellence.* Homewood, Ill.: Dow Jones-Irwin, 1987.

HERNANDEZ, ARNALDO. *Just-in-Time Manufacturing: A Practical Approach.* Englewood Cliffs, N.J.: Prentice-Hall, 1989.

HERSEY, PAUL, and KEN BLANCHARD. *Management of Organizational Behavior. Utilizing Human Resources.* Englewood Cliffs, N.J.: Prentice-Hall, 1982.

MERLI, GIORGIO. *Total Manufacturing Management: Production Organization for the 1990s.* Cambridge, Mass.: Productivity Press, 1990.

# 16★

# *The Challenge for Quality: The Search for Perfection*

The concept of quality as meeting a goal for the reduction of defects is old fashioned. Quality is an evolutionary process that always strives to advance from whatever level has already been achieved. A modern quality system uses goals as stepping stones to advance a product along the road of constant improvement. This is a lesson that many U.S. manufacturers are having difficulty learning. Quality is not reaching a particular defect yield or perfection. Quality is a continuous process for product improvement.

A successful quality system requires planning and focus to make commitments happen. Quality programs that try to achieve too much while lacking proper focus and resources will languish for years and are doomed to failure. Quality programs should avoid concentrating on areas that are less relevant while ignoring more critical ones that greatly influence customer satisfaction. Quality should be properly attuned to the company's needs and strategy. The responsibility for this belongs to management. Management's job is to set up objectives and priorities and keep them advancing to the next level once they have been achieved. A successful quality program shows constant evolution and progress.

## 16.1 ZERO DEFECTS

Zero-defect programs have been used for years to achieve quality improvements. In this program, a company makes a commitment to produce products with no defects. The problem is that most companies hope the simple fact of having the program will help them to reach the zero-defect goal. Then, when quality doesn't reach goals within the time allotted, management stops the program, or even worse, it starts paying lip service.

A zero-defect program is nothing but a quality improvement program with a different name. All quality programs should have zero defects as a goal. That is what quality is about—no defects. The problem with a zero-defect program is that it is too product oriented; it pays no attention to other areas of the company that either affect quality or affect customer satisfaction. A broad-based quality program covering all areas of a company should have zero-defect output in every department. The same program should strive for the reduction of waste in all forms in every organization.

## 16.2 THE SEARCH FOR PERFECT PARTS

Many cynics long involved in the manufacturing business claim that perfection in quality is not attainable. Real life has proven many times that nothing is 100 percent perfect, even when it looks that way. The search for perfection should be viewed as a challenge to do the job right the first time. Perfection is not to waste time and effort redoing a job that should have been done right. Perfection is eliminating wasteful tasks producing no results and defects.

There is no specific formula for reaching perfection. There is not even a formula for knowing when you are there. The approach for pursuing perfect quality is to stop doing business as usual and implement changes that will improve the system, eliminating errors that stand in the way of perfection. This searching for perfection should be embedded at all levels of the organization, down to the individual. Teaching by example will help nonbelievers to join the effort and start the search.

Just-in-Time and quality programs force the organization to search for practical ways to do things that eliminate waste. It also impresses on everybody the real responsibilities of their jobs.

Success in the search for perfection can be achieved by making things simple and practical. When there is no apparent better way to do things, challenge the organization not to quit and to keep looking for a better solution.

## 16.3 CONTINUOUS IMPROVEMENT PROGRAMS

Continuous improvement programs are crucial to reaching perfection in quality, but these programs have to be improved upon themselves or they will grow stale and wasteful. Quality programs should have a broad scope that reaches areas involving product design and support. They should also be self-critical and goal oriented, or the system will not measure progress properly. People involved in managing the program have the responsibility for keeping pace, driving the system. But they should not set goals and make commitments. It is important that people directly involved in implementing the program participate in goal setting, so that they feel ownership of the goals.

Another aspect of continuous improvement programs is that they tend to become ineffective with time, growing complacent. If this happens, it is better for management to scrap the program and start fresh with new people and new goals. Very few companies have the guts to take this step, because it implies failure in the effort to improve quality. In today's market environment, starting from scratch is a must if you are losing the war to improve your product. Companies whose efforts to improve quality have grown stale are doomed to failure unless they have the courage to start from scratch.

## 16.4 WAR AGAINST POOR QUALITY

Many managers believe that business is a war against the competition. These people see business as an effort to put the competition out of commission. But they don't realize that to win the external war, they should fight and win many internal battles to eliminate waste and poor quality.

Excellent quality is an effective weapon against the competition. When used correctly, quality is a very effective weapon that in most cases is enough to win a customer away from the enemy—the competitor. When not owned, lack of quality is self-destructive and needs no competition to put the company out of business.

## 16.5 TRAPS TO AVOID IN A QUALITY SYSTEM

The approach to perfect quality is full of traps. Many of these traps can easily be avoided by involving people in the effort. The most important ones are:

1. *Commitment.* People involved in a quality program should be genuinely committed to making the system work. The commitment should be evident at all levels of the organization and should include all employees. The commitment should include honest self-appraisal and a willingness to change when something is not working.

2. *Responsibility.* One of the first things a quality program needs to implement is the assignment of responsibilities for quality. Workers cannot expect to improve quality if they are not responsible for it. This assignment of responsibility should be specific and clearly identified. General quality responsibilities not focused on specifics will fail. Workers need to identify with them personally in order to feel a sense of ownership.

3. *Accountability.* Quality programs need to implement a system of goals, measurements, and accountability. The program needs all these measurements to monitor progress. Clear goals are a necessity. Too many goals will cause the effort to lose focus.

## 16.6 TEN RULES TO REMEMBER

There are many important rules that influence the implementation of a Just-in-Time quality program. These rules are not complete by any means, but they serve as a foundation. The rules are general, so they can be applied to different businesses. Most of the rules are commonsense, practical advice.

1. A Just-in-Time system must be implemented with a parallel quality system that embraces the same principles. The converse is not true. You can implement a Just-in-Time quality system without implementing Just-in-Time. The odds for success, however, will decrease; Just-in-Time corrects much of the operational waste that causes poor quality. Just-in-Time also drives operational people to improve quality.

2. Implement a Just-in-Time quality system as soon as possible. Don't delay because of lack of resources, low volume, or a belief that your quality is good enough. Quality is never a steady-state condition that reaches a perfect-product plateau. There is always room for improvement, and the competition is working hard to do just that.

3. Select a team to drive the quality program not for their experience and knowledge, but for their enthusiasm and commitment to succeed. The quality team needs drivers who believe in what they are doing. These people will infuse their enthusiasm and belief in the rest of the organization.

4. Senior management should support the program by deed, not words. Management involvement is necessary for success. The best way for management to show support is to allocate enough resources to support the effort. Management should also participate in the program in some form or another.

5. Worker participation should be accomplished by involvement, not by imposition. Workers should participate in the goal-setting sessions in order to feel ownership in meeting goals.

6. Educate all participants on the principles of Just-in-Time and quality, including management and workers. Training is key during the program; there can never be enough of it. Managers should also participate in training programs. Extend training to suppliers involved in the program.

7. Ask management to get involved with suppliers' management at the beginning of the program. Educate them in the new concepts and clearly explain the new partnership concept. Make sure presentations are not overly optimistic, setting expectations too high. The new program will require resources, time, and effort before it becomes productive.

8. Limit the scope of the program to the resources available. If resources are limited, don't choose an easy area to start the program. Select those areas that are already in trouble, challenging the effort.

9. Set up a parallel effort to put into writing new systems and procedures the quality system is going to follow. Train everyone who will use them until they are clearly

understood. When procedures are being used, encourage feedback based on experience and change those that need improvement. Nothing should be cast in concrete.

**10.** Constantly measure goal progress and move to the next level after goals are reached. If the program does not show progress after a period of time, scrap it and start a new one. Never quit running a quality improvement program, even when you think you have achieved perfect quality. There is always a better way to do the same job and you have already gained experience proving it. Try again.

## 16.7 SUMMARY

Just-in-Time is a discipline that wages a war against waste in its many forms. Just-in-Time quality is a discipline that searches for perfection in products. Both systems help each other and the company to achieve a key goal: *customer satisfaction*.

Two great challenges lie ahead of the reader. The first one is to implement both systems successfully, using an organization and a group of suppliers that might not believe in the principles and changes. The best way to overcome this problem is to get them involved, so they can share successes. The second challenge is to keep the program going, even when nothing seems to be working and progress is minimal. The best solution to this problem is to be persistent and honest enough to accept temporary failure, then to keep working hard to avoid mistakes, improving the system so it can succeed. If after a second attempt the system still does not improve, you have to be ready to scrap the program altogether and start again. The key to success is never to quit.

Success turns people into believers; words will not. Get the quality system implemented, show results. Then get a group of committed workers behind a program that will always search for perfection no matter how perfect the product already is. If that process is repeated, you will be working for a very successful company.

## REFERENCES

Ernst and Young Quality Improvement Consulting Group. *Total Quality: An Executive's Guide for the 1990s.* Homewood, Ill.:, Business One Irwin, 1989.

GITLOW, H., and S. GITLOW. *The Deming Guide to Quality and Competitive Position.* Englewood Cliffs, N.J.: Prentice-Hall, 1987.

HAYES, ROBERT H. and STEVEN C. WHEELWRIGHT. *Restoring Our Competitive Edge: Competing Through Manufacturing.* New York: John Wiley & Sons, 1984.

JURAN, J. M. *Juran on Planning for Quality.* New York: The Free Press, 1988.

WINCHELL, WILLIAM. *Continuous Quality Improvement: A Manufacturing Professional's Guide.* Dearborn, Mich.: SME, 1991.

# *Appendix A*

---

## RELEVANT
### TECHNOLOGIES

### Just-in-Time (JIT)
### Manufacturing Agreement

Contract No. _____

Original Issue Date _____

## 0.0 PREFACE

This agreement is hereby made this _____ day of _____ 19____ between _____ having its place of business at _____ (hereinafter "Buyer") and RELEVANT Technologies, Inc. having its place of business at 2241 Lundy Avenue, San Jose, CA 95131 (hereinafter "Seller").

## 1.0 SCOPE

The intent of this agreement is to define a long term partnership between _____ and Relevant Technologies where both parties can benefit in having a mutually successful business relationship. Relevant's goal is to provide highest quality, cost-effective, Just-in-Time Manufacturing services to support _____ to further enhance its position as being a leader in the industry. We think that this goal will be achieved by working together in an open and honest environment as partners in success.

The product(s) to manufacture will be as described in the appropriate purchase order.

## 2.0 REQUIREMENTS FOR PURCHASING

### 2.1 Forecast Purchase Order

All services provided by Seller shall be against written purchase orders issued by Buyer ("Purchase Orders"). For each separate product to be manufactured by Seller, Buyer shall issue an initial written Purchase Order. This initial Purchase Order shall contain the following information:

**a.** Buyer's Part Number, description and revision level of Product to be shipped, together with a bill of materials, product specifications (including all drawings, tapes, documentation and other material necessary to manufacture the Product), and test procedures and specifications of all such materials (herein called the "Specifications").

**b.** Three (3) month firm delivery requirement.

**c.** Four (4) month rolling forecast.

**d.** The unit price.

**e.** Reference to this Agreement.

**f.** Seller's quotation.

**g.** Method and destination of shipment and carrier.

For products to be delivered after the first 3 month period, Buyer will issue a written Purchase Order containing the same information provided above by the end of each month for a firm delivery schedule for the next 3 months as well as a revised forecast for the 4 month period following. The portion of each Purchase Order for 3 months firm delivery shall be noncancellable.

## 2.2 Changes to Purchase Orders

Buyer may cancel or reschedule delivery of Product only in accordance with Section 4.

## 2.3 Acceptance/Rejection

All Purchase Orders issued by Buyer shall not be binding on Seller until accepted by Seller at its discretion. Seller shall notify Buyer of rejection of any Purchase Order within five (5) working days of receipt of such order.

## 2.4 Terms of Purchase

The Buyer's Purchase Orders and any other specially negotiated terms set forth on the face of the Purchase Order shall govern for quantities ordered. Any other preprinted terms and conditions on the Buyer's Purchase Orders shall be disregarded. In all other respects, this Agreement shall govern.

## 2.5 Implied License

Seller shall be deemed to have been granted by Buyer a nonexclusive, royalty-free license during the term of this Agreement to use all of Buyer's patents, trade secrets and other intellectual property required for Seller to perform its obligations under this Agreement.

# 3.0 PAYMENT TERMS/ADDITIONAL COSTS AND PRICE CHANGES

## 3.1 Invoices and Payment

Seller shall invoice Buyer upon shipment of Product. Payment shall be net thirty (30) days from the date of invoice and shall be made in lawful U.S. currency.

Seller may delay subsequent shipments and/or require prepayment by Buyer or other payment arrangements satisfactory to Seller. Overdue payments will be subject to a service charge of $1\frac{1}{2}\%$ per month or the maximum permitted by law, whichever is less if payment is not received within 45 days from date of shipment.

## 3.2 Buyer's Responsibility for Additional Costs

*Product Price.*    The price for Products to be manufactured will be the amount set forth in Seller's quotation, except as set forth below. This price does not include additional costs as provided in this Section 3.2 or as provided elsewhere in this Agreement.

*Taxes.*    The quoted price is exclusive of federal, state and local excise, sales, use and similar taxes. Buyer shall be liable for and shall pay all applicable taxes, which shall be invoiced to Buyer by Seller, unless Buyer provides Seller with a valid tax exemption certificate prior to delivery.

*Price Changes.*    Seller reserves the right to change the price for Products upon 30 days' prior notice to Buyer for any reason, including, but not limited to, changes in vendor pricing, changes in duties or taxes payable by Seller, changes in Buyer's requirements from the amount upon which Seller based its quotation, or other changes in overhead and materials costs. Such changes shall apply to the portion of accepted Purchase Orders to be delivered more than 60 days from the date of the notice and to all Purchase Orders received after the date of the notice.

*Volatile Commodity Pricing.*    Commodities with volatile price changes such as DRAMS will be subject to changes within 30 days of written notification to Buyer by Seller. Such changes shall apply to the portion of accepted purchase orders to be delivered more than 30 days from the date of notice.

*Expediting Charges.*    Seller will promptly notify Buyer after acceptance of any Purchase Order if, in order to meet Buyer's delivery dates, it will be necessary to incur any expediting charges for materials, labor or shipment. Seller will obtain Buyer's approval prior to incurring any such charges.

*Additional Costs.*    In addition to any other prices and costs invoiced to Buyer under this Agreement, Buyer shall be responsible for certain additional charges incurred by Seller as a result of Buyer's actions. These charges shall be negotiated by Seller and Buyer. Examples of such charges are:

   **a.** Overtime or downtime charges and actual expenses incurred as a result of delays in the normal production or interruption in the workflow process where such delays or interruptions are caused by: (1) Buyer's change in product specifications or product test, or (2) Buyer's failure to provide sufficient quantities or a reasonable quality level of consigned materials where applicable to sustain the production schedule.

**b.** Any inventory rendered obsolete as a result of an engineering, field, manufacturing, design, test or other change; provided, however, such obsolete inventory shall be delivered, if requested, to Buyer by F.O.B. shipping point, at Buyer's expense and risk.

## 4.0 SHIPMENTS/CANCELLATION AND RESCHEDULING

### 4.1 Shipment

All Products delivered pursuant to the terms of this Agreement shall be suitably packed for shipment in accordance with Buyer's specifications, marked for shipment to Buyer's destination specified in the applicable Purchase Order and delivered to a carrier or forwarding agent chosen by Buyer. If Buyer does not specify carrier or method of shipment, Seller will select carrier and method in accordance with good commercial practices. Shipment will be F. O. B. Seller's facility in San Jose, California, at which time risk of loss and title will pass to buyer. All freight, insurance and other shipping expenses, as well as any special packing expenses not included in the original price quotation for the Products, will be paid by Buyer.

### 4.2 Security Interest

Until the purchase price and all other charges payable to Seller hereunder have been received in full, Seller hereby retains and Buyer herby grants to Seller a security interest in the Products delivered to Buyer and any proceeds therefrom. Buyer agrees to promptly execute any documents requested by Seller to perfect and protect such security interest.

### 4.3 JIT Kanban Scheduling

Seller will implement a JIT Kanban system to coordinate the delivery of products to Buyer based on the actual consumption of the product in Buyer's production line. The system will work as a means for Buyer to request delivery of Seller's products in a JIT pull system. The system will work as follows:

Buyer will provide Seller with a 3 month firm delivery schedule plus a 4 month Forecast that the Seller will use to plan and procure the material needed to support the Buyer's product needs. Only the 3 month firm portion of the Purchase Order will be used by the Seller for procurement. The 4 month forecast will be used to purchase long lead items per paragraph 5.2.

Seller and Buyer will mutually agree on the optimum withdrawal Kanban size and the number of Kanbans required to support Buyer shipments on a product by product basis.

Buyer will fetch the withdrawal Kanbans on a need basis (pull) and will communicate to Seller the delivery requirements by some agreed protocol. Ex: electronic, Fax, phone, etc. Seller will deliver the Kanban within a 4 hour time limit.

Buyer will be committed to take all the Kanbans that correspond to the firm released products. The maximum time frame for this consumption will be 120 days.

Seller will set an internal production Kanban system to manufacture and feed the withdrawal Kanbans, so there is always a full set of withdrawal Kanbans available to Buyer.

When Buyer consumes a withdrawal Kanban, this action will trigger the Seller to produce a replacement Kanban. Seller's production runs will be only to fill the empty withdrawal Kanbans.

Seller will set an external JIT system with the main component suppliers of the Buyer's product and use a similar withdrawal Kanban system to operate the complete system in a Just-in-Time mode.

Any request by buyer to move up delivery times will be reasonably considered by Seller, subject to availability of supplies and to expediting charges. Any request by Buyer to delay deliveries where Seller has already purchased supplies will be subject to Buyer's reimbursement of Seller for the reasonable financing costs of carrying such inventory or, if necessary, direct payment by Buyer to Seller's third party vendor for materials previously accepted or noncancellable. In addition, in connection with any cancellation or rescheduling, Buyer shall be responsible for and pay to Seller reasonable cancellation or rescheduling charges based upon costs incurred by Seller from any third party vendors for similar charges or for materials that cannot be returned, together with reasonable labor actually expended plus other out-of-pocket expenditures. The total of such charges will not exceed the value of material on order consistent with the authorized noncancellable releases under accepted Purchase Orders.

## 5.0 INVENTORY MATTERS

### 5.1 Consigned Inventory

If the bill of materials provided to Seller by Buyer calls for Buyer to furnish any materials, Buyer agrees to deliver to Seller such quantities of materials at such times as shall be necessary for Seller to meet its delivery obligations, without need of further testing of such materials by Seller. Buyer may, at its option, furnish Seller on a consignment basis with any other parts or materials required for the manufacture of the Products, subject to renegotiation of the price of the Products to reflect such consignment. Seller agrees to segregate any materials belonging to Buyer from its own property. Buyer agrees to pay any insurance required to insure Buyer's property kept on Seller's premises.

## 5.2 Long Lead time Inventory

Buyer understands that in order to meet the delivery schedules set forth in Buyer's Purchase Orders, Seller may be required, due to its vendors' lead times or its own manufacturing or handling lead times, to commit to purchase materials from vendors for a time frame up to the longest lead time. If Buyer cancels orders the Buyer will be fully responsible for all costs associated with such materials in accordance with Section 10.3.

## 6.0 PRODUCT ACCEPTANCE AND WARRANTIES

### 6.1 Product Acceptance

The Products delivered by Seller will be subject to inspection and test by Buyer promptly upon delivery to Buyer. Buyer agrees to test all Products within 30 working days of receipt. If Buyer finds any Products to be defective in material or workmanship, Buyer has the right to reject such Products during the acceptance period. In this case the Buyer may ask the Seller, at Buyer's option, to replace or repair defective material at the Buyer's location. If upon evaluation it is determined that the Buyer induced the defect the Seller may invoice the buyer for cost incurred as mutually agreed to between Buyer and Seller. Buyer will be deemed to have accepted any Products not rejected during such 30 day period. Products rejected by Buyer to be returned to the Seller shall have a failure report attached, and shall be forwarded to Seller freight collect. Such rejected Products will be repaired or replaced at Seller's option and returned to Buyer freight prepaid. Seller shall use its best efforts to repair or replace returned defective Products within 30 days of their receipt. In the event Seller is unable to repair or replace such defective Products, Seller shall refund the purchase price paid by Buyer for such defective Products.

### 6.2 Express Warranty

   **a.** Seller warrants that the Products will conform to their applicable Specifications and will be free from defects in materials and workmanship for a period of ninety (90) days from the data of shipment to Buyer. This express warranty does not apply to (a) any materials consigned by Buyer to Seller; (b) any defects resulting from Buyer's design of the Products; or (c) any Product that has been abused, damaged, altered or misused by any person or entity other than Seller after delivery to Buyer.
   **b.** Before returning any defective Products, Buyer shall first obtain a return material authorization number from Seller to be displayed on the shipping container. Buyer shall then send Products with defects covered by this warranty to Seller's facility postage prepaid in the original shipping container. If the defective Products are received by Seller during the applicable warranty period, Seller, shall at its sole option and expense, repair or replace such Products, and shall ship the repaired or replaced Products to Buyer freight prepaid.

**c.** In the event that any Products are returned after the expiration of the warranty period, or are not otherwise covered by Seller's warranty, Seller shall repair such Products at Buyer's request at a charge to be mutually agreed upon by the parties, with the costs of transportation to be paid by Buyer.

### 6.3  No Other Warranties

**a.** EXCEPT FOR THE ABOVE EXPRESS LIMITED WARRANTIES, SELLER MAKES AND BUYER RECEIVES NO WARRANTIES OR CONDITIONS ON THE PRODUCTS, EXPRESS, IMPLIED, STATUTORY, OR IN ANY OTHER PROVISION OF THIS AGREEMENT OR COMMUNICATION WITH BUYER, AND SELLER SPECIFICALLY DISCLAIMS ANY IMPLIED WARRANTY OR CONDITION OF MERCHANTABILITY OR FITNESS FOR A PARTICULAR PURPOSE.

**b.** Seller does not warrant that the Products will receive the approval of or meet specifications not set forth in this Agreement which are promulgated by Underwritten Laboratory, and federal, state or local government agency, or any other person or entity, and seller assumes no responsibility for obtaining such approvals or meeting such specifications.

## 7.0  ENGINEERING CHANGES

### 7.1  Engineering Changes Proposed by Seller

Seller shall notify Buyer of any proposed change to any Product (an "Engineering Change") and shall supply a written description of the expected effect of the Engineering Change, including effect on delivery schedule, price, and any cost savings permitted by the Engineering Change. Buyer may elect to evaluate parts and designs specified as part of the proposed change. Buyer shall approve or disapprove the proposed changes within 15 working days or as negotiated after receipt of a written request. Seller may not change or modify the Product without Buyer's prior written consent.

### 7.2  WIP Engineering Changes Requested by the Buyer

Buyer may request, in writing, that Seller incorporate an Engineering Change into the Product. Such request will include a description of the proposed change sufficient to permit Seller to evaluate its feasibility. Within 7–10 working days or as negotiated after receiving such a request from Buyer, Seller will advise Buyer the terms and conditions under which it would make the Engineering Change requested by Buyer. Seller's evaluation shall be in writing and shall state the impact on delivery schedule as well as any cost savings or increase, if any, expected to be created by the Engineering Change, and its effect. If Buyer requests Seller in writing to incorporate an Engineering Change into the Product, the Product Specifications, Delivery Schedule and Pricing Schedule will be amended as required. Seller shall not unreasonably refuse to incorporate Buyer's Engineering Changes into the Product when requested by Buyer.

A documentation fee of $200.00 (plus cost) will be charged to Buyer to update engineering and in-process documentation.

### 7.3 WIP Emergency Engineering Changes

If Buyer notifies Seller of safety or emergency Engineering Changes, Seller shall expedite its efforts to give Buyer the information required by Section 7.2 hereof. Seller shall respond to Buyer within 1–3 working days after receipt of written change request. A documentation fee of $500.00 (plus cost) will be charged to Buyer to update engineering and in-process documentation.

## 8.0 TOOLING/NON-RECURRING EXPENSES

Seller shall provide all of the Non-Product specific process tooling in accordance with the terms of the appropriate Buyer's Purchase Order and corresponding Seller quote. The exception will be Product specific assembly tools which may be consigned by Buyer. Both parties agree that the quantity of Non-Product and Product specific process tooling as described in the corresponding quotes will be sufficient to insure that the process tooling will produce the required quantity of Product units.

Seller shall invoice for and Buyer shall be responsible for all NRE charges relating to Product specific tooling including, but not limited to, process tooling, in-circuit programming and fixturing charges in accordance with the Seller's quotation.

Seller shall provide reasonable maintenance of the process tooling, at no additional charge, for as long as such equipment remains in its possession.

All software which Buyer provides to Seller is and shall remain the property of Buyer. All software developed by Seller to support the process tooling shall be and remain the property of Buyer. Seller shall have a license to copy, modify and use this software, but only for the purposes intended under this Agreement, and then only while this Agreement is still in effect.

## 9.0 TERMS AND TERMINATION

### 9.1 Term

The initial term of this Agreement shall commence on the first date written above and end on _____ and shall be renewed for separate but successive one-year terms unless earlier terminated by the parties as follows:

 a. At any time upon the mutual written agreement of the parties;
 b. At the end of the Initial Term or any subsequent one-year term by either party upon written notice to the other party received not less than ninety (90) days prior to the expiration of any such term;
 c. By Seller upon ninety (90) days' prior written notice to Buyer;
 d. By either Party at any time upon the occurrence of any one or more of the following Events of Default: (1) failure of the other party to perform any payment obligation or covenant and to cure such failure within five (5) days of receipt of written notice from the non-defaulting party of each failure; (2) failure of the other party to perform any performance obligation or covenant and to cure such failure within thirty (30) days after receipt of written notice from the non-defaulting party of such failure; or (3) the seeking of an order for relief under the bankruptcy laws of the United States or similar laws of any other jurisdiction, a receivership for any of the assets, a composition with or assignment for the benefit of creditors, a readjustment of debt, or the dissolution or liquidation of the other party.

## 9.2  Effect of Termination

Upon termination of this Agreement, all rights and obligations granted under or imposed by this agreement (including the licenses granted herein) shall immediately cease and terminate, except for the rights and obligations set forth in Articles 5 (Long Lead Time Parts), 6 (Product Acceptance and Warranties), 10 (Indemnification), 11 (Proprietary Information), and 12 (Limitation of Liability) of this Agreement, and except for any cause of action which arises prior to the time of termination.

Notwithstanding the foregoing, and subject to the provisions of Section 10.3, upon termination of this Agreement Seller shall be entitled, at its option, to fill all accepted Purchase Orders to the extent that they are noncancellable.

The sale of any Product by Seller to Buyer after the termination of this Agreement shall be governed by the terms and conditions of this Agreement. Nevertheless, the acts of either party in consummating such sales shall not waive the termination of the Agreement or renew the Agreement.

## 10.0  INDEMNIFICATION

### 10.1  Patents/Copyrights/Trade Secrets/ Other Proprietary Rights

Each party will, and reserves the right to, defend, at its own expense, any claim, suit or proceeding brought against the other party to the extent it is based upon a claim (a) in the case of Seller, that the manufacturing process used by Seller and not specified by Buyer in the manufacture of any Products purchased from Seller, or (b) in the case of Buyer, that any

Products purchased from Seller, infringe upon any patent, copyright or trade secret of any third party. The party entitled to indemnification under this Section agrees that it shall promptly notify the indemnifying party in writing of any such claim or action and give the indemnifying party full information and assistance in connection therewith. The indemnifying party will pay all damages, costs and expenses finally awarded to third parties against the indemnified party in such action, other than in connection with a compromise or settlement of such claim made without the indemnified party's consent. The indemnifying party shall have the exclusive right to settle or compromise any such claim or action.

**THE FOREGOING STATES THE ENTIRE LIABILITY OF THE PARTIES TO EACH OTHER CONCERNING INFRINGEMENT OF PATENT, COPYRIGHT, TRADE SECRET OR OTHER INTELLECTUAL PROPERTY RIGHTS.**

### 10.2  Product Liability

Buyer agrees that, if notified promptly in writing and given sole control of the defense and all related settlement negotiation, it will defend Seller from any claim or action and will hold Seller harmless from any loss, damage or injury, including death, which arises from any defect in design of any products or from defective material supplied by Buyer.

### 10.3  Inventory Indemnification

The parties recognize that this Agreement may require Seller to purchase materials unique (in specification or quantity) to the production and manufacture of the Products. Therefore, in order to provide assurance that Seller will recover all of its investment in materials, the parties agree that in the event Buyer fails for any reason, including termination of this Agreement, to purchase Products for delivery during the term of this Agreement, Buyer shall purchase from Seller, at Seller's cost plus reasonable materials handling expenses (to be negotiated on a case by case basis), such materials remaining in Seller's inventory.

Seller shall purchase material with appropriate lead times as required to provide deliveries in accordance with Buyer's Purchase Orders.

### 11.0  PROPRIETARY INFORMATION

Buyer and Seller agree to keep in confidence and not disclose to others all knowledge, information and data furnished to it by the other party and claimed by the other party to be proprietary, provided such information is given in writing and such writing is marked to indicate the claims of ownership. Buyer and Seller agree that neither shall use, or reproduce for use, in any way any proprietary information of the other except in furtherance of the relationship set forth. Buyer and Seller agree to protect the proprietary information with the same standard of care and procedures used by each to protect its own proprietary information of similar importance. This paragraph shall not be applicable and shall impose no obligation on either party with respect to any portion of proprietary information which:

a. Is at the time received or which thereafter becomes, through no act or failure on the part of either party, generally known or available to the public;

b. Is known to either party at the time of receiving such information as evidenced by documentation then rightfully in the possession of either party;

c. Is furnished to an other by either party without restriction on disclosure;

d. Is thereafter rightfully furnished to either party by a third party without restriction by that third party on disclosure; or

e. Is released from restrictions imposed hereunder by written release given by the owner of the information,

f. Has been disclosed pursuant to a requirement of a United States governmental agency or of United States law without restrictions or other protections against public disclosure, or is required to be disclosed by operation of United States law; provided, however, that each shall have first given written notice of the such required disclosure to the owner of the information and have made a reasonable effort to obtain a protective order requiring that the proprietary information so disclosed be used only for the purposes for which disclosure is required; or

g. Is independently developed by a party without use of the proprietary information received from the other party.

The convenants of confidentiality set forth herein shall continue and be maintained from the effective date hereof until termination of this Agreement and for a period of three (3) years thereafter.

## 12.0 LIMITATION OF LIABILITY

EXCEPT FOR THE EXPRESS WARRANTIES CREATED UNDER THIS AGREEMENT AND SELLER'S INDEMNITY OBLIGATIONS HEREUNDER, IN NO EVENT SHALL SELLER BE LIABLE TO BUYER FOR ANY INCIDENTAL, CONSEQUENTIAL, SPECIAL OR PUNITIVE DAMAGES OF ANY KIND OR NATURE ARISING OUT OF THIS AGREEMENT OR THE SALE OF PRODUCTS BY BUYER, WHETHER SUCH LIABILITY IS ASSERTED ON THE BASIS OF CONTRACT, TORT (INCLUDING THE POSSIBILITY OF NEGLIGENCE OF STRICT LIABILITY), OR OTHERWISE, EVEN IF SELLER HAS BEEN WARNED OF THE POSSIBILITY OF ANY SUCH LOSS OR DAMAGE, AND EVEN IF ANY OF THE LIMITED REMEDIES IN THIS AGREEMENT FAIL OF THEIR ESSENTIAL PURPOSE.

## 13.0 MISCELLANEOUS

### 13.1 Entire Agreement

This Agreement constitutes the entire agreement between the Parties with respect to the transactions contemplated hereby and supersedes all prior agreements and understandings between the parties relating to such transactions. Buyer shall hold the existence and terms of this Agreement confidential, unless it obtains Seller's express written consent otherwise.

Each party agrees that information to be furnished by it to the other hereunder will to the best of its knowledge and belief, be correct. Each party agrees to notify the other promptly in the event it determines that information provided by it contains an error or omission or at such time that information is modified in any respect by the furnishing party.

### 13.2 Amendments

No modification, termination, extension, renewal or waiver of any provisions of this Agreement shall be binding upon either party unless made in writing and signed by an authorized officer or representative of each of the parties.

### 13.3 Third Party Beneficiary

This Agreement is intended for the benefit of the parties and their permitted assigns, and no other person shall be entitled to rely upon this Agreement or be entitled to any benefits under this Agreement.

### 13.4 Independent Contractor

Neither party shall, for any purpose, be deemed to be an agent of the other party and the relationship between the parties shall only be that of independent contractors. Neither party shall have any right or authority to assume or create any obligations or to make any representations or warranties on behalf of any other party, whether express or implied, or to bind the other party in any respect whatsoever.

### 13.5 Advertising

No advertising by Buyer or Seller shall display any of the Buyer or Seller's trademarks or refer to the other as the manufacturer of the Products without the prior written approval from the other.

## 13.6  Expenses

In the event a dispute between the parties hereunder with respect to this Agreement must be resolved by litigation or other proceeding or Seller must engage an attorney to collect any amounts due and owing to it, the prevailing party shall be entitled to receive reimbursement for all associated costs and expenses (including, without limitation, attorney's fees) from the other party.

## 13.7  Notice

Unless otherwise specified in this Agreement, all notices and other communications permitted or required by the provisions of this Agreement shall be in writing and shall be mailed, telecopied, telegraphed, telexed or delivered to the other party at the address shown on the signature page hereof (or at such other address as either party may designate in writing to the other party during the term of this Agreement in accordance with this Section) and shall be effective and deemed received (a) if mailed, when received by the addressee; (b) if telecopied, when received by the addressee; (c) if telegraphed, when delivered by the telegraph company to the addressee; (d) if telexed, when dispatched and confirmation of message received by the sender; or (e) if personally delivered, when delivered to the addressee.

## 13.8  Non-Hiring Employees

For a period of twenty-four (24) months after the termination of this Agreement or any renewal thereof, Buyer and Seller agree not to employ any person who is, or has been within the most recent twelve months, an employee of the other party without the other party's prior written consent.

## 13.9  Governing Law

This Agreement shall be governed by and construed under the laws of the State of California, excluding its choice of law principles.

# 14.0  FORCE MAJEURE

In the event that either party is prevented from performing or is unable to perform any of its obligations under this Agreement due to any Act of God, fire, casualty, flood, earthquake, war, strike, lockout, epidemic, destruction of production facilities, riot, insurrection, material unavailability, or any other cause beyond the reasonable control of the party invoking this section, and if such party shall have used its best efforts to mitigate its effects, such party shall give prompt written notice to the other party, its performance shall be excused, and the time for the performance shall be extended for the period of delay or inability to perform due to such occurrences.

      Regardless of the excuse of Force Majeure, if such party is not able to perform within 45 days after such event, the other party may declare such party to be in default without regard to any applicable cure period.

# ACCEPTED AND AGREED TO:

FOR BUYER: _____    FOR SELLER: _____

By: _____    By: _____

Title: _____    Title: _____

Date: _____    Date: _____

Address: _____    Address: _____

_____    _____

_____    _____

_____    _____

Attn: _____    Attn: _____

Fax No. _____    Fax No. _____

# Index